FANGIO

'I simply expressed what I had in me: respect for others, a love of machinery, and a passion for speed.'

JUAN MANUEL FANGIO

FANGIO
The Life Behind the Legend

Gerald Donaldson

Published by Virgin Books 2009

2 4 6 8 10 9 7 5 3 1

First published in Great Britain in 2003 by
Virgin Books
Random House, 20 Vauxhall Bridge Road,
London SW1V 2SA

www.virginbooks.com
www.rbooks.co.uk

Addresses for companies within The Random House Group Limited can be found at:
www.randomhouse.co.uk/offices.htm

The Random House Group Limited Reg. No. 954009

A CIP catalogue record for this book is available from the British Library

ISBN 9780753518274

The Random House Group Limited supports The Forest Stewardship Council [FSC],
the leading international forest certification organisation. All our titles that are
printed on Greenpeace approved FSC certified paper carry the FSC logo.
Our paper procurement policy can be found at www.rbooks.co.uk/environment

Typeset by TW Typesetting, Plymouth, Devon
Printed in the UK by CPI Bookmarque, Croydon, CR0 4TD

CONTENTS

A Tribute

When asked to nominate my Top Ten, the man I unhesitatingly put at the top of the list was a quiet Argentinian with cool, piercing eyes called Juan Manuel Fangio. The statistics don't tell half the story, but on their own they are devastating. In seven full seasons in Formula 1, Fangio was world champion five times and runner-up twice. During his career I had admired him from afar, but in 1987 I filmed a long interview with him. Even in old age, those eyes hadn't dimmed. I was astounded by his total recall, and also, I have to say, somewhat overawed in the presence of so charismatic a hero. More than anyone, Fangio represented the sporting ethic of a period of motor racing that is now long past. He was an artist in the cockpit, tremendously fast, and a daunting competitor. But he wasn't flamboyant. He didn't play to the gallery. He always said the best way to win a race was by going as slowly as possible. But if in order to win he had to go faster than anyone had gone before, he always seemed to be able to do it. And as his former team-mate and lifelong admirer Stirling Moss points out, you never heard anything bad about him; from his fellow drivers you never heard anything but admiration and respect. Out of the car he was calm and courteous, a unique blend of charm, humility and tough acumen.

Murray Walker, *Murray Walker's Formula One Heroes*

Acknowledgements

Thanks is due first of all to Roberto Carozzo, who worked with Juan Manuel Fangio to write *Fangio, My Racing Life*, his official autobiography, and who generously gave permission to use quotations from that book and assisted with research for this one. For providing other research material, advice and assistance, my thanks also go to the motorsport editor and journalist Quentin Spurring, to the journalists and authors Nigel Roebuck and Richard Williams, to the text's editor Daniel Balado and to my editors at Virgin Books, Jonathan Taylor and Vanessa Daubney.

A special thank you as well to Stirling Moss and Jackie Stewart, who went out of their way to make sure the driver they consider to be the greatest of all time was accurately depicted, and to everyone else who gave interviews and whose names are listed herein.

While speaking to Roberto Carozzo, Juan Manuel Fangio said, 'A book should be about a boy, from a humble family, born in a small town. I want it to deal more with people than with cars and races. Bring out the human side.'

That is what this book attempts to do.

Part I: El Chueco

1911–49: A Lifetime Already Lived

Chapter One

Boyhood in Balcarce

'We were a humble family, but we never lacked anything, we never missed anything.'

AMONG HIS EARLIEST, and happiest, memories were those evenings when as a small boy he sat around with his five brothers and sisters in their home in Balcarce, Argentina, listening with wide-eyed fascination as Papa Fangio told enchanting tales about his own boyhood, long ago and far away. Loreto Fangio told his children that he had been born in the small Italian village of Castiglione Messer Marino, in Chieti province, among the rugged mountains of the Abruzzi region east of Rome and south of Pescara. There, he explained, the Fangios – Loreto, his sister Francisca, his brother Alfonso and their parents – had a home that was little more than a hut. Their father was a tenant farmer who laboured from dawn to dusk trying to eke out a modest living from soil that was exhausted after centuries of cultivation. Life was very hard, but grandfather Giuseppe Fangio was adventurous, courageous and ambitious, and in 1887 he took the bold decision to search for a better life in the new world – in South America.

Leaving his family behind, Giuseppe sailed on a ship across the ocean to Buenos Aires, then took a train heading south-east towards the coastal town of Mar del Plata. The train tracks ran through the pampas, the flat, fertile plains where immigrants from Italy, Spain and other parts of the world were beginning to settle. The pampas seemed monotonous compared to the mountains of Abruzzi, but Giuseppe's mind was alive with possibilities. He got off the train at a lonely station called Coronel Vidal, from where he travelled by road deep into a remote area of scrub forest. There he began to cut and burn tree branches, transforming them into charcoal fuel for which there was a ready market among the settlers who were establishing farms in the region. In just three years, Giuseppe Fangio had saved enough to buy a farm of his own, a 25-acre section of land six miles from the nearest major town, Balcarce. There was just enough money left to pay the boat fares to bring his wife and family over from Italy.

And that, Loreto told his children, is how he arrived in this part of the world at the age of seven.

Little Juan Manuelito and his brothers and sisters particularly enjoyed hearing how their papa and mama had met. Loreto said he was only about fifteen years old and working as a farm labourer when he first saw Herminia Deramo, the girl who would become his wife and their mother. Taking up the story, Herminia explained that though her family had also originally come from the Abruzzi region in Italy, she'd been born in the town of Tres Arroyos, about 75 miles from Balcarce, where her father had established a contracting business. One day, two young men on horseback rode up and dismounted at the Deramo home. They introduced themselves as the Fangio brothers, Alfonso and Loreto. In fact, Loreto revealed, Alfonso, who was working for Herminia's father, had arranged the visit so that his brother could meet this most attractive girl.

It was love at first sight, and four years later, on 24 October 1903, when he was nineteen and she was seventeen, Loreto and Herminia were married. At first they lived on farms where

Herminia helped with the housework and Loreto continued to work as a labourer. Then he became an apprentice stonemason and began to learn the building trade. Like his father, he saved his money and bought a plot of land in instalments, on the busiest street in the middle of Balcarce, where he began to build a house – the very place where they now lived: number 321 on Calle 13. When the first room was finished, Loreto and Herminia moved in. She sewed and made garments for the local tailor (and later opened her own clothes shop) while he added plastering and painting to his growing list of skills which soon earned him a reputation for excellent house-building workmanship (Loreto would continue working until he was well into his seventies, by which time he had built over a hundred houses in Balcarce.) As and when the money became available, more rooms were added to accommodate their growing family. All six of them were born there, in Casa Fangio, three boys and three girls: first Herminia, then José, Celia, Juan Manuel, Ruben Renato (nicknamed Toto) and finally Carmen.

From his mother, Juan Manuel learnt that he was born ten minutes after midnight on 24 June 1911. She chose the name Juan because 24 June was St John's day, while Loreto, a fervent admirer of the monarchy, decided on the second name in honour of the Italian king, Manuel. Juan at first needed more care and attention than his siblings for he was a frail and weak little boy and his mother constantly worried about his health. But he was an eager and fast learner, and it soon became obvious that he had inherited some of the Fangio family traits, particularly their industriousness and capacity for hard work. Juan had an aptitude for working with tools, and at a very young age he became surprisingly skilled at improvising repairs to worn-out household items. His parents were impressed by the way such a young boy was able to solve complex problems with practical solutions. By the time he was little more than four years old, Juan was given his own bench in Loreto's workshop in the back yard, and there he spent many happy hours. It was also around this time that he became entranced by the first motoring machine he ever saw, a neighbour's horseless carriage powered by a single-cylinder internal combustion engine. With the other children, he took great delight in helping to push-start this, to them, wondrous device.

His parents, to whom Juan was devoted – even late in his life he referred to them as Papa and Mama – watched proudly as their fourth-born child's admirable character developed. From the beginning he was especially warm and considerate. One Sunday, Herminia remembered, Loreto gave Juan a few centavos to attend the local cinema. On the way he met a small boy from a poor family who had never seen a film; unbidden, Juan took him by the hand and paid for his cinema ticket. 'Yes, as a child he was kind-hearted,' Herminia confirmed. 'He always avoided doing anything that might come to my ears to worry me, though I began to quake when he became fascinated by cars.'

Juan enjoyed going to school, where he got good marks, particularly in mathematics. He also regularly attended the Catholic church, where he took his first communion at the age of eleven. Before his twelfth birthday he had finished the first six years of school, which was the extent of education then available in Balcarce; further formal study would require a move to Buenos Aires, nearly 250 miles to the north, but the Fangios had no money for that, nor did his mother want him to leave her care. Besides, the tradition in Balcarce was for boys to learn a trade, so before he left school Juan began working as an apprentice blacksmith, a profession much in demand since horsedrawn wagons and carriages were still the main mode of transport in this agricultural region.

To accommodate what was quite a heavy workload for a young boy, Loreto would wake his son at four o'clock in the morning. His long days, spent preparing his lessons before attending school in the morning, then working as an apprentice in the afternoon at Cerri's blacksmith shop, extended through-out the week to Saturday, sometimes even Sunday. One of Juan's proudest accomplishments as a budding blacksmith was transforming a piece of scrap metal – by heating it on the forge then hammering and bending it on the anvil – into a useful tool, a machete, which everyone agreed was expertly made and with which he was able to cut an impressive swathe through the unruly undergrowth in the Fangios' garden.

Juan spent what little spare time he had watching the work being done in a nearby garage by mechanics whose expertise he greatly admired. To him, they seemed like brilliant surgeons performing delicate operations on ailing machinery with deft applications of their tools, though these were rudimentary in the extreme. Everything was done by hand (there were no power tools), and Juan marvelled at the way in which the mechanics came up with clever solutions to keep well-used machinery operational – a necessity, since new machinery, let alone spares, was in short supply. By the time he was twelve he was working in the garage, having exchanged the blacksmith's hammer and tongs for spanners and drills, which he learnt to use by emulating his superiors. He worked on tractors, harvesters and other farm machinery, but the real attraction at the Capettini garage was the automobiles that were brought in for repair.

It was in one of these, a chain-driven Panhard Lavassor, that he first experienced the thrill of driving, albeit at the most sedate pace possible. One day, in order to sweep the floor beneath the car, Juan started the engine by climbing on to the crank handle and jumping on it. He then clambered up into the cockpit, carefully depressed the clutch, selected reverse gear, grasped the steering wheel and gingerly backed the sputtering machine to the doorway. The sweeping done, he eased the Panhard back into its former position. Though he had travelled for a total distance of little more than 30 feet, it was a fabulous journey that gave Juan a tremendous sense of accomplishment. 'With my foot on the accelerator I could call as much as forty horsepower into play,' he said. 'Had I dared, I could have driven off and made two tons of metal answer my will. I was shaking with excitement.'

Soon, his mechanical skills had improved to a point where he became indispensable to Señor Capettini, who wanted to take Juan with him when he moved to set up a garage in another town. But his mother, still worried about her boy's health, forbade it, and he continued his apprenticeship at other garages in Balcarce. His first exposure to racing machines came while he was working for the Carlini brothers, who modified Rugby cars by stripping them down, fine-tuning the engines and fitting them with handcrafted aluminium coachwork, then competed in them at the races that were now a major attraction throughout the country.

Automobile racing in Argentina, which began at the turn of the century on horse-racing tracks, had by this time branched out to include long-distance events on the open dirt roads between towns. With few purpose-built racing cars available, most of the participants used ordinary road models that were cobbled up into competition cars, such as those prepared by the Carlinis. Juan was struck by the raw, purposeful beauty of these racing machines and greatly admired the exploits of the heroic drivers and the riding mechanics who accompanied them. His duties at his next job, with the Estevez Ford agency, included taking trips with the chief mechanic to fix machinery at farms in the surrounding countryside. Occasionally on these journeys Juan was allowed to take the wheel while his boss, an avid hunter, blasted away at any game flushed out by their noisy passage.

At the age of thirteen, Juan moved to the Viggiano Studebaker agency where he was employed as an assistant mechanic. He eagerly volunteered for the weekly chore of carting accumulated debris from the garage to the nearby dump. This great adventure, Juan's first experience driving alone on the open road, was conducted behind the wheel of a rough wooden chassis powered by a sputtering motorcycle engine. With typical self-deprecating humour, Juan later recalled that while he felt on top of the world, as proud as a conquering Roman general riding in a splendid chariot, nobody took the slightest notice of him phut-phutting along in Viggiano's primitive rubbish hauler.

'Juan was a good boy – as we say, *muchacho*. He worked hard and learnt fast,' Loreto Fangio remarked, and by the age of fifteen Juan had become a fully-fledged mechanic working on customers' road cars and also helping to prepare competition machines for clients as well as the proprietor, who was himself a local racer of note and, as it turned out, a driving instructor for his teenage employee, who accompanied him on business trips as far away as Buenos Aires. During these journeys, Miguel Viggiano regaled his young passenger with thrilling anecdotes about his racing exploits. Juan hung on to his every word, while also watching intently the considerable expertise with which his boss drove the car. Señor Viggiano was particularly adept at handling cars in the muddy conditions they often encountered. When rain turned the dirt roads into quagmires, Juan noted how Viggiano, always a fast driver, hardly slowed down, instead changing his technique to maintain control of the car on even the most slippery surface. Hardly ever touching the brakes, he would slow down by changing to lower gears while working constantly on the steering wheel and the accelerator with great sensitivity, responding immediately to feedback from the four wheels to counteract threatened slides with seemingly improvisational yet absolutely precise movements. Witnessing firsthand these skilled demonstrations of a man mastering a contrary machine filled Viggiano's passenger with awe. The experience also further fuelled in Juan Manuel Fangio a growing desire to develop such skills himself.

For that, he needed a car of his own, and one duly came his way from Viggiano in lieu of past wages that remained unpaid. To settle the outstanding debt, Viggiano presented Juan with a Harley-Davidson motorcycle. However, it quickly became apparent that his boss's expertise on four wheels did not necessarily extend to handling the idiosyncrasies of this two-wheeled device, a pristine Indian model. While demonstrating it to his employee, Viggiano used the accelerator instead of the brake as he rounded a corner. The bike flew off the road, hit a rock and was reduced to a pile of scrap. Unhurt, though embarrassed, possibly to the point of over-compensating for the loss, Viggiano came up with a well-used though welcome substitute: a four-cylinder Overland car. Juan received it with delight, and in his spare time he streamlined the bodywork, fine-tuned the engine, changed the springs and modified the suspension with a view to improving its sporting capabilities. For in his mind's eye Juan saw the Overland as a potential racing car, and himself as a racer.

This vision came closer to fruition one day when a customer of Viggiano's, Manuel Ayerza, invited the Fangio boy to act as his riding mechanic in a race on the dirt road between the towns of Coronel Vidal (where grandfather Giuseppe Fangio had set up his charcoal operation) and Maipu. After some hesitation, for he knew his parents would forbid it, Juan agreed to take part. Their car, a much-modified 1928 Chevrolet coupé, did not feature prominently in the race, which was conducted in a huge cloud of dust that prevented Juan from seeing much of what went on. But the emotional roller-coaster ride left an indelible impression on his mind, and for the rest of his life Juan was able to recall the sensations vividly.

Acute anticipation mixed with considerable apprehension meant he didn't sleep a wink the night before the race. In the morning, his body trembled involuntarily, and just before the start he was overcome by a fever of excitement so thrilling he could scarcely contain it. As the cars roared away he was immediately plunged into a state of terrible fear; gradually, as the race progressed, this gave way to a growing sense of cautious confidence. Soon, Juan became intoxicated by the sheer speed of it, and by the finish he had been transported from delight to previously unimagined heights of euphoria. 'I loved the idea of motor racing,' he said. 'I was attracted by the spirit of adventure that is an inseparable part of it. I already felt I was a racer. It put me on the right track.' His driver, Señor Ayerza, went on to become the Argentine pre-war champion, but was later killed. Still, for Juan the pleasures of racing far outweighed its perils and he was filled with resolve to somehow make it part of his life.

Juan's other passion at this time was football, an activity in which driving his Overland car also came into play. (Briefly, he had also tried boxing at the gym in Balcarce, but this experiment had ended in his seeing stars from a knockout blow delivered by a much larger opponent.) As a footballer, Juan developed into an excellent playmaker and was noted as a dedicated and unselfish team man. Despite his still slight physique and suspect health, he had surprising stamina and was well co-ordinated and agile. On the football pitch he found himself able continually to dart among his opponents while maintaining control of the ball. From his midfield position as an inside-right he became particularly skilled at setting up goals for his team-mates, who began to call him 'El Chueco', the bandy one, because he had slightly bowed legs that churned furiously as he zig-zagged up and down the pitch. El Chueco was much in demand as a driver when his team travelled to matches outside Balcarce, especially when the roads were muddy and Juan was able to take advantage of Viggiano's expert tuition. While other cars got bogged down, El Chueco's Overland could be relied upon to keep going, and if they broke down he could fix them.

His footballing forays to destinations outside Balcarce also gave rise to an increasingly independent streak that at the age of sixteen led him to run away from home to seek his fortune. With two friends, he drove 40 miles to the coastal town of Mar del Plata to look for work. Five days later his father, driven by Miguel Viggiano, found Juan working in a shop near the harbour and living with his friends in an abandoned house. Loreto Fangio was deeply hurt and explained that Herminia was distraught at the absence of the son to whom they were so devoted. The adventure ended on the spot, and the wayward boy sheepishly returned to the family fold.

The comforts of home became a necessity when Juan was forced to stay there for most of his eighteenth year. The first sign of a serious illness had been a sharp pain in his chest when he was running hard in a football game. Soon, his mother's worst fears were realised: Juan was diagnosed as having a severe bout of pleurisy, a lung affection that for a time threatened to escalate into tuberculosis. He was bed-ridden for two months during which time his distressed mother often wept at his plight, but she nursed him with great care and, rigorously following the advice of doctors, saw to it that he avoided any strenuous activity, though her discipline wasn't really necessary since even the slightest work or exercise brought back the pain in his chest.

Gradually he recovered, and by the time Juan was 21 he was pronounced fit enough to do his compulsory military service. He spent 1932 at the Campo de Mayo cadet school near Buenos Aires. There, his confinement to barracks was made more tolerable when word of his prowess behind the wheel prompted his commanding officer to appoint Private Fangio as his official driver. The enforced discipline of serving with the 6th Artillery Regiment was no hardship for a youth accustomed to hard labour as a way of furthering his personal ambitions. He now also learnt more about the value of working for the common good; always self-aware, he came to understand the limitations and conceit of his self-centred teenage years. Among his peers he had been a natural leader, controlling play on the football pitch, impressing his friends with his skill and daring behind the wheel, driving his boisterous gang to matches and parties and generally acting as the ringleader in mischievous escapades and youthful pranks from which it was sometimes necessary for them to make hasty exits, with Juan in charge of the 'getaway car'. But there was no place for such high jinks in the army. As an army cadet he was just another cog in the wheel, and the strict regimentation made Juan realise that the best way forward was to share responsibilities and respect the rights of others.

The army made a man of him. He thrived on the canteen fare and benefited physically from the endless marching drills conducted in all weathers. By the end of his 21st year he had put on over twenty pounds and was now a strapping young man with a powerful physique. In his final military physical examination the doctors found him to be five feet nine inches tall, and the scales showed that he weighed 187 pounds. Moreover, his resting heart rate registered a mere 44 beats per minute, which was impressively slow compared to the average rate of 72. In terms of endurance fitness, this put Juan on a par with the most tireless athletes, and also served as a pointer to a placid disposition and natural state of calmness that would serve him well in times of stress.

After his discharge from military service, Juan returned to Balcarce where an opportunity to further his footballing career soon beckoned. Juan and his close friend José Duffard, who shared his passion for fast cars and also loved working on engines, received an offer to play for a club in Mar del Plata. But then their Balcarce team-mates, who wanted desperately to keep them on the home side, suggested that the two players should turn Juan's hobby of working on his own car and those of friends in front of the Fangio house into a proper garage business, and they volunteered to help them do it. Loreto and Herminia Fangio heartily approved and donated a small section of the front yard where Juan and his footballing friends, several of whom were expert tradesmen, built a rudimentary shed in which they dug a pit for servicing vehicles. Soon, Fangio, Duffard & Co., as they called their enterprise, developed a reputation for honest and reliable yet inexpensive repair work on both cars and trucks. To help with the increasing workload Juan's younger brother Toto and Duffard's older brother Bernard joined the company, as did other friends and acquaintances including Francisco Cavalotti, a trained accountant who also played on the football team.

Besides being a great believer in remaining loyal to friends and working with people he knew, Juan also proved to be a good judge of character, and was always generous and kind to those less fortunate than himself. One of those he hired was a boy whom others refused to employ because he had a criminal record, having been convicted and served time in jail for taking part in a railway robbery. Yet Juan placed his trust in him, giving him the reponsibility of running the company office and handling all the money, not a peso of which went missing. Another acquaintance, an orphan who had worked in a bakery and provided the football team with post-match refreshments, later became a political activist and was imprisoned as a potential anarchist. Juan and his friends arranged for his release and helped him move to 'exile' in Mar del Plata, where he was unfortunately shot and killed by extremists. Terribly upset by their friend's fate, Juan and the others arranged for his funeral and paid all the costs.

After suffering through some lean times in the economic depression of the early thirties, Fangio, Duffard & Co. began to thrive again, and in 1934 the need for expansion was accommodated by a move to a rented garage in the centre of Balcarce. Six years later the business had prospered to a point where even larger premises were required, so the partners bought an abandoned store across the street which, again with the help of friends, they demolished and rebuilt as a proper garage complete with a YPF (the Argentine national oil company) petrol station in the forecourt. The funding for this expensive exercise came from their own savings, loans guaranteed by impressed Balcarce businessmen, and from prize and appearance money earned by the increasingly well-known race driver Juan Manuel Fangio.

Chapter Two

Fast Cars, High Spirits

'I went racing in tremendous spirits. I felt like another person when I was behind the wheel. I felt ecstatic. I often used to sing to myself.'

I T WAS ON 24 OCTOBER 1936 that Juan first tried to combine business with pleasure by going racing to gain publicity for the garage, though his driving debut was a failure on all counts. Indeed, the event – 25 laps around a five-mile road course at Buenito Juarez, a town west of Balcarce – was not officially sanctioned, his means of conveyance was not a proper racing car, and he didn't drive it under his own name. The car, a 1929 Model A Ford taxi loaned by the father of a friend, was driven by a certain 'Rivadavia' which was the name of the football club for which Juan played and whose squad members had encouraged him to compete. Calling himself Rivadavia, he decided, would be an appropriate reward for his loyal team-mates who would be able to ride with him vicariously in his first experience as a racing driver.

As the cars roared away at the start, great clouds of dust and flying clods of earth obscured the vision of all but those in front, which did not then include Rivadavia, who wisely chose to proceed with caution into the maelstrom. On the chaotic first lap a less prudently driven car overtook Juan, who watched in horror as it clipped a culvert and somersaulted high into the air, pitching out its driver, who was instantly killed. But the race continued and Juan pressed on, gaining confidence and speed; soon his number 19 Model A Ford was running an impressive third. Then, with just two laps to go, an engine bearing seized and Rivadavia's mount ground to a halt. His enforced exit left Juan weeping with exasperation, though before long his determination took over and the setback only strengthened his resolve to try again.

For his second attempt, on 13 December at a course near the town of Adolfo González Chavez, Juan drove another borrowed Model A Ford, a 1930 car that had been stripped down and prepared for racing. In practice on the Saturday before the race the car's ignition system failed and Juan spent nearly all that night repairing it. On Sunday morning, exhausted and covered in grease and oil, he arrived at the start only to find the race already in progress. Before the organisers could stop him, Juan charged out on to the track, assuming a solitary position well away from the main pack so that spectators in the grandstands wildly applauded his passage in the mistaken belief that he was leading the race. His moment of glory lasted only one lap, after which the organisers commanded him to stop and promptly disqualified him.

Bitterly disappointed, and also embarrassed by his reckless stupidity for contravening the rules, Juan returned to Balcarce where news of his day of infamy had reached his parents. Loreto Fangio had known about Juan's racing efforts and was quietly proud of him, but Herminia was plunged into a state of near hysteria at the thought of her boy, even though he was now 25 years old, risking his life in such a dangerous sport.

Her fears were put to rest, for a while at least, as Juan temporarily shelved his racing ambitions and concentrated on his business. But a few months after the disqualification débâcle a race at his home track, the La Chata circuit on the outskirts of Balcarce, proved too tempting for him to resist. Although Juan's failures so far made him wonder if he might possibly be permanently jinxed as a driver, he gathered his courage together and gained a last-minute entry. The car, again loaned by friends whose faith in his potential remained undiminished, was an eight-cylinder Buick, from which Juan removed the bodywork. Somewhat apprehensively, he took his position on the start line, from where the Buick promptly refused to budge. Unfamiliar with the car's gearbox, Juan had roughly tried to engage first, whereupon the gear lever flopped ineffectually in his grasp. Solving the problem with a screwdriver, he set off at a furious pace to make up for lost time. He passed several cars before paying the price for his haste. The car ran wide in a turn and sideswiped a bridge; the impact twisted the chassis to the point of no return and he was forced to retire.

With the car, his pride and his bank balance dented (he couldn't charge for the several days' work necessary to repair the damage to the borrowed Buick), Juan began a self-enforced sabbatical from racing that lasted for over a year. 'If it hadn't been for my friends,' he stated later, 'I might not have continued. One of the main things about motor racing is the friendships you make and keep.' Encouraged by those friends, and finally persuaded by his brother Toto, at the end of March 1938 he agreed to enter a race at Necochea, a coastal town south of Balcarce. The event, officially sanctioned by the Automóvil Club Argentino, the country's sporting authority, was for both purpose-built racing cars imported from Europe and for the 'Mecánica Nacional' category of home-built machines in which the Balcarce boys decided to compete.

The 'Fangio Special' was a basic 1934 Ford two-seater chassis into which was stuffed a 1938 Ford V8 engine that developed 80bhp. Bought with borrowed money from a previous winner of a race at La Chata, it was primitive in the extreme, with a rock-solid suspension that sent it juddering and bouncing down the unmade road like a bucking bronco. Nevertheless, by hanging on to the reins with the will of a fiercely determined gaucho, Juan was able to coax from the contrary contraption a somewhat terrifying top speed of 106mph, though this was about 50mph less than the speed the fastest cars could achieve in a straight line. Astonishingly, by making up time in the twists and turns of the circuit's four-mile-long configuration, the number 23 Fangio Special qualified fifth fastest among the 24 entrants. The strength of the frontrunners was testimony to the worth of this achievement: on pole position was a 330bhp Alfa Romeo racer imported from Italy and driven by Carlos Arzani, then one of the top drivers in Argentina; second and third on the grid were a Mercedes-Benz with a supercharged seven-litre engine and a Chrysler-engined Oro that had competed in the USA's famous Indianapolis 500 race. In the first of two heats, with the much more powerful cars spinning their wheels at the start, Juan leapt into the lead. Inevitably, he was eventually passed by Arzani, who went on to win, but Juan finished third in the first heat, and after some mechanical problems he was seventh in the final. These results, against seasoned drivers in better cars, whetted the novice driver's appetite for more racing, and there was plenty of it in his next event.

Throughout Latin America there remained a strong tradition of long-distance races on open roads that had long ago been banned for safety reasons in most of Europe, where they had been the earliest form of automobile competition. Rallying, with cars competing for several days over longer distances on public roads closed for the occasion, was still a popular form of European motorsport, and events such as the Mille Miglia (Thousand Miles) and the Targa Florio (44 miles to the lap) were still held on everyday roads in Italy, but racing on much shorter, purpose-built circuits was now the norm in the rest of the world. In fact, the rest of the world had never seen the monstrous marathons conducted over vast distances that made the mighty pan-American epics the longest, most gruelling and most dangerous test of men and machines in the history of racing. 'The roads were very bad,' Juan recalled, 'no asphalt, full of holes, always mud or dust. Some people thought we were mad. And they were right. Every now and then one of us got killed.'

From 12 to 30 October 1938, acting as mechanic and co-driver for a Balcarce friend, Luis Finochietti, Juan took part in the Gran Premio Argentino de Carreteras, a twelve-stage cross-country race that took competitors to the country's northern border with Bolivia and back again. At the end of their 4,590-mile journey, which included traversing Andean mountain passes over 11,000 feet in altitude and stopping several times to effect makeshift repairs, the battle-scarred Finochietti-Fangio 1937 Ford sedan was classified an impressive seventh overall. Juan's first long-distance event, which tested both his mechanical and driving abilities to the extreme (Finochietti was soon exhausted and Juan drove most of the way), was valuable experience in the type of racing that was to become Juan's forte.

The perils of the profession to which he aspired became grimly apparent in his next race a fortnight later at Tres Arroyos, the town where Juan's mother was born and where five people were destined to perish on a five-mile track a lengthy heatwave had turned into a deadly dust bowl. In spite of the infernal heat, thousands of spectators had crowded up to the wire fences that surrounded the scorched circuit. From the seat of his trusty Ford V8 Fangio Special, Juan did not see the tragedies unfold, though fortunately he avoided them himself.

The dust raised on the opening lap remained suspended in the still air and grew thicker with every passage of the cars so that after a few laps the 400 Kilometres of Tres Arroyos was being conducted in conditions resembling a fully-fledged desert sandstorm. Visibility steadily worsened, to such an extent that the sweat-soaked, dust-covered drivers were forced to navigate mainly by sound (judging their distance to other cars by listening to their engines) and blind faith. Juan was running fifth when he heard the grinding crunch of metal and the tortured scream of uncontrolled engines that signified the chain reaction of crashes occurring in front of the main grandstands opposite the pits. He smelt the acrid smoke of burning fuel and rubber, then through the gloom he finally spotted frantic officials waving red flags. Juan brought his Fangio Special safely to a stop amid desperate scenes of carnage. The death toll included two mechanics and two drivers, one of whom burnt to death along with a spectator who had tried to help him extinguish the flames. Juan went to the victims' wakes, where he mourned the needless waste of lives in a race he had begun to realise should never have taken place because of the atrocious conditions.

His first race of 1939, on 7 May, was his last outing in the Ford V8. In the La Plata race at the El Bosque circuit near Buenos Aires he qualified fifth and finished eighth. Riding with him was Hector Carlos Tieri, a trusted mechanic from Juan's garage who was a specialist in repairing Fords.

Though his relatively mediocre results to date after so much effort had left Juan's morale rather low, the citizens of his home town had become infatuated by the racing adventures of the local hero whose exploits were covered live by the Balcarce radio station and reported in detail in the newspaper. In the opinion of most townspeople, 'El Chueco' only needed a better car to really put Balcarce on the map. To capitalise on this burgeoning civic pride, an influential councillor organised a collection campaign to buy a car for El Chueco to carry the Balcarce colours in the forthcoming Gran Premio Argentino de Carreteras. Donations poured in, ranging from 500 peso contributions from prosperous businessmen to a few centavos from humble labourers who eagerly gave all they could to help fund a driver whose family background was similar to their own. Juan, who had been at first embarrassed and sceptical about the scheme's likelihood of success, was overwhelmed by the display of generosity. He felt deeply indebted to the people of Balcarce and his resolve to repay their faith in him provided extra inspiration to do well in the Gran Premio, a long-distance race whose planned route would take the competitors zig-zagging through some of the worst terrain to be found in the rugged Argentinian landscape.

Given his familiarity with the make, Juan's first choice of car was a Ford, but no suitable vehicle could be found. With the race date fast approaching, a brand-new black 1939 Chevrolet coupé was purchased from the showroom floor of a local General Motors dealer and taken back to the Fangio garage to be prepared. Since stock six-cylinder Chevrolet engines were then notorious for using a surfeit of oil at high speeds, Juan, assisted as usual by eager friends, replaced it with a modified Chev engine obtained from a potato farmer. The car's interior was gutted of all surplus trimmings, and tools and vital spare parts were packed into the rear seat area and stowed in the boot. The suspension was strengthened and the chassis jacked up to provide greater ground clearance. Finally, in recognition of his loyal benefactors, Juan painted the name BALCARCE in large letters above each door.

Accompanied by his mechanic Tieri, he set off for Buenos Aires where the ten-day-long Grand Premio de Carreteras would start and finish. The Balcarce entry was designated number 38 among the 133 cars that took the midnight start and roared off into the darkness, heading north-west toward Sante Fe, where the first stage was to end after over 600 miles. Back in Balcarce, despite the lateness of the hour, many lights were still on as the inhabitants sat listening to the radio commentary and checking off the names of the towns 'their car' passed through.

After only 90 minutes, the listeners were disturbed to hear about a major delay to the Fangio-Tieri car at Pergamino, little more than 100 miles beyond Buenos Aires. Their enforced halt came when the Chev's oil pressure gauge suddenly dropped to near zero. Juan pulled over under a street lamp and found that a seized connecting rod bearing was responsible for the loss of oil. Working feverishly, they set about effecting makeshift though far from foolproof repairs, then resumed the chase, with Juan driving the Chev at a furious pace between stops to add more oil. Many hours later, with its occupants all but exhausted and its engine all but out of oil again, the Balcarce car struggled into Sante Fe, three hours behind the leader and 108th overall among the 119 cars that survived the first stage.

From Sante Fe, the cars were ferried across the Paraná river to the start of the next stage, which ran east in a circuitous route from the town of Paraná to Concordia on the Uruguayan border, a distance of nearly 200 miles, much of it through the notoriously swampy Entre Rios region. In Paraná, Juan devised an ingenious if primitive system intended to replace lost oil without having to stop the car: he drilled a hole through the dashboard and connected a length of spare radiator hose to the oil filler cap, through which Tieri could top up the vital fluid, many tins of which were stored in the footwell.

The second stage began in torrential rain that was to fall for hours, turning the run into something of a nightmare for everyone, but especially for the Balcarce car. The oil replenishing system worked well enough, but it worked both ways, backfiring oil, thick smoke and noxious fumes from the engine compartment into the cockpit, leaving Fangio and Tieri blackened, red-eyed and fighting off asphyxiation. It was worse for Tieri, whose periodic attempts to stem the flow by blowing into the hose meant he ingested some of its volatile contents. But Juan had problems of his own, having to manhandle the Chev through the worst driving conditions he had ever experienced. The incessant rain turned what was little more than a cart track through a swamp (at the best of times) into a steaming bog of glutinous mud. 'It seemed impossible to continue,' Juan recalled. 'Then I had a vision of all those who had contributed to getting me here. I felt it was up to me to defend the honour of Balcarce.' As they lurched through the thickening quagmire the smell of burning clutch was added to the sickening mix of odours in the car. Juan skidded the Chev to a halt and they jumped out to investigate. On discovering that the mud-caked wheels were causing the clutch to slip, they began the laborious task of removing each wheel and scraping off the offending substance.

On the road again, Juan changed his approach to incorporate lessons he had learnt long ago while driving with his old employer Viggiano. To avoid the mud he took to the water, driving down the ditches on either side of the road, a detour that was often necessary anyway since the main route was strewn with marooned cars. On one occasion the Balcarce car also became bogged down. While helping a group of spectators heave it back on to higher ground, Juan's shoes sank so deeply into the mud that they remained there when he hopped back into the car. The barefoot boy from Balcarce pressed on, finally slithering the sputtering Chevrolet into Concordia, where the muddy, smoke-stained, oil-soaked occupants fell out of their seats gasping for breath. To their amazement, they were told they had finished ninth fastest in the stage, and among the 70 cars still running they were now 18th overall. The leaders were the Galvez brothers, with Oscar driving and Juan the riding mechanic, in a Ford.

After a day's rest, the third stage began, but the persistent downpour had made the roads completely impassable and the organisers cancelled what remained of the race. When the final results were tallied the Fangio-Tieri car was classified 22nd overall in the Gran Premio Argentino de Carreteras.

But their adventure was not yet over, for the survivors of this extraordinary race were invited to take part in a new event. Hastily arranged to try to salvage something from the shambles of the Carreteras, it was aptly called the Gran Premio Extraordinario. It would start a week later, from the city of Córdoba, 400 miles west of Concordia, from where the cars were transported by railway. From the station in Córdoba, Juan drove the clanking Chevrolet, its oil-starved engine on its last legs, to the General Motors depot that was also servicing the cars of the official Chevrolet racing team. In the garage, Fangio and Tieri were welcomed by the mechanics who, greatly impressed by the perseverance and determination of these gritty private entrants, willingly pitched in to help them take out the engine to see if it could be repaired. But their work was interrupted by an angry GM official who insisted that only the team cars, over which he presided, could be worked on in the garage. Furthermore, the blustering bureaucrat declared, the crankshaft in the Balcarce car's engine was scored beyond repair and must be replaced by a new one, which Fangio and Tieri would have to buy. When they pleaded poverty a vociferous argument ensued, the normally mild-mannered Fangio becoming increasingly incensed at the disdainful attitude of the red-faced GM official, who finally shouted that if the dishevelled, grease-covered occupants of the battered Balcarce car continued to race it would bring nothing but negative publicity to General Motors products. Juan retorted that it would indeed demonstrate to all the considerable deficiencies of Chevrolet cars.

The heated exchange only gave Juan a greater incentive to do everything in his power to get his car raceworthy again. Aside from the slight to his personal pride, he again felt motivated by a deep need to defend the honour of Balcarce, to repay the debt he owed to the friends who had helped him prepare the car and especially to those townspeople who had invested their hard-earned pesos to buy the car. He explained this worthy cause to the sympathetic proprietors of two Córdoba garages, where modifications were made to the crankshaft (including the fitting of a gasket cut from the brim of an old felt hat) to prevent the oil loss that had so seriously impeded progress in the earlier race.

On 29 October 1939, the refettled Fangio-Tieri car took its place among the 123 entries that set off from Córdoba on the first stage of the new race. Once the rebuilt engine had covered the first few miles of the 275-mile journey without drama, Juan's confidence in it grew and he pushed harder and harder; by the time they got to the stage finish in Santiago del Estero, the Balcarce car was in a highly commendable eighth place. Moreover, in a field dominated by the more powerful Ford cars, it was the leading Chevrolet, having impressively outperformed those of the official GM racing team. But the achievement had come at a cost, literally, since Juan had bought the parts and paid the mechanics who had helped him with the repairs in Córdoba. Hotel rooms, fuel and oil for the car and food for himself and Tieri, though they skimped on meals, had further depleted cash reserves that now needed replenishing if they were to continue. Overcoming his shame and embarrassment, Juan reluctantly sent a telegram back to Balcarce informing his friends of the financial plight and asking if they might somehow find additional funds.

News of their car's impressive result in faraway Santiago del Estero had been broadcast by radio back to listeners in Balcarce, who celebrated the achievement, though it was a while before they heard from their reluctant celebrity of a driver. In Santiago, having several times heard his name mentioned by the radio commentator, Juan finally plucked up enough courage to introduce himself and agree to be interviewed. The experience of speaking to his loyal followers back home raised his spirits and reinforced his commitment to put Balcarce even more prominently on the map of Argentina.

He really made his mark on a second stage that took the competitors 300 miles north into the province of Jujuy and the foothills of the Andes near the border with Bolivia. By the finish, at San Salvador de Jujuy, only two Fords stood between the Balcarce car and first place overall. Instead of bringing infamy to Chevrolet, the Fangio-Tieri car had glorified its name, though the unexpected result also brought a degree of shame to the official four-car Chevrolet entry which had been comprehensively outpaced and whose team boss now performed a complete U-turn. Heaping praise on Señor Fangio, as he now called him, the GM bureaucrat who had tried to stop him in Córdoba presented Juan with a contract that in effect made the Balcarce car part of the official Chevrolet team. On learning that Juan was broke, the team boss told him that henceforth General Motors would supply him with new parts and tyres and pay all his expenses, whereupon the grateful recipient of this good fortune dashed off another telegram to Balcarce cancelling the request for funds and informing the townspeople that their car was now also representing one of the world's largest companies in competition.

As the Gran Premio Extraordinario sped onward, so did Juan's upward mobility in the standings. Second fastest on the 300-mile run south to Catamarca, he then moved into a tie for first with a Ford on the 100-mile dash from Catamarca to La Rioja. Traversing nearly 200 miles through swamps and salt marshes, he steadily made up time, and at the stage finish at Guandacol he was fastest by ten minutes. The next stage, from Guandacol to San Juan, was about 200 miles south as the crow flies, but much further and slower on the Extraordinario route. The competitors travelled at a snail's pace between Guandacol and the village of Hueco on a surface of fine sand that buried the cars to the axles. With stranded vehicles impeding his progress, Juan veered off course and cut through the scrub forest. He was soon lost, but fortunately the dust storm raised by another car revealed the route of the race. For nearly two hours, in soaring temperatures that overheated both the car's engine and its occupants, Juan was forced to keep the Chev coupé in first gear. 'A car is not just a piece of metal,' he remarked later. 'It is like a living being, with a heart that beats, which can feel well or ill, depending on how you treat it.' Relief for all concerned finally came at Cuesta de Miranda, where the Chev paused in the middle of a ford through the river and both occupants jumped fully clothed into the welcome coolness of the water. Refreshed from this brief immersion, they pressed on and arrived in San Juan with a fastest stage time that elevated them to first overall in the race. That evening, on the podium in the main square, town dignitaries and race officials presented race leader Juan Manuel Fangio with a cheque for 200 pesos, his first ever prize money.

On the straightforward 100-mile run south from San Juan to Mendoza the Balcarce car remained in the lead, though it came to grief just 25 miles further on. During a brief stop in Mendoza Juan had tried and failed to procure a pair of tinted glasses to improve a vision impairment caused by abruptly alternating bright sunshine and deep shade as he drove flat out between the rows of poplar trees that lined the road. Squinting through the windscreen, Juan maintained a furious pace, though the flickering light played havoc with his concentration. Especially important was the need to judge distances properly, and his inability to do this caused a crash. Just outside the village of Palmira, a sharp S-bend suddenly materialised and Juan reacted too late. The Chev careered into a ditch, spun backwards and thumped hard into a solid bank of unyielding earth. As the dust settled, Juan noticed that their misfortune had been witnessed by a large group of ghoulish spectators, who confessed that the S-bend was notorious for having been the scene of crashes in previous races. Juan filed that information away, and would from then on regard an unusual concentration of bystanders on an unfamiliar road as a sign of the need for increased caution.

Juan and Tieri immediately set about trying to make their sorry state of a Chev roadworthy. A wheel was broken, the rear of the chassis sagged on broken springs and the propeller shaft was twisted. They removed the broken wheel, mounted the spare and regained the road, where they quickly discovered that all the brake lines had been severed, though the absence of stopping power was no real handicap given the sedate pace made necessary by the unsprung chassis drooping on to the rear wheels, one of which fell off about 60 miles down the road. The rearward bias had caused an axle shaft to break, and they could go no further without a replacement. Hitching what seemed to Juan far too slow a ride in a spectator's Model A Ford, they drove to the nearest town, where Juan persuaded a Chevrolet owner to let them borrow an axle shaft from his car. Working feverishly, they removed the part, and with Juan commandeering the controls of the spectator's Ford and thrashing it at racing speeds they tore back to their coupé only to find that the cannibalised axle shaft was too big to fit.

Juan simply refused to give up. Though almost delirious with fatigue, he somehow found the mental fortitude to overcome the deep despair that was certainly warranted by their seemingly hopeless plight. He rushed out on to the road, flagged down the car of a passing competitor and asked him to have the GM team send a spare back from San Luis, the end of the stage, which was only 18 miles away. Many hours later the repaired Balcarce car made it to the finish line in San Luis, where it was classified 44th among the 47 cars that remained from the 123 that had started in Córdoba.

Only two stages remained, and these Juan tackled with renewed conviction, having proved to himself that tenacity and willpower could triumph over mechanical misfortune. However, the problem of exhaustion remained, and this he kept at bay by having the faithful Tieri slap his face hard whenever he noticed Juan nodding off at the wheel. Though the 450-mile stage southward from San Luis to Bahía Blanca was run on relatively straight roads, it also meant that less intense concentration was required, a factor that brought driver fatigue dangerously to the fore. Several times the speeding Chev swerved drunkenly before a slap in the face put it back on course. It continued at unabated speed to Bahía Blanca, where it was rewarded with the seventh fastest stage time. The final stage, which took the competitors 200 miles north to La Plata near Buenos Aires, took the Fangio/Tieri Chev less time than all but three other cars. When their fourth place at La Plata was combined with their other stage finishes they were classified an impressive fifth overall and presented with a 2,000 peso prize. Though the four-week-long Gran Premio Extraordinario was won by the Galvez Ford, with three more Fords following, it was Fangio's fifth-place Chevrolet that captured the public's imagination, especially in Balcarce where Juan was hailed as the hero who had put the town on the map.

In December, Juan entered the Mil Millas Argentinas, a race held on straight roads that put a premium on pure horsepower rather than the extraordinary driving skill, pure perseverance and mechanical ingenuity that had enabled Juan to overcome the odds in the previous race. Nevertheless, the underpowered underdog of a Chevrolet from Balcarce finished a commendable 13th in a race Juan treated as a 1,000-mile tune-up for a forthcoming event that would dwarf anything he or anyone else in South America had undertaken before.

Chapter Three

Mountain Highs and Lows

'It was not stupid to be fearful where we went. Only a very wild man went alone without God through those lonely places. The things that happened to us!'

THE 1940 GRAN PREMIO INTERNACIONAL DEL NORTE was organised by the Automóvil Club Argentino to publicise their ambitious project to link New York City with Buenos Aires via a Pan American Highway; the ACA hoped that its pioneering trial run through Argentina, Bolivia and Peru would start the ball rolling. The first objective for the competitors in the much-publicised race was to travel the nearly 3,000 miles between the capital cities of Argentina and Peru in just seven days, a tremendously ambitious time limit given the immense geographical hurdles that lay between Buenos Aires and Lima. Yet at the Peruvian capital the journey would be only half over, since the Gran Premio Internacional del Norte would require the cars to turn around and retrace the route back to Buenos Aires in only six days.

In all, for those brave – some would say mad – men who chose to enter it, this epic automotive adventure involved a total distance of 5,868 racing miles. The outward-bound route, running in a north-westerly direction from Buenos Aires, included vertical climbs to altitudes of nearly 14,000 feet among the soaring peaks of the Andes, the mighty snow-capped mountain range that runs like a spine down the western side of South America. The first and longest of the thirteen stages covered 847 miles from Buenos Aires to San Miguel de Tucumán, longer than any single stage yet run in cross-country racing, though it was only a warm-up for the mountainous ordeal that followed. From Tucumán, the road conditions deteriorated rapidly while climbing steadily to 11,385 feet at Villazón on the Bolivian border. From 12,200 feet at Pulario the route then plunged over 5,000 feet into a valley at El Puente, only to rise again to nearly 12,000 feet at Polcomayo. Another descent of several thousand feet was followed immediately by a climb to just over 13,000 feet at Potosi, the end of another stage. None of the running was straightforward, nor were the corkscrewing tracks perched precariously on the sides of sheer cliffs thousands of feet above rock-strewn gorges really suitable for cars. Often they were little more than meandering switch-back trails where even Andean llamas – ungainly creatures related to camels and used as pack animals by native Andean tribes – had difficulty remaining sure-footed. Yet the Gran Premio cars, driven by men whose judgement would surely be impaired by altitude sickness, were expected to negotiate the tortuous terrain at racing speeds.

From Potosi to the Bolivian capital La Paz was by far the most daunting section, the majority of its 325 miles complicated by serpentine twists and turns among vertiginous peaks so remote that even the hardiest Inca tribes had not conquered them. Tiny villages of rude stone huts that were few and far between became major destinations. Beyond Potosi an alpine pass would bring the cars up to Tolapalca, at 13,609 feet the highest point of the route. From there it wound for many miles through heights that seldom ventured below 10,000 feet, before arriving at La Paz, itself lying at 12,200 feet, making it the highest capital city in the world. From La Paz, the three remaining stages provided a gradual descent to sea level, which would finally be reached at Lima on the Pacific coast, though it would be a long time coming since the route covered over 1,000 miles of scarcely less arduous motoring. There would be no time to enjoy the spectacular scenery as they sped along the shores of mighty Lake Titicaca, the 3,000-square-mile body of water lying at over 10,000 feet in the Andean plateau between Bolivia and Peru. The penultimate stage, between Arequipa and Nazca, wound treacherously along steep mountainsides that towered above the surf crashing wildly on to the rock-strewn Pacific shore. For those who had made it this far, the last dash to the finish line would be even more hazardous: the roller-coaster ride of sickening switchback curves that comprised the run into Lima would test the mettle of fatigued drivers to the limit.

For Juan, the ultimate challenge presented by the 1940 Gran Premio Internacional del Norte was simply too much to resist, though his resolve to enter it was again hampered by the absence of a suitable car and the money to buy it. To pay off debts incurred in his 1939 races his trusty Chevrolet had been sold, and the help given him previously by GM would not now extend to providing him with a new car. With Argentina beginning to experience an economic slump occasioned by the war that was raging in Europe, there was no chance of getting adequate private contributions from the good citizens of Balcarce either – nor would Juan have had the temerity to ask them. However, some of his more entrepreneurially minded friends came up with a scheme to raise the necessary funds by organising a raffle. The response was disappointing, and with the September start of the race fast approaching, Juan swallowed his pride and went further afield in search of a saviour.

In Mar del Plata, he explained the situation to a wealthy potato broker, Francisco Polio, whose Chevrolet cars and trucks were often serviced in the Fangio garage. Polio, who had also been impressed by Juan's performances in 1939, eagerly agreed to invest in his racing future, then applied his business mind to setting the wheels of the raffle scheme in motion. For 3,500 pesos Polio bought a nearly new 1940 Chev coupé for Juan and told him to bring it back to his Balcarce garage and put it on display as the prize for the winning raffle ticket. Only 1,000 tickets would be sold at ten pesos each, giving quite favourable odds to those who wished to take a chance on the worthy cause of helping the up-and-coming Fangio contest the Gran Premio Internacional del Norte. Polio's idea worked like a charm. He personally sold tickets in Mar del Plata and also arranged for their sale at the Central Potato Market in Buenos Aires. In Balcarce, with the car itself as inspiration, tickets flew out of the garage. Within a few days the full 10,000-peso pay-off was realised and the money handed to Juan, who promptly paid off Polio.

But Juan the grateful recipient had little time to thank his benefactors since the lottery prize needed much work to prepare it for the race in which it was registered as a last-minute entry. Helped by his loyal friends, Juan laboured through the few days and late into the nights that remained before the start. To transform the stock Chev coupé into a raceworthy Turismo de Carretera (TC) car they performed the permitted higher-performance alterations to the engine. Particular attention was paid to adjusting the carburettor, which would struggle for breath in the high altitudes. To prepare it for battle with rock-strewn surfaces the suspension was strengthened, more spring leafs were inserted and the chassis raised to an ungainly height above the beefed-up wheels. The interior was stripped bare, the narrow rear seat replaced by an oversize fuel tank to augment the original tank, and the front bench seat thrown out in favour of two handmade bucket-style seats to hold Juan and his mechanic, Hector Tieri again, in place for the ordeal that lay ahead.

At one minute past midnight on Friday, 27 September 1940, the cars set off at timed intervals from a podium erected in the River Plate football stadium in Buenos Aires, where a huge crowd cheered on their heroes. The starting order, determined by a draw, had the light-green Balcarce Chev starting 26th, which number Juan painted on its doors. Among those starting earlier was the official Ford team entry with the Galvez brothers, Oscar and Juan, whose wins in both the 1939 Gran Premio Argentino and the Gran Premio Extraordinario made them race favourites. But the field also included other champions from Argentina, Bolivia, Chile and Uruguay as well as private entries from unknown hopefuls eager to test themselves against the established stars. There was a team of Plymouth cars, and the offical Chevrolet team was headed by the exuberant youngster Tadeo Taddia. It did not include 29-year-old Juan Manuel Fangio, whom GM considered an ageing dark horse whose moment of glory had surely come and gone.

The cars tore through the dimly lit streets of Buenos Aires and out into the dark void of the great unknown, their headlights probing into the inky blackness in search of faraway Tucumán, the end of the first stage. As the field flashed through the first major town, Córdoba, excited radio commentators informed their thousands of listeners that the Galvez brothers' Ford was in front; there followed two other cars, then came the Fangio-Tieri Chevrolet. Back in Balcarce, most of the population sat wide awake by their radios, though inside 'their car' its busy occupants knew nothing of their meteoric rise. Instead, their attention was riveted on a rapidly falling needle on the petrol gauge that could signify an early end to their journey.

The problem had arisen because Juan had chosen to forgo a planned refuelling stop in Concepción, where the floodlit town square was full of crowds and confusion. His decision not to waste time there might have cost them dearly. Now, with the 50-gallon rear-seat auxiliary tank empty, they were speeding through the dawn on whatever dregs remained of the thirteen gallons in the car's original tank. With his heart in his mouth, Juan kept his foot to the floor and blasted into Tucumán well ahead of schedule having averaged 78mph over the 847-mile distance, a scintillating pace that made him the outright winner of the first stage.

Forever afterwards the town of Tucumán in the Andean foothills of north-western Argentina held a special place in Juan's affections. Yet the pleasure he felt at the time was tempered by caution because of a prevailing notion that the first-stage winner would not win the race. Though he was not by nature superstitious, Juan's wariness was rooted in the realisation of potential trouble ahead, as well as in his solid belief in the dangers of letting success go to his head. 'You must always believe you will become the best, but you must never believe you have done so,' he would say, and even at this early stage of his career he was putting into practice this personal dictum.

The Galvez Ford regained its expected supremacy by winning the next two stages, by which time the cars were well and truly up among the Andes and altitude sickness was rearing its ugly head. With precious little time between driving stints of up to eight hours, the crews of several cars became too ill to continue. Even the short stoppages between stages afforded no respite since these intervals were filled with a frenzy of work to repair damage inflicted by the uncompromising terrain. Those in the team cars with personnel to service them had it easier, but for those in the independent category, as exemplified by the

Balcarce car, the problems were multiplied. Fangio and Tieri struggled with opposite extremes, trying to proceed with maximum haste while heeding doctors' – some of whom were competing – orders: take things calmly and unhurriedly, and breathe deeply and slowly to extract as much oxygen as possible from the rarified air. Many years later most competitors racing in this environment carried oxygen tanks with them, but in 1940 they were left to their own devices. To combat fatigue, altitude sickness and whatever other ailments might come their way, Juan and his companion had a secret weapon in the form of a possibly medicinal, certainly smelly, concoction. Throughout the race they chewed a heady salad of pungent cloves of garlic spiced with liberal quantities of narcotic coca leaves that were used as a stimulant by South American Indian tribes.

It was the Fangio-Tieri duo that conquered the giddy heights of the first Bolivian stage, averaging just over 43mph for the 325-mile distance. But the formal recognition of their achievement resulted in a disastrous setback. In the offical box at the finish at La Paz stood the Bolivian president, General Penaranda, whose duty it was personally to present a laurel crown to the winner. For Juan, it proved to be a crown of thorns.

The rules allowed just ten minutes for the crews to get from the arrival checkpoint to the parc fermé, the closed parking area where the cars were impounded until the fifth stage began. At the checkpoint, leaving his mechanic in charge of the Chevrolet, Juan leapt out and ran off to the official presentation. It only took a few minutes, but Tieri became nervous about the delay and took it upon himself to drive the car to the parc fermé. However, Hector was unfamiliar with the Bolivian custom of driving on the right side of the road (a situation that was not yet in effect in Argentina) and promptly crashed head-on into a private car. The Balcarce Chev came out of this exchange much the worse for wear, its front axle twisted, its steering askew and the chassis bent badly out of shape; Tieri had trouble manoeuvring the crippled car even the short distance to the parc fermé. With Juan fighting off his considerable agitation and Hector his acute embarrassment, and both of them panting with exhaustion, they frantically set about some makeshift repairs in the all too brief hour that remained before the start of the next stage. Sweating profusely, Juan attacked the salvage operation with his customary steely determination and swiftly applied his improvisational skills, and with just seconds to spare they made it to the start of what soon became an agonising ordeal.

In the deeply rutted roads the wheels danced about to a wobbly tune that was dangerously out of harmony with that required to make fast progress. Juan's sweat ran cold, his efforts to control the unruly car punctuated by muttered insults directed towards his guilt-ridden passenger. Many desperate hours and 365 hard-earned miles later they struggled into Arequipa, where they continued the damage repair exercise. Once they were reunited in a common cause the atmosphere between them became less tense, and Tieri's mishap was soon shoved into the background.

Halfway through the next stage, from Arequipa to Nazca in Peru, Juan felt a vibration emanating from the front of the car, then spotted a growing pool of steaming water beneath his feet. A glance at the red-lined temperature gauge confirmed his worst fears: the engine was overheating. He stopped, and the source of the problem was quickly found: the car's constant juddering had dislodged the radiator from its mounting brackets and a fan blade had broken off and pierced the radiator. While Tieri balanced the fan by breaking off the opposite blade, Juan stuffed pieces of torn rag into the gaping hole in the radiator. They resumed the chase, though at a greatly reduced pace since their spares did not include reserves of water to top up the now dangerously low supply in the cooling system. At this point, high in an arid and desolate mountain plateau, water was hard to come by. Finally, with the temperature needle soaring off the top of the gauge, they came upon a remote Indian settlement where a group of curious onlookers surrounded the steaming Chevrolet. The locals did not speak Spanish, so Juan made their requirements known by making drinking motions with his hands. In response to his gesticulations, two glasses of the precious liquid were offered to the dishevelled and obviously very thirsty tourists. Juan cleared up the misunderstanding by emptying the glasses into the radiator.

They continued the race, but even their slower speed failed to prevent the radiator from boiling away all its coolant again, and there was no choice but to stop for a second time. Though they were only about 60 miles away from the end of the stage at Nazca on the Peruvian coast they feared their isolated position must surely be the end of the line. As they stood disconsolately kicking the dust beside their stranded vehicle, Juan spotted what he at first thought might be a mirage conjured up in the shimmering heat haze rising from the parched landscape. On closer inspection, however, it proved to be an abandoned road works depot where, to their great joy, they discovered a large water cistern and an earthen jug lying beneath its slowly dripping spout. Whooping with delight, they quickly quenched their car's thirst, then their own, and gingerly resumed the journey to Nazca.

There, working all night, they repaired the radiator with lead reduced to a molten state by heat from a burning candle. They installed a new battery and reconnected dynamo cables that had been cut by the flying fan blade. By dawn, everything was relatively shipshape save the tyres, which were badly worn, but no new ones could be found. By the time they got to Lima, 350 miles later, the rubber casing on the tyres had worn through to the fabric, but at the end of this seventh stage they were credited with the tenth fastest time. Moreover, their perseverance had paid off in the best possible way in a race that had become a survival contest during which many competitors had fared even worse than the Balcarce car. Despite their assorted trials and tribulations, after nearly 50 hours of desperate motoring from Buenos Aires to Lima the Fangio-Tieri partnership was classified first overall at the halfway point of the Gran Premio Internacional del Norte.

After a 24-hour halt in Lima, where Juan and Tieri worked flat out at a Chevrolet dealership to refettle their car, the last half of the race commenced. Starting again at midnight, the cars accelerated away, none at more furious a pace than Oscar Galvez, who was determined to restore the balance of power in favour of Ford and take the lead from the Chev driven by the upstart Fangio. For four hours they raced through the Peruvian night separated by scant seconds at each checkpoint. Just before five o'clock in the morning, Juan was waved to a halt by a driver standing in the middle of the road. Juan recognised him as Julio Perez, a member of the Chevrolet team, and saw that he was in a state of considerable agitation. Perez was excitedly pointing a spotlight down into the dark void beyond the roadside precipice where they stood. There, at the bottom of a ravine, beyond his own crashed Chev which dangled precariously on a stony outcrop, lay the wreckage of the Galvez Ford.

Other drivers stopped, one of them forgetting to put on the handbrake; his car rolled backwards and smashed into a rockface. The Galvez brothers, both of whom had been thrown out of the tumbling Ford, yelled for help. While Juan Galvez had miraculously escaped without serious injury, Oscar lay in a heap, bloodied from a deep head wound and suffering great pain from a broken shoulder. Their concerned rivals made the unfortunate brothers as comfortable as they could before resuming the race, leaving them in the care of a group of Indian spectators. Had not Perez also come to grief on the same corner, the Galvez brothers might not have been found for some time. Perez himself was destined to die a few months later in the Mil Millas.

As dawn rose over the Andean peaks, those that remained in the Gran Premio Internacional del Norte quickly distanced themselves from the accident scene, none faster than the number 26 entry from Balcarce. Juan pressed on harder than ever, keeping his foot to the floor to maintain an astonishing average speed of 52mph that, after 13 hours, 20 minutes and 41.2 seconds, made him the winner of that 700-mile stage from Lima to Arequipa. Juan's stage prize, a solid silver trophy in the shape of a racing car, was added to a collection that grew as the race went on. Despite having an overall lead of nearly 90 minutes by the end of the ninth stage, he refused to back off and play it safe. He kept his competitive fires stoked by overtaking other cars, even those that were far behind him in the standings. He was fastest again on the tenth stage, from La Paz to Potosi, 325 miles that took him over seven hours, extending his aggregate race advantage over the next best car, a Ford driven by Daniel Musso, to an hour and 40 minutes. Also making the running for Ford was the veteran driver Domingo Marimón, whose son Onofre would later become a Fangio protégé and would unfortunately lose his life at the 1954 German Grand Prix, which Juan won. But in 1940, between Potosi and Villazón, Domingo Marimón became embroiled with Juan in a furious fight for the eleventh-stage honours. They traded positions throughout the 310 miles, with Marimón eventually declared the victor.

Though he was still in the overall lead by a substantial margin, Juan continued to attack what remained of the course with considerable aggression, motivated by the need to build a sufficient time interval to allow for any mechanical misfortune that might come his way over the long and winding road back to Buenos Aires. Sure enough, he had to cash in on this insurance policy on the twelfth stage, between La Quiaca and Tucumán. Due to either over-confidence or inattention, Juan's powersliding Chev ran wide on a curve and hit a rock; the impact bent the right rear wheel, twisted the propeller shaft and caused the universal joint to seize. The car refused to budge until the seized joint cooled down. Frequent applications of grease helped free it up, but progress was exasperatingly slow on the journey to the next checkpoint, at Jujuy. There, in the 30 minutes available for servicing, a new differential was hastily installed and the carburettor adjusted for lower altitudes. The run into Tucumán was completed without incident, and Juan arrived there for the overnight stop with his race lead comfortably intact.

Now that he was back in Argentina, the importance of his position was brought home. In Tucumán's main square he was mobbed by crowds of jubilant well-wishers who clamoured for the autograph of the gallant conquistador from Balcarce. 'It was the first time I heard my name being shouted by people,' Juan reflected. 'I could hardly believe it was my name on everyone's lips. I thought how marvellous it would be if my family could hear this.' Though a touch embarrassed by his first real exposure to demonstrations of unrestrained adulation – his uncertainty about being worthy of it was fortified by an apprehension that the celebrations might be premature; after all, the finish line in Buenos Aires was 845 miles away and there was every chance he might still let his countrymen down – Juan accepted the accolades with the combination of good grace and humility for which he would later be renowned.

He approached the rest of the race with more circumspection. From the midnight start at Tucumán, Juan slotted in behind another car and used its headlights as a beacon to point the way. At dawn they arrived in Rosario, where an hour was allotted for the cars to cross the city and where the highly partisan Fangio faction went into high gear. Shouts of 'Fangio, Fangio, Fangio!' echoed around the streets. The crowd pursued him, clutched at him, and showered him and his co-driver with bouquets of flowers and offerings of food, a freshly grilled chicken among them. From Rosario, Juan carefully paced himself over the remaining 150 miles to Buenos Aires, though he still averaged the 71.5mph that gave him the fifth fastest time in the thirteenth and final leg of the race. The four cars that beat him were Fords, and in all 32 cars crossed the finish line. When the final results were tabulated, the winner, averaging 53.6mph for the 109 hours, 36 minutes and 16.8 seconds it took him to complete the Gran Premio Internacional del Norte, was Juan Manuel Fangio.

For his victory, Juan received a total of 43,400 pesos (20,000 for winning, 3,400 for stage wins and placings and 20,000 in bonuses from sponsors and advertisers). He also received an impressive number of trophies, though the one he treasured most he paid for himself. The battle-scarred, grime-covered number 26 Chevrolet coupé with 5,868 hard-earned miles on the clock belonged to the holders of the winning raffle ticket, a group of twenty mechanics who worked in the Mar del Plata Chevrolet dealership where the car originated. Juan paid the mechanics 3,500 pesos for the car and drove it proudly home to Balcarce.

Word of the champion's impending return had preceded him. Along the road, at intersections and farm entrances, groups of people gathered to cheer and wave at the passing hero. By the time it arrived on the outskirts of Balcarce, the Chev's raucous exhaust note was being drowned out by the hullabaloo. Crowds lined both sides of what was now a victory parade. The jostling throng surged around the car, forcing Juan to slow down to the point where the engine began to boil over. The delighted mob hauled El Chueco out of the car, pumped his hand, thumped his back and kissed his face. No politician or dignitary had ever received such a welcome, but then no one had ever brought such great honour to Balcarce. No longer was it just a remote potato town somewhere in the pampas. It was the home of El Chueco, the boy from Balcarce.

To officially confirm this fact, Juan was ushered up on to a podium erected in the town square, around which it seemed the entire population of 40,000 people had gathered. There on the podium, his eyes shining and his face beaming with pride, stood Loreto Fangio, dressed in his best, and only, Sunday suit. Beside him stood the mayor, who ceremoniously unfurled a magnificently decorated scroll and held it up for all to see. This, the mayor announced, is the Balcarce roll of honour, and here, he pointed out, is the most important name on it: Juan Manuel Fangio. The mayor's short speech was met with thunderous approval, not least from the proud Fangio family.

'As a person and a brother, there was no one to touch Juan,' said Juan's brother Toto. 'It was always him putting his shoulder to the wheel for the sake of the family. He won for all of us.'

To his ecstatic family and audience it seemed the bashful boy from Balcarce was a bit bewildered and perhaps not fully appreciative of the magnitude of the occasion. Or perhaps Juan's faint smiles and subdued expressions of thanks were simply in keeping with his down-to-earth character. In truth, Juan was completely worn out, mentally and physically, after driving himself so hard for so long. He lost fifteen and a half pounds in weight during the race and only later did he reveal the degree of emotional stress he had suffered. At one point in the Andes his mind had begun to wander dangerously. A few

45

feet, sometimes mere inches, had separated his car's wheels from the edge of a chasm that fell untold thousands of feet into the dark depths below. Juan had nearly succumbed to a terrible temptation to venture closer and closer to the edge, to launch himself into that fearful void, to finish everything.

Juan always maintained that the 1940 Gran Premio Internacional del Norte win was the most satisfying of the 78 major race victories he scored. It was his first big win, and it was achieved against all the odds, over very strong opposition in the most difficult circumstances imaginable. Yet at the time he wondered if it might have been just a one-off result, a fluke. To prove it wasn't, to continue his momentum, he felt he had to win again. 'Once you have won, you feel an obligation to prove yourself by continuing to win,' he said. 'But this is easier said than done.'

Preparations were made to contest the traditional end-of-season race, the Argentine Mil Millas, but in Juan's estimation they were inadequate and the Fangio-Tieri Chev finished only eighth. Despite a growing tension between them in the Gran Premio, Juan had given Hector Tieri a generous share of the prize money. Though he'd done all the driving and most of the mechanical repairs, he felt he owed Tieri a ride in the 1,000-mile event, but he had thought the car was capable of winning and insisted that the reason it didn't was a caruburettor fault that was Tieri's responsibility. Tieri argued the reverse, and before long a continuation of their relationship became untenable. Tieri left his job at the Fangio garage and went away to open up his own shop in another town.

Meanwhile, El Chueco was the toast of his town, indeed the whole country. With his Gran Premio Internacional del Norte win and his eighth place in the Mil Millas he was officially declared the 1940 Road Racing Champion of Argentina. As such, he was one of the first to be invited to compete in the 1941 Gran Premio Presidente Getulio Vargas, a 2,423-mile race run over seven stages in Brazil. To replace the departed Tieri, Juan made what seemed a rather surprising choice, a Basque immigrant named Antonio Elizade who was not a mechanic; he worked in a Balcarce service station washing cars. Juan, always a shrewd judge of character, saw in Elizade an inner strength that would enable him to remain cool under fire; he also sensed in the Spaniard an ability to learn quickly and to improvise on the spot. In their first runs together, Elizade also proved to be conscientious and reliable, and he had a photographic memory that would be invaluable on the open road, starting with the Brazilian event. The Fangio-Elizade Chev coupé actually got lost during one stage of the Gran Premio Presidente Getulio Vargas, but managed to finish first in three stages and second in four others. Juan's old adversary, the now-recovered Oscar Galvez, also brought glory to Argentina by winning three of the seven stages, but Juan was declared the overall winner of the event that looped in a north-easterly direction between the cities of Rio de Janeiro and São Paulo. His prize money proved to be a godsend for Juan, who still did not have any support from General Motors; he had spent nearly 1,000 pesos, all the cash he had, on a reconnaissance mission before the race began. With his winnings, Juan was able to ship his car back to Buenos Aires on an ocean steamer.

Five months later, in December 1941, Juan won the Mil Millas for the first time (on his third attempt) and was again declared his nation's road racing champion.

Juan's 1942 season began with the Gran Premio del Sur, a new event intended to bring publicity to southern regions as the Gran Premio Internacional del Norte had done for the north. Run in ten stages, it started in Buenos Aires and went south through the pampas deep into Patagonia, close to Tierra del

Fuego at the southern extremity of the continent. After a brief excursion into Chilean territory, the route returned north again and finished at Bahía Blanca on the Atlantic coast. Juan only managed a tenth-place finish in the Gran Premio del Sur, though he at least finished, an achievement he considered as satisfying as an overall win.

After winning the second stage he remained among the frontrunners until the fourth stage, a rock-strewn stretch of road that peppered the underside of the Chev with flying stones. The constant barrage shattered the shackles that held the springs in place. To prevent further damage, Juan and Elizade stopped and covered the bottom of the car with heavy felt sacking, then set off again into the face of what was now a howling force ten gale. Sweeping unhindered across the flat pampas, the violent windstorm pushed the cars off course, and several of them rolled over on to their sides. A flying rock smashed a hole in the Chev's windscreen, filling the eyes of the occupants with dust and grit. Throwing caution to the wind, blinking tearfully and spitting out sand, Juan speared onward into the teeth of the maelstrom. The cracks around the hole widened until the entire left side of the windscreen began flapping in the wind. Whipping off his shoes and socks, the resourceful Elizade tied his hosiery to what remained of the panel of glass and fixed it to the spotlight on the side of the car. Thus equipped, the Balcarce car made it to the finish of the stage, albeit two and a half hours behind the winner.

They began the next stage with unimpaired vision, having replaced the shattered windscreen, but just six miles after the start Juan saw the needle on the oil pressure gauge sag alarmingly. A quick inspection revealed that the plug in the sump had come partly undone and almost all the oil had trickled out. They screwed the plug back into place and continued at a slower pace, but the damage – a seized big-end bearing and a broken connecting rod that smashed a hole through the engine block – was done. In the next town, Juan found a garage where, with the help of a group of Fangio fans, he removed the damaged motor. His travelling stock of spare parts included a rod, piston and piston rings, but there remained the considerable problem of patching the gaping hole in the block. The solution, an aluminium cooking pot, was acquired at a nearby hardware store; a section of the pot was cut out, hammered into the required shape and soldered into place. The engine was put back in and the repairs worked well enough to bring the car to the end of the stage before a deadline that was met by just thirteen other cars.

Though Juan was now second last overall, he tore into the next stage with such a vengeance that he made it to the first checkpoint in the fastest time. However, his exertions proved to be more than the mended motor could bear, and on the next section, in the middle of nowhere, it announced its objections in no uncertain terms by emitting an almighty bang. The repair job still held, but another over-stressed and under-lubricated con-rod had exploded through the side of the block.

Juan's usual fierce determination to try to continue come what may was in this case reinforced by a wish to finish a race with an engine which for the first time had been prepared by Ruben Renato Fangio, his younger brother who was now a stalwart in their Balcarce garage. It wasn't Toto's fault that the oil had been lost, nor was Juan about to abandon his brother's handiwork. He flagged down a passing truck driven by a farmer, and they attached the crippled coupé to the truck with a length of rope. With Elizade steering the car and Fangio behind the wheel of the commandeered farmer's truck, they set off in search of the stage finish. Before long, flying stones had once again smashed the Chev's windscreen to smithereens, and poor Elizade, hanging on to the wheel for dear life, disappeared in clouds of dust and debris. Sixty miles later they arrived at the finish line, where their reward took the form of not being disqualified. Though the rules prohibited towing, the growing absence of competitors in what was obviously a car-breaking event (only twelve remained) forced the organisers to do all they could to keep the Balcarce entry in the running. For that to happen, major engine repairs were required, which this time were accomplished in a Chevrolet dealer's garage. Juan then decided to go for broke, and he pushed the rebuilt engine as hard as it was capable of going. Indeed, it went all the way, and fast enough for him to win the last stage of the Gran Premio del Sur, in which he was classified tenth overall.

Juan's next chance to resume his winning ways came in the spring of 1942, in the Gran Premio Circuito Mar y Sierras, an almost local race in comparison to the previous events that had probed such geographical extremes. The 'sea' and 'mountain' race took place in the appropriate terrain, ranging from Argentina's Atlantic coast to the Andean foothills and back. Starting and finishing in Mar del Plata, the route also passed through Balcarce, where Juan was particularly keen to do well. Perhaps this was why he took even more risks than was his custom.

In the draw for starting positions at Mar del Plata he was given the number 16. At that time of year, in the month of April, the climate tended towards early-morning fog from the ocean, while the absence of a breeze meant there was also day-long dust on the roads. Added to this dangerous mix was the darkness occasioned by the starting time of six a.m. Moments after his start, Juan found himself driving through a visually impenetrable combination of darkness, swirling fog and dust raised by previous cars. Keeping his foot to the floor, he switched off his headlights and began to navigate by focusing on a halo of light made by a car in front. Then, by flashing his headlights he announced the need for the car to move over and let him by. In this way he made rapid, if perilous, progress through the ranks, which were being rapidly depleted by the crashes of other, less sure-sighted (or misguided) drivers.

Juan's growing suspicions that he was being foolhardy in the extreme were confirmed when he homed in on yet another beacon of light with nearly disastrous consequences. Once again he flashed his lights to inform the driver of his intentions, then pulled out of the frontrunning car's slipstream. At the last second, Juan spotted the frightening fact that the other car was at that moment in the middle of a narrow bridge bordered by unforgiving iron and cement parapets. Only an instant stood between the Balcarce car and catastrophe. Juan just managed to avoid it by slamming on the brakes with terrific force. His split-second reaction time prevented an almost certain calamity that had arisen from his imprudence. It was a very close shave, one of the closest of his career. It was also a lesson learnt. The actions of his right foot, Juan now fully understood, must always be governed by his head.

Of course, no small amount of good luck had also been involved, and more of it would soon come his way in the form of the misfortune that befell the race-leading car. Following his narrow escape, Juan had managed to get into an overall lead which he held for several stages. Suddenly, the speeding Chev's steering went askew and Juan skidded to a halt. One of the main leafs of a spring had broken, causing the chassis to distort. As they crawled crabwise through the rest of the stage, Juan's lead was steadily eroded; by the finish line they were three minutes behind the new leader. Working hand in hand with Elizade, Juan wrenched the rear bumper off their coupé. By banging, levering and bending it they fashioned it into the approximate shape required and used it to replace the broken leaf. Their handiwork proved entirely adequate for what remained of the race. Meanwhile, the race leader had suffered a gearbox failure he was unable to repair, so Juan Manuel Fangio, master mechanic and champion driver, won the Circuito Mar y Sierras, whereupon his racing adventures came to an abrupt halt.

Chapter Four

The Businessman Racing Driver

'*When driving a racing car, I became another person. I forgot everything. I was in a different world, with only the car and the race.*'

THE FALLOUT FROM World War Two had now arrived in Argentina, where strict austerity measures were introduced. Fuel was rationed, as was rubber, and the increasing scarcity of the latter commodity meant that tyres were hard to come by. Eventually, none were available for the comparatively frivolous pursuit of racing; no tyres were being imported either, so before long there were none for new cars or trucks, barring special circumstances – a situation that brought Juan's forte as a businessman even more to the fore.

By now the Fangio garage had become a mecca for motorsport fans and the repair depot of choice for more and more customers. The famously indomitable Balcarce coupé was on display, and Juan's original intention to go racing to publicise his business had paid off handsomely. Yet the garage's biggest attraction was the presence of the illustrious driver himself, who despite his heroic stature was invariably charming and always willing to chat to visitors, even when he was flat on his back working beneath a customer's vehicle. He regaled his awestruck audience with tales of his harrowing driving experiences in far-flung outposts, though he stopped well short of revealing more intimate details about some of his off-track escapades.

His passion for racing might have been an open book, but Juan was much less forthcoming about his consuming interest in the opposite sex. Despite his invariable discretion about the subject, the permanent twinkle in his eye hinted at the well-developed romantic side to his life. His first carnal experiences came during nocturnal visits with his teenage friends to 'ranchos' operated by ladies of the night on the outskirts of Balcarce. As a youth he also enjoyed occasional trysts with non-professional girls, and was one night caught *in flagrante* in the warm embrace of a maid whose employers returned unexpectedly. By the time he began racing he was well versed in the ways of seduction, a process that became easier, even unnecessary, as admiring women sought to consort with the macho racing driver.

One unwelcome souvenir he brought back from his successful conquest of the Gran Premio Internacional del Norte came from a dalliance in a dance hall with a girl whose infectious charms proved to be double-barrelled. As a result of their coupling, accomplished on a wooden bench in a dark corner of the dance hall, Juan became infected with a nasty social disease that took several weeks of agonising treatment to cure. Another, much more rewarding liaison took the form of a birthday present. A stage victory in the 1941 Gran Premio Presidente Getulio Vargas coincided with Juan's 24 June birthday. At the finish line his well-wishers included a ravishing Brazilian beauty who kissed him passionately on the lips. That evening, while he was enjoying a celebration dinner with friends, she sent the 30-year-old a message requesting his company at her home. Juan immediately obliged, and their assignation continued well into the dawn of the following morning, when he had to force himself from her bed to stagger to his Chev for the start of the next stage – which he also won.

But now, with no racing in the foreseeable future, Juan applied his energies to finding ways to help his business survive the war. He did this by astutely taking advantage of the shortage of fuel and tyres, a situation that had also led to an abundance of vehicles for sale. Only those truck owners who could get fuel coupons could keep their trucks and trailers on the road, and coupons were only obtainable for enterprises the government considered vital. As a result, those hauliers who couldn't get fuel were forced to sell their vehicles at cut-rate prices. The shortage of tyres meant they were often available for the cost of the tyres alone, and Juan began to buy trucks and trailers.

He had no problem financing these ventures. His business had by this time accumulated a bank balance of some 20,000 pesos, and it also benefited from the largesse of the potato growers who continued to prosper in the war years and needed both tyres and trucks. The growers, who got only a low rate of interest from the Argentine banks, began to invest in the operation run by one of the country's most famous citizens. In addition to his racing fame his reputation as an honest businessman stood Juan in good stead, and either cash or credit was readily available over the few years that remained of World War Two. During that time Juan roamed far and wide around Argentina, picking up bargain vehicles and arranging to have them delivered back to his partners in Balcarce. On his solitary excursions he drove hard, keeping himself in racing trim in the hope that competition would soon resume, and that he wouldn't be past his prime when it did.

When the global conflict finally ended he found another way to capitalise on its aftermath. By late 1945 surplus military vehicles were being sold off for next to nothing. There was a ready market for them in Argentina, where the economy quickly recovered with the help of exports of grain and beef to war-ravaged Europe. The farmers and ranchers needed more vehicles, so Juan began to supply them. With two new partners, one of them the owner of a Studebaker agency in Balcarce, he began to import war-surplus Studebaker and GMC trucks from North America. Juan's first sale was to a coal haulier who had a contract to transport coal from a mine in the far south of the country, near the Chilean border. To persuade the at first sceptical customer that a four-wheel-drive war-surplus truck would make an ideal coal-hauling vehicle, Juan offered to demonstrate its capabilities. At the Balcarce garage, he fitted sturdy wooden racks on the truck's chassis. Overnight, accompanied by an employee of the coalman, Juan drove to the mine, loaded up the truck and returned it fully laden twelve hours later. Suitably impressed, the coalman bought five trucks from Juan.

On 24 February 1946, Argentina elected a new president, General Juan Domingo Perón, whose government embarked on an ambitious campaign to promote the country to the rest of the world. While his glamorous wife, Maria Eva Duarte de Perón, popularly known as Evita, toured the capitals of Europe, the president, a keen motorsport enthusiast, encouraged a movement to put Argentina into the limelight as a racing nation. The slogan 'Perón Supports Sport' was applied to the effort to find ways for the country's relatively primitive and insular forms of motorsport to become more worldly. With government financial assistance, the Automóvil Club Argentino organised for 1947 a series of races for Grand Prix cars, the sophisticated, purpose-built single-seater machines that had competed in Europe prior to the war.

Having begun in France early in the twentieth century, Grand Prix ('Big Prize') racing had evolved into what was regarded as the highest expression of automotive competition. With cars and drivers mainly from France, Italy and Germany, the pinnacle of motorsport also became a battleground for national prestige. In the late 1930s it was successfully used for propaganda purposes by Adolf Hitler, whose Nazi government funded the Auto Union and Mercedes-Benz teams. The German cars, though their drivers came from several countries, tore through the opposition like a blitzkrieg right up until war was declared. Soon after the end of hostilities in Europe, in May 1945, the surviving machinery was dusted off and racing resumed, with Alfa Romeo and Maserati cars from Italy leading the way.

For the Argentine series, held in February and March 1947, the invited Europeans were led by the Italian stars Achille Varzi and Luigi Villoresi. To fill out the field among the famous drivers in their exotic imported machinery, examples of which would also be raced by favoured South American drivers, the ACA included a category for Argentine-built Mecánica Nacional cars.

Juan, who had been concentrating on his business, found out about this opportunity only a few days before the first race. From Bahía Blanca, where he was staying at the Grand Hotel, he placed an urgent telephone call to the garage in Balcarce and asked his brother Toto if there was enough time to cobble up a car for him to race. The basis of the car he had in mind was a venerable Ford Model T chassis, powered by a hybrid Chev engine that sat among the bits and pieces at the back of the garage. Juan suggested to Toto that the installation of a four-litre war-surplus truck motor would provide a more suitable means of racing power. Toto eagerly agreed and presided over an enthusiastic workforce that began the laborious task of stuffing the oversize engine into the Ford chassis. The rather ungainly result, with the truck engine protruding into the cockpit and extending beneath the chassis, was painted black and christened 'Negrita'. It eventually became even more of a mongrel assemblage when an overheating problem was solved by the addition of an extra radiator in front of the engine and another in the tail of the chassis. A single large radiator would have done the job properly, but there was no money for it, nor was there enough time to get the car ready for the first race.

Negrita's delayed debut, in the second race at the Retiro circuit in Buenos Aires, was only made possible when another entry failed to show up. Juan himself was not particularly race-ready, having worked non-stop on his car for 48 hours. The Fangio-Negrita combination managed third places in the two preliminary heats, from which only the winners were allowed to compete in the main event with the Grand Prix cars. Unfortunately, the exhausted Negrita driver was unable to take advantage of his enforced role as a spectator and study the driving techniques of the great Varzi and Villoresi. At the start of their race he lay down on the grass beside the track and fell into a deep sleep.

Face was saved in the next and last race of the series (the third race was cancelled because of poor weather), at the Parque Independencia circuit in Rosario. There, Juan manhandled Negrita to victory in a heat and thus booked a place in the final, which Varzi's Alfa Romeo won, ahead of Villoresi's Maserati and the Alfa Romeos driven by Oscar Galvez, Chico Landi (a Brazilian) and Juan Galvez. The latter three, well connected with the ACA establishment and thus given prime examples of the superior European machinery, acquitted themselves admirably, yet those whose sentiments lay with the underdog were more impressed by the Fangio-Negrita combination that finished in sixth place. Juan was again hailed as a hero, and his ugly duckling of a car became a symbol of Argentinian know-how.

When a car dealer in Rosario wanted to exhibit Negrita in his showroom, Juan decided that the only good-looking cars are the ones that win.

Negrita was not put on show because Juan needed it for forthcoming races. In the first of these Negrita failed to finish, and while it then managed to transport him to a third place in a subsequent race, his car's shortcomings sent Juan on a search for a less cumbersome, more highly evolved machine. He found it in Buenos Aires, a sleek Volpi single-seater with an American-built Rickenbacker engine. With the help of his first major sponsor, Suixtil, a men's clothing manufacturer, Juan bought the Volpi. After two races he decided to add more power and replaced the Rickenbacker with a modified Chevrolet motor. In four races that summer, though the Volpi-Chev retired twice with mechanical problems, it won convincingly on two occasions.

The resumption of long-distance road racing in South America in the autumn of 1947 meant Juan had to find a suitable coupé in which to defend his championships of 1940 and 1941, and especially to maintain his reputation as the winner of the last previous race of this type, the Mar y Sierras in 1942. Two weeks before the first race of the new series, the Doble Sierra de la Ventana, he acquired a 1939 Chev coupé and spent ten days preparing it for the competition that would take place on roads not far from Balcarce. During the last few days before the race, Juan drove the Chev around the roughest section of the route at least ten times, even at night. His groundwork on the severely rutted roads paid off to the maximum degree. Bounding over the undulations like a skipping stone, Juan left everyone in his dusty wake, including his old rival Oscar Galvez, whom he overtook in a shower of dirt.

His less satisfactory showing in the next event, a new version of the Gran Premio Internacional del Norte, made it seem as if either his eight-year-old Chev or his 36-year-old self was not up to the task of tackling marathon races. While this time confined to Argentina and Chile, and about half the length of the original race, the route of the 1947 Gran Premio Internacional de Carreteras included Andean stages at heights close to 16,000 feet. Though his rivalry with other competitors was as keen as ever, Juan remained generous when it came to helping them out, especially those he liked, but his generosity sometimes cost him. For the race Juan loaned his friend and rival Domingo 'Toscanito' Marimón a special camshaft. During the first stage, from Buenos Aires to Santiago in Chile, Juan and Oscar Galvez were fighting for the lead in the middle of the night when to their surprise the headlights of another vehicle suddenly appeared in their mirrors. As it roared by, Juan recognised the car as the one in which his camshaft had been installed. Marimón won the stage by averaging 70mph for just over twelve hours. Galvez finished seven minutes behind him, leaving the camshaft donor in third, a further eight minutes in arrears.

Marimón crashed and retired from the race on the second stage, which Juan won. Accompanied for the first time by his good friend Daniel Urrutia (Elizade had moved away from Balcarce to start his own business), Juan was the overall leader by the end of the fourth stage, even though their Chev was relatively underpowered. This became more of a disadvantage as the route climbed ever higher into thinner air. To compensate, Juan began to straighten out the bends on the little more than a llama track that served as the road. On one of these shortcuts the Chev buried itself in soft sand and no amount of furious wheel-spinning would budge it. There, in below-freezing temperatures at 13,000 feet, Juan kept warm by trying to jack the marooned car back on to a firm footing while Urrutia ran off in search of rescue. Two hours later, with the help of a truck driver Urrutia had found, they managed to manoeuvre the Chev back on to the road, but all hope of a victory had been lost. Though they still managed to finish tenth on that stage, sixth overall in the Gran Premio Internacional de Carreteras (which was won by Oscar Galvez) was quite a comedown for Juan. In the annual season-ending Argentine Mil Millas he fared even worse, the Chev failing to go the distance.

Juan had scored barely enough points to finish third in the 1947 Argentine Road Racing Championship. People began to whisper that the war had robbed him of his best years at the wheel.

Chapter Five

Meetings with Remarkable Men

'There they were, the giants from Europe we had all heard about. It was their game, and now we had a real chance to play in it.'

JUAN'S FIRST CHANCE to redeem himself and prove any doubters wrong came early in 1948 in the second edition of the Argentine international series, which the ACA was now calling La Temporada ('The Season'). This year the entry was confined to thoroughbred Grand Prix cars only, two of which the ACA would make available to Argentine drivers to test themselves properly against the European establishment. The man in charge of selecting the lucky drivers was the head of the ACA's motorsport committee, Francisco Alberto 'Pancho' Borgonovo, who was besieged with requests from many hopefuls. Interviewing the eager aspirants one by one, Borgonovo soon found that they had a common denominator: nearly every driver asked him for an appearance fee. After all, they said, the imported foreign drivers were paid handsomely to perform, so why shouldn't the local heroes get similar treatment? The ACA official's conversation with the driver Fangio from Balcarce was different. Borgonovo was impressed by his quiet and sincere manner, and was particularly pleased by his only financial query: Juan wanted to know how much he would have to pay the ACA to hire a Grand Prix car.

The line-up for the Temporada opener in January included the Argentinians Oscar Galvez in an Alfa Romeo and Juan Manuel Fangio in a Maserati. Among their rivals were the returning Italian stars Varzi and Villoresi, who were joined by their esteemed countryman Giuseppe Farina and the great Frenchman Jean Pierre Wimille, whom many considered to be the best driver in the world.

The Premio Ciudad de Buenos Aires took place on the Circuito de Palermo, a course comprising twisting streets in the city's fashionable residential district. In qualifying for the first heat, Villoresi's Maserati set the fastest time ahead of Wimille's Alfa Romeo and Fangio's Maserati. Though others were greatly impressed that in his debut in a Grand Prix car Juan was at the front of the starting grid with the superstars, he was less than impressed with his supercharged 1500cc Maserati 4CL, a well-used pre-war model. His suspicions about its shortcomings seemed to be confirmed in practice when the gear lever came off in his hand. Still, given that he was accustomed to manhandling beefed-up, home-built vehicles, perhaps he was treating this comparatively delicate machine too roughly. Indeed, Juan noticed, the fluid and smooth way the Europeans handled their cars made his own style look brutal and clumsy. Nonetheless, the Maserati held together long enough and he drove it hard enough to finish fourth, after a pit stop, in the opening heat, which was won by Villoresi over Varzi.

Juan was surprised when the great Achille Varzi generously took time out to give him some tips about driving Grand Prix cars. As Juan had already discovered, everything happened very quickly in the car, including the sudden surge of power that came when the supercharger kicked in. Varzi told Juan to keep a close watch on the instrument panel, especially on the rev counter, which must not drop below 3,500rpm or the engine's sparkplugs might foul up, and it was important to keep changing gears to maintain optimum engine revs. Though Juan hung on to the esteemed Varzi's every word, his unfamiliarity with the Maserati later caught him out. In the second heat, he circulated for only four laps before his failure to heed the rev counter warning caused the Maserati's plugs to stop sparking.

Though he had trouble resisting the urge to get his hands dirty and work on the car with the Maserati mechanics, the perks of having others labour on his behalf soon became apparent. Instead of having to find the parts and make repairs to the car himself, then arrange its transportation, which usually meant driving it to the next race himself, all he had to do now was show up for the next race, which in this case was the Premio Ciudad de Mar del Plata. There, only a few miles from Balcarce, several thousand Fangio fans watched him impressively hold his own in exalted company. He qualified fourth, behind Villoresi, Farina and Wimille, and in the race El Chueco held third place for eighteen laps until the engine started to sputter after another plug foul-up. Juan realised his mistake – he had again let the revs drop too low while taking a slow corner – and after a quick visit to the pits, where the Maserati mechanics cured the problem, he regained enough lost ground to finish fifth.

For the final two races in the Temporada series, Juan was invited by the French constructor Amedée Gordini to drive one of the two 1220cc Simca-engined cars he had brought over for Wimille. It was felt that the nimble little Gordinis, which were about half the size of the Italian Grand Prix cars, would be ideally suited to tackle the twists and turns of the tight, mile-and-three-quarter-long Circuito Parque Independencia where the Premio Ciudad de Rosario was held. There, Gordini thought, Wimille would fly the French flag in style, while Fangio would add some local colour. In fact, Fangio overshadowed his illustrious team-mate, outqualifying him by a second and a half and fighting him for the lead for many laps in the race. They repeatedly overtook each other, setting such a pace that Juan's fastest race lap was nearly a second quicker than he had gone in qualifying. However, the pressure Juan put on his Simca engine became too great for it to bear. A cracked cylinder head sent him backwards in the running order and he finished eighth, behind the winner, Wimille. Juan was at first worried that the European champion might resent the audacious attempts of an unknown newcomer to dethrone him, but Wimille shook him by the hand and told Juan that if he could get himself into a first-class Grand Prix car he would surely go places.

This prophecy did not come to fruition in the Premio Dalmiro Varela Castex, a race held on the wider, more open spaces of the three-mile-long Palermo Park track in Buenos Aires, where the lengthy straight especially left the underpowered Gordini seriously disadvantaged. Still, Juan impressed with his perseverance, never letting up and flogging the Gordini for all it was worth to the chequered flag, where his unstinting effort was rewarded with eighth place in the last race of the 1948 Temporada series.

When the Europeans returned home, the Argentinians went back to their own types of racing, with Juan doing most of the winning. From late February to early May 1948 he won four times in six races, twice in closed-track events with his Volpi-Chev and twice in open road races with the Chevrolet coupé. Meanwhile, preparations were underway for him to travel further afield. Part of Pancho Borgonovo's brief from the Perón government was for the ACA to undertake a detailed study in countries where the automotive industry, and motorsport in particular, were well developed, with a view to investigating ways for Argentina to make progress in these fields. To further this aim, Borgonovo organised a group to travel abroad on a fact-finding mission. Included in the entourage were the leading Argentine drivers Oscar Alfredo Galvez and Juan Manuel Fangio.

Their first port of call was the USA, where they visited the Ford, General Motors and Kaizer operations in Detroit. From the Kaiser-Fraser assembly line they bought a car and drove it to New York via Indianapolis, where at the end of May they attended 'America's Greatest Race', the Indianapolis 500. Juan was struck by the uniqueness of this type of racing, with the purpose-built cars using only one gear and seldom the brakes as they roared round and round the 2.5-mile banked oval track in an anti-clockwise direction for 200 laps. The Argentine travellers also took in some of the smaller dirt-track races, where the sight of cars constantly sliding sideways in showers of dirt was more familiar.

Their European tour began in Italy, the homeland of Juan's ancestors, where they visited the automobile factories in Turin and Milan, then the race-car manufacturers and teams located in and around Modena. These included an enterprise run by Enzo Ferrari, a former race driver who had gone on to operate teams for Alfa Romeo and was now starting his own racing business. To Juan, the Italian way of going about racing was a revelation. Compared to his humble little headquarters in the Balcarce garage, the premises he visited seemed pillars of superbly organised industrial efficiency. In their spacious, bright, clinically clean workshops, the crisply uniformed employees were led by learned engineers armed with complex detailed drawings and skilled craftsmen and mechanics who wielded finely made tools with deft precision. In the cramped, dimly lit Fangio garage, Juan and his amateur crew of grease-covered friends had only the most rudimentary tools with which to improvise often crude solutions to mechanical problems.

Sometimes, to celebrate a particularly clever technical achievement, the Balcarce amigos burst into song accompanied by a wheezy old accordion. Juan did wonder if the sophisticates in the European workshops got as much personal satisfaction as the peasants in Balcarce, and if state-of-the-art automotive competition came at the expense of the human side of the sport that was so important to him.

One of his boyhood idols, a driver who exemplified the man-over-machine aspect of racing Juan so much admired, was the legendary Tazio Nuvolari. The daredevil little Italian from Mantua was near the end of a long racing life that had featured several heroic victories scored over much faster cars, simply because he refused to be beaten. His iron will and determination were universally admired, and though he was now ill with a lung disease believed to have been caused by inhaling noxious fumes from too many engines, Nuvolari was still racing, wearing his famous leather helmet, a tricoloured Italian flag for a scarf, a yellow shirt and blue trousers (on his death in 1953 he was buried in this racing costume). When he called to pay his respects, Juan was surprised and delighted that the racing world's greatest hero should single him out for special treatment. Nuvolari invited him on a sightseeing tour of his home town. As they drove through the streets, the populace cheered and waved at their idol. Juan wondered if the adulation of his fans was why the 55-year-old Nuvolari was still racing, though he also understood that race organisers still sought out Nuvolari precisely because of his crowd-pulling power. 'When I met Nuvolari,' Juan said, 'he was being used by organisers and the young guys were beating him. I was really displeased by this fact, and thought that when I retired I would do so before arriving at the point Nuvolari did.'

The ACA group's itinerary also provided for visits to several European circuits to see the latest Grand Prix machinery in action. The first race took place at San Remo on Italy's Mediterranean coast, where they were to evaluate the latest Maserati cars as possible investments for the ACA. In a restaurant the night before the race, Juan was delighted when Achille Varzi recognised him and invited him to join his table. Varzi, from a wealthy Italian textile family, had originally gained racing fame in the early 1930s for his intense rivalry with Nuvolari. Noted equally for a smooth driving technique and ruthless ambition, in 1936 Varzi became addicted to the morphine given to him to ease the pain after an accident. His health deteriorated and he was fired by the Auto Union team. After the war, having dropped his drug habit, he re-established his racing career with several notable victories for Alfa Romeo, where he was now Wimille's team-mate. In the San Remo restaurant, the usually austere and often grim-faced Varzi warmed to the quiet charm of this refreshingly uncomplicated character Fangio, who was seven years his junior and miles away in terms of social sophistication. Varzi confided that he was considering retiring from racing and setting up a driving school, perhaps in Argentina. Varzi then invited Juan to his sumptuous home in Galliate, near Milan, where Juan met Achille's father Menotti Varzi, an engineer by profession, with whom Juan quickly developed a rapport. Sadly, they would meet again only a few days later, at the funeral of his son, whose death Juan had the misfortune to witness.

Juan and his ACA entourage were spectators at the Swiss Grand Prix, held on the outskirts of Berne in Bremgarten Park, a venue that was made both picturesque and dangerous by the large leafy trees through which the track wound for four and a half very fast miles. Overhanging branches created a tunnel effect, changing the light and interfering with the driver's vision, and when it rained the leaf-laden track surface became especially treacherous. The day before the race, in the final moments of practice, it was raining heavily. His Alfa Romeo team-mate Wimille had set the fastest time, and Varzi was trying to beat it. As he descended a downward-sloping S-bend at considerable speed, his Alfa lost adhesion on the slick surface, slid broadside into an earth bank and overturned, killing its driver instantly. On race day there was more tragedy when the young Swiss driver Christian Kautz also had a fatal crash. In another accident the Frenchman Maurice Trintignant's Gordini somersaulted and threw him out on to the track, where he lay badly injured and was almost hit by onrushing cars.

The European cars and tracks might have been more highly evolved than those to which he was accustomed, but Juan now fully understood that they were no less dangerous. Yet the pitfalls of the sport by which he remained consumed also created opportunities. At Reims, to where the ACA group travelled next for the Grand Prix de L'Automobile Club de France, Juan found himself a participant instead of a spectator. With his driver Trintignant lying in a hospital in Switzerland, Amedée Gordini, influenced by Juan's memorable battle with team leader Wimille in the Rosario race of the Temporada series, invited Juan to replace him. Gordini knew neither of them was likely to do nearly as well on the almost five-mile-long Reims circuit in France's champagne region. Composed of a triangulated section of closed-off public roads, the straightforward layout enabled high-horsepowered cars to attain speeds of nearly 190mph, far beyond the reach of the Simca-engined Gordinis. Though beautifully made, the little blue French cars also tended to be as unreliable as they were underpowered. Given these disadvantages, his friends questioned Juan's wisdom in accepting Gordini's invitation, but they knew his answer: he would race anything, anywhere, any time.

Though it would ultimately prove to be quite inauspicious, his European race debut took place amid a gathering of most of the greatest names the sport then had to offer: Ascari, Villoresi and Nuvolari; Sommer, Etancelin, Chiron and Schell; Prince Birabongse, Baron de Graffenreid and Prince Troubetskoy. None of them – professional or playboy, legend or loser, aristocrat or amateur – took much notice of the unknown newcomer, though it was observed that he was being shown around the paddock by their esteemed colleague Jean Pierre Wimille. In fairness to the disinterest shown in him, it must be said that his sartorial shortcomings gave Juan a rather less than commanding presence. While the stars of the establishment were nattily attired in freshly pressed blue overalls, and each would race with a personalised helmet well known to the 100,000 spectators, the aspirant from the Argentine seemed to have dressed down for the occasion. Juan wore a faded yellow short-sleeved shirt over a well-creased pair of trousers (the bottom half of his one and only suit) from the turn-ups of which crumpled socks sagged loosely around a pair of well-worn dress shoes. Completing his ensemble was a tattered light-blue linen cloth cap with a chinstrap, and a pair of battered aviator goggles that might have seen service in a war, and not necessarily the most recent one. In short, had anyone cared to pin a label on him, the balding, short, stocky 37-year-old with the broad shoulders and hefty forearms looked like a mechanic, or possibly a potato farmer.

Race day at Reims, 18 July 1948, afforded Juan two opportunities to test the European racing waters. Though the black storm clouds that glowered low in the sky above the vineyards all afternoon did not unload any precipitation, neither did Juan greatly exceed the admittedly low expectations. He did, however, manage to set the second fastest time in qualifying for the preliminary event, which was for cars with small-capacity engines. This not insignificant achievement, in a four-cylinder 1430cc Simca-Gordini versus the two-litre V12-

engined Ferrari with which Raymond Sommer secured pole position, came to nothing in the race. While Sommer, one of the French stars from before the war, went on to win for the glory of France in a car that represented the future of Italian race-car engineering, the venerable French car driven by the unknown Argentine mechanic lasted only four laps before it was forced to stop by a split fuel tank.

Restricted to the same car for the main event, for full-blown Grand Prix cars, Juan's top speed of 130mph was about 60mph short of what was required to be a frontrunner. Among the twenty cars on the starting grid, Juan's Gordini was separated from the polesitting Alfa Romeo driven by Wimille by eighteen cars. After ten laps of racing, Juan pulled his stuttering machine into the Gordini pit where the remedying of an ignition problem took eleven minutes. After another 25 laps of racing he was up to twelfth when his Gordini gave up the ghost, the fuel tank having split itself irreparably. Wimille's victory was toasted liberally with the Reims region's famous product, but for Juan there was no champagne, nor was there any fame, since his name was hardly mentioned in the race reports. However, the Grand Prix winner, whom Juan thought of not only as 'the best French driver at the time, but also a gentleman, and that was most important', maintained that Juan Manuel Fangio's time would come. At a press conference in Paris, from where the ACA group was about to fly home, Wimille introduced the South American driver who had had the audacity to overtake him in Argentina. This man, Wimille insisted to the gathering, will one day make a name for himself.

Chapter Six

Disaster in the Andes

'*Enormous concentration was necessary if you wanted to press ahead. All this must have sapped my energy and caused me to make the mistake that caused the accident.*'

HAVING FINISHED HIS FIRST European tour, Juan now started preparing for the longest journey of his or anyone else's racing life. The 1948 Gran Premio de la America del Sur would traverse nearly the entire length of the South American continent, a distance of 9,174 miles. The competition, another effort to pave the way for a Pan American highway, was divided into two sections which were further subdivided into nineteen stages. The first section, over fourteen stages and 5,950 miles, which became known as the Race to Caracas, went from Buenos Aires to the Venezuelan capital by way of roads through Argentina, Bolivia, Peru and Ecuador; the second, five-stage, 3,224-mile section started in Lima and finished in Buenos Aires. The organisers, quite rightly as it turned out, arranged for this section to be shorter so that some of those who failed to complete the Race to Caracas might regroup and compete in the final section.

Before the start, Juan and his friend Domingo Marimón made a private arrangement to share equally whatever prize money they won. The amount could be considerable, since the spoils of victory on offer included cash for stage, section and overall wins as well as 10,000 pesos and solid gold plaques to be awarded by the government's Eva Perón Foundation to the two best-placed entries from Argentina. As a reward for his previous open-road successes, Juan's Chevrolet coupé was given the number 1 to signify its prime starting position, which was no small honour since 138 cars lined up for the start in Buenos Aires.

At ten o'clock on the night of 20 October, the Balcarce car, with Fangio and his friend Daniel Urrutia on board, tore away from the start as if the race was a sprint. The others, following at ten-second intervals, immediately began fighting to improve their positions with a ferocity and velocity that belied the vast distances and enormous challenges that lay ahead. Oscar Galvez, who started third, soon overcame his Ford's twenty-second disadvantage and caught up Juan's Chev at a level crossing where they had to wait for a passing train. When the barrier lifted they roared away side by side, the Ford's slightly superior acceleration enabling it to inch ahead of the Chev, which slotted in behind and stayed glued to the Ford's rear bumper for nearly 300 miles. Ultimately, their private race was resolved in favour of Galvez by a massive margin: while Galvez averaged 74.5mph in winning the 990-mile first stage, his long-term rival struggled over the finish line at Salta in 79th place. Juan's head-long pursuit of Galvez had met with a series of protests from his over-taxed Chev that in total caused nearly four hours of delay en route to Salta. A misfiring engine was eventually cured by roadside repairs to the distributor; then a serious vibration signalled trouble in the differential, where the crown and pinion were chewing each other up. Juan's attempts to replace the offending parts met with failure because the spare crown and pinion, procured by Urrutia, proved to be for a truck and wouldn't fit in the Chev. The laborious task of dismantling then reassembling the differential ate up valuable time, more of which was lost when the continuing vibration became so serious that they had to stop at a checkpoint, remove the differential again and replace it with one borrowed from a local garage.

Fired up by the setbacks, Juan attacked the second stage with a vengeance and overtook some 60 cars. The retirements of others meant he finished fourth, but the rules required competitors to start each stage according to their overall classification in the race, which was now being led by Domingo Marimón. No matter how hard he drove, Juan's handicap of having to start each stage well back in the pack remained, and it irked him in the extreme. For once, his calm and reasoned approach deserted him, and while his relentless flogging propelled him past car after car, day after day, the satisfaction was diminished by the fact that he had also overtaken most of them the day before. His despair deepened when his rapid progress was delayed by yet more mechanical problems. Rear axle shafts broke on the third and sixth stages, which were run through intense heat. While replacing the first broken halfshaft, Juan became so thirsty that he drank from pools of muddy water that had collected in the hoofmarks left by horses.

To Juan, it seemed that their continuing misfortunes were undermining the resolve of Urrutia, who became increasingly detached, perhaps because he felt guilty about causing more delays. When the second halfshaft broke, Urrutia neglected to fit a vital component in the replacement, forcing Juan to take the halfshaft apart and install it all over again. At the end of the fourth stage, at La Paz in Bolivia, the Chev's engine refused to fire up. Urrutia, whose responsibility it was, had forgotten to drill a hole in a new exhaust gasket that had been put in. Juan, who couldn't understand how anyone could make such an elementary mistake, was again forced to waste time making up for his friend's forgetfulness. Though he was a most compassionate man, Juan could not hide his increasing exasperation and their friendship was severely strained.

Juan channelled his mounting frustration into a sensational attack on the fifth stage. Familiar with the route from the 1940 race, over the Andes from La Paz to Arequipa in Peru, he knew his best chance would be to coax his underpowered Chev up to the 15,500-foot peak at Alto de Torova, then pull out all the stops and descend at the maximum possible speed. His downhill drive was the stuff of legend. Careering sideways around corners and bouncing several feet into the air over bumps, the streaking Chev tore through the lunar landscape like a tornado. In all, Juan left 33 cars in his wake, one of them parked by its driver who said he stopped deliberately to watch the fantastic Fangio. Juan completely dominated the 340-mile stage, finishing it in just over seven hours – eight minutes ahead of the next fastest driver, Oscar Galvez.

But on the following 832-mile stage to Lima, the Balcarce car was again overtaken by mechanical failure. In fact, it was overtaken by its own rear wheel, which detached itself when yet another halfshaft broke. Juan managed to wrestle the car to a safe halt, but the ensuing repair work cost him an hour of the valuable time he had made up after the previous delays. Nor was there any time during the rest day in Lima to recover from his mounting exhaustion. Besides scurrying around to find spares then fixing his own car, Juan was also responsible for looking after two other cars. His pre-race pact with Domingo Marimón included Juan lending a mechanical hand to his friend and another driver, Eusebio Marcilla, a protégé of Marimón's. Late that evening, the bleary-eyed driver-mechanic fell into his hotel-room bed to get a few hours' fitful rest before the start of the next stage, which was scheduled for a five a.m. start. Juan had scarcely dozed off when there was a loud hammering on the door. 'Someone knocked on the door and said we had to leave immediately because there was a revolution,' Juan recalled.

As the competitors scrambled into their cars, tanks were rumbling through the streets of Lima and gunshots could be heard. Troops loyal to the government were fighting another army faction led by a disaffected general intent on taking over the country. The considerable confusion at the floodlit startline was compounded by dense clouds of fog swirling around the 60 cars that remained from the 138 that had started in Buenos Aires. In their haste to get out of Lima, several anxious competitors ignored the correct starting order and left before they should have. One of those who lost his place in the shuffle was a leading Peruvian driver, who had to start behind Juan. Once they were underway, Juan slowed down and allowed the Peruvian to pass, with a view to taking advantage of his familiarity with the local roads. In tandem, they ripped through the curtain of fog, overtaking many cars. By the time they reached a checkpoint 85 miles out of Lima, Juan was in fourth place in the stage. A few miles further on the fog became even thicker and the Peruvian's speeding car ploughed head-on into a donkey. The impact sent the unfortunate though blessedly instantly killed beast flying high into the air and the out-of-control car cartwheeling off the road. The driver and his companion were lucky to escape with only minor injuries, but Juan's guide-dog of a car was gone.

Juan scarcely slackened his speed, though maintaining such a pace through the nearly impenetrable murk required tremendous concentration that severely sapped his dwindling reserves of mental strength and alertness. To sharpen his focus he began to discourage a closely following car by cutting corners, driving off the edge of the asphalt surface and throwing up dust that combined dangerously with the fog to impair the vision of his pursuer. His companion shouted at Juan to stop playing dirty, pointing out that Juan had had no compunction about sitting on the tail of the departed Peruvian's car. Juan quickly obeyed his friend's command; he knew that Urrutia was above all a decent man. And despite their recent estrangement, Juan now welcomed his friend's insistence that he should conduct himself with the sense of fair play that usually governed his driving.

His restored scruples did not slow him down, and for nearly 200 miles Juan fought a tooth-and-nail battle with Oscar Galvez for the stage lead. But by now Juan's critical faculties were seriously impaired. Accumulated fatigue, exacerbated by the debilitating demands of driving so hard in such difficult conditions, interfered with his judgement. In the dark and fog, he sped blindly past a vital refuelling point in the town of Trujillo. The realisation of this error added exasperation to his confusion. Somewhere ahead they would have to find petrol. Urrutia consulted his watch and predicted that in a few minutes' time dawn would start breaking and they should at least be able to see where they were going.

But it was still foggy and black as they sped through Huanchasco, a tiny Peruvian mountain village crowded with typically whitewashed houses. The Chev's headlight beams bounced off the white walls and back into Juan's eyes. Dazzled and disoriented, he fought to control the car as it slid sideways around a sharp left-hand curve. Beyond the curve he glimpsed only a black void. Interpreting it as an abyss to be avoided at all costs, Juan cut the corner more sharply than centrifugal force would allow and the car started to skid on the asphalt. Juan fought desperately to regain control, but the Chev slid wider. Instead of a precipice, the side of the road was bordered by a sandy embankment, which the sliding car hit. 'I felt what fear was at that moment,' Juan said, 'because I believed it was the end for me.' With shocking ferocity, the Chev flipped over and over. Inside the tumbling car, flying tools and spare parts banged and crashed around the occupants as they tried desperately to hang on. There were no seat belts, nor were the safety straps fastened to the doors. Juan gripped the steering wheel with all his might. After what seemed an eternity, the tumbling wreckage came to rest and there was silence. The car lay on the driver's side with its door ajar and Juan lying in a heap under the steering wheel, with one leg jammed against the open door and the other tangled in the pedals. There was no sign of his passenger, whose door had been ripped off.

Oscar Galvez, who had been following closely and had nearly suffered the same fate as Juan, had managed to slow his car and safely stop it part of the way down the embankment, below which was a cane field. There, about 50 yards away, Galvez saw headlight beams piercing skyward at odd angles. Shouting at some villagers to come and help him, Galvez ran down to Juan's car. They heaved it on to its wheels and pulled Juan out. He was dazed and winded, but seemed otherwise unhurt. Gasping for breath, he whispered to Oscar about how lucky it was the car hadn't caught fire. It was also fortunate, Juan added, that the roll cage installed by his brother Toto had held up, otherwise it could have been a lot worse. But it would have been better had Daniel fastened the safety straps to hold the doors in place. And where, Juan wondered, was Daniel?

They found him lying on the ground about fifteen yards away; he had been thrown out as the car overturned. In the gathering dawn, as Oscar and Juan crouched beside Daniel's unconscious body, another car stopped. It was Eusebio Marcilla, Marimón's protégé. Marcilla told them there was a hospital in Chicama, a town about ten miles away, and that he would drive them there. They carried Daniel up to Marcilla's car and put him in the back, where Juan, sitting on top of the fuel tank, cradled his friend's head in his arms. Juan thought he felt warmth returning to Daniel's body but was worried about a slight indentation on the back of his neck. At the hospital, Marcilla wanted to stay with them but Juan insisted he should continue racing. By now shock had set in, and Juan was trembling uncontrollably; he was also badly bruised, in considerable pain and utterly exhausted. The hospital nurses sedated him and put him to bed.

When Juan woke up, another driver, Manuel Montes, was sitting beside his bed. Montes, who had retired from the race, had insisted he would keep Juan company and do whatever he could to help. When they asked the doctors and nurses about Daniel Urrutia they were told that he had a fractured skull but was in no great danger. Later, when Juan asked to see him, he was told that Daniel had been taken to Lima for further treatment.

When he was released from hospital in Chicama, Juan was driven by Montes to the city of Trujillo where they spent several days making arrangements to transport the crashed car to Lima. There, Juan would visit Urrutia in the hospital and have their car repaired. When Urrutia was fit enough, they would drive back to Argentina. On their way out of Trujillo, with the Chev loaded on the back of a hired truck, they pulled into a service station for petrol. The boy who served them recognised the great Fangio and expressed his sincere condolences for the loss of Urrutia. Juan, realising that the terrible news had been kept from him so as not to impede his own recovery, was struck dumb. His great friend was dead. Juan's grief was deepened by the despair he felt for being responsible for the accident that had taken his companion's life. 'The blame for his death rested squarely on me,' he would say later. 'With his death I got the true measure of the sense of tragedy.'

When the car was repaired, Juan set off on the long return journey to Balcarce; beside him, where Daniel Urrutia used to sit, was Manuel Montes. Juan drove gingerly at first but found that the slow pace only set his mind in motion with recurring thoughts of the accident. He became fearful that he might never be able to race again. Remembering that when pilots survived an air crash they immediately flew again, he pressed his foot to the floor, but Montes told him to slow down and Juan did so. To purge himself of the memory he began to reflect on the accident in more detail. As the car had begun to roll he remembered thinking that this is how one might die. There was no overwhelming feeling of impending doom, only momentary fear before his senses left him. However, Juan did recall feeling fearful for Daniel, and a kind of premonition that had occurred before they left Balcarce. When Daniel had asked him to visit his beloved wife and two children, Juan had felt uneasy for his friend and suggested it might be unwise for a man with family responsibilities to risk taking part in the Gran Premio de la America del Sur. But Daniel's passion for racing ran deep and Juan could not persuade him to stay behind. During the race he had appeared not to have his mind fully on the job, and the mistakes he had made had led to harsh words between them. Juan felt guilty about that, too. It was only when he returned to Balcarce that he found out why his friend had been so distracted: almost at the moment when the fatal accident happened, Daniel Urrutia's wife was in hospital giving birth to their third child.

Juan's friends gathered round to console him. He was particularly touched by the kindness and generosity of two of them. One was Manuel Montes, who stayed with him for over a week. On their long return journey from Peru they had slept huddled together for warmth in the freezing mountains. They became firm friends, and Montes eventually became a trusted business partner. Juan also found he could place complete faith in Domingo Marimón, who had gone on to win the Gran Premio de la America del Sur and insisted on honouring their pre-race pledge to share whatever prize money they won. This was some consolation for Juan, but the ill-fated race remained his most traumatic experience, until it was matched by another tragedy involving his friend Domingo's son.

As he mourned the loss of Daniel Urrutia, Juan tried to lessen the burden of grief by pitching himself into his business enterprises. About his future as a driver he was less sure. During his worst moments he doubted he would ever race again, but towards the end of 1948 it was announced that the ACA had bought two Maseratis for the forthcoming Temporada series, and one of them was for Juan Manuel Fangio.

To prepare himself for the mental test of racing again, Juan entered the annual Mil Millas. Usually the country's classic road race marked the end of the season, but organisational problems had delayed it until January 1949. It was with some trepidation that Juan prepared the Chev coupé, and he invited Antonio Elizade to accompany him. Elizade, who had ridden with him in the pre-war long-distance races, assured Juan he still had complete confidence in him and eagerly accepted the chance to join his old friend for another 1,000 miles of racing. As usual, the route from Buenos Aires out into the pampas and back was almost entirely on dirt roads. A drought meant that the later a car started the more dust it would face, and the luck of the draw for starting positions did not favour the Balcarce car, which started 125th among the 177 entrants that took off at fifteen-second intervals.

By the first checkpoint, in the village of 9 de Julio, Juan had overtaken 100 cars. Nineteen more had eaten his dust by the time they got to Pehuajo, where, after 633 miles of very hard driving, he was classified sixth overall. During the last third of the race conditions got much worse: a pampas cyclone whipped up the flat landscape in a terrific dust storm. For the competitors, the advantage of having a tailwind was wiped out by the addition of the even worse impediment to their vision. Yet Juan sped blindly on – at speeds of over 90mph he was travelling even faster than the weather. He could hardly see the dust-covered Elizade sitting beside him, let alone the cars in front he was determined to overtake. Whenever he managed to discern the silhouette of a car in front he informed its driver of his wishes by firmly tapping its rear bumper with the front of the belligerent Balcarce Chev. At the finish line, Fangio and Elizade emerged from their sand-blasted car as white as ghosts, though obviously not from fear. When the dust settled, Oscar Galvez, who had started 30th, was declared the winner. Second overall, and obviously back on top form, was his old rival Fangio.

Galvez and Fangio were chosen to represent their country in the 1949 Temporada series against the European elite, who were this year led by Ascari, Bira, Farina, the Englishman Reg Parnell, Villoresi and Wimille. For Fangio, the latter was now something of a role model. At 43, Jean Pierre Wimille was five years older than Juan and a veteran of nineteen years of European Grand Prix racing, and the previous year he had shown considerable kindness to the unknown from Argentina. One of Juan's prized possessions was a photo taken in 1948 with Juan in his car and Wimille leaning over him, smiling and offering advice and encouragement. In Europe, Wimille had praised him and informed the press that Juan was a future champion. Juan admired the way the gallant French champion conducted himself in public. Unlike many racing heroes he did not flaunt his celebrity, but was quiet, self-effacing and reserved – qualities not dissimilar to the calm, tactical approach he took behind the wheel. Though Juan attacked the open roads with vigour and bombast worthy of the fabulously flamboyant Nuvolari, he thought Wimille's much less exhibitionist, apparently effortless style was the way to go about handling the more sensitive Grand Prix cars. In his cockpit, Juan noticed, Wimille seemed completely relaxed, keeping his head rock steady and grasping the steering wheel with fully outstretched arms.

Changing direction, braking and shifting gears were accomplished with great precision and unvarying regularity, lap after lap. His economy of movement and unflustered manner made it appear as though Wimille, who had been racing since 1930, could keep control of his car for ever.

But even the great French stylist, whom many regarded as the greatest driver of his time, was not immune to losing control of a racing car at speed. Jean Pierre Wimille was killed when his Simca-Gordini crashed on the Buenos Aires Circuito Palermo in practice for the Gran Premio Internacional Juan Domingo Perón. Practice had begun early in the morning, and Wimille's was one of the first cars on the track. His little blue Gordini, its 1430cc engine less than half the size of the bellowing behemoths in the Maseratis, Ferraris and Alfa Romeos, needed to corner as quickly as possible to make up for time lost on the straights. At 7.30 a.m., on its first lap of the day, the Gordini came to grief on one of the fastest corners. Eyewitnesses reported that Wimille had had to take sudden evasive action to avoid a female spectator running across the road. The Gordini spun sideways, flipped over, somersaulted several times, landed on its wheels, then hit a tree. The unconscious and obviously dreadfully injured driver was prised from the wreckage and rushed to a nearby hospital. There, suffering from crushed ribs and a fractured skull, he died a few minutes later in the arms of his distraught wife Christine, with Amedée Gordini standing by, wringing his hands in anguish.

Wimille's widow, a former champion ski racer, requested that the mourning in Buenos Aires be kept low-key and out of the public eye. The wake, held in the ACA headquarters, was attended only by dignitaries from the French embassy, race officials and selected drivers. The honorary pallbearers included Luigi Villoresi, Alberto Ascari, Giuseppe Farina, Juan Galvez and Juan Manuel Fangio. Wimille had also been a wartime resistance hero, and he was later buried with full state honours in France and awarded posthumously the Légion d'Honneur. The memorial service in Paris was attended by celebrities such as the Duke and Duchess of Windsor, and among those paying their respects, though he was unaccompanied and unnoticed, was Fangio.

When practice resumed at the Circuito Palermo, Juan remembered how his late mentor had cautioned him about how a Grand Prix car had to be treated with the utmost respect. Even then, as had been proved by Wimille's sad fate, the car could turn around and bite the hand that drove it. 'Wimille used to say there is a whole school up to 125mph; after that there is a black hole,' Juan recalled, but if one was to race, one had to enter that dark void wherein lurked danger, and Juan did this in qualifying for the Gran Premio Internacional Juan Domingo Perón. Reaching speeds of just over 125mph, he put his ACA Maserati on the front row of the grid beside the similar machines of Ascari and Villoresi.

For Juan, his first experience in a thoroughbred, state-of-the-art Grand Prix car was a revelation. He marvelled at the precision of the steering, the responsiveness of the controls, the willingness of the engine. In the cockpit, it seemed the car was an extension of himself, an animate object willing to obey his every command, and this chimed perfectly with his driving philosophy: 'I never considered a car as an instrument to achieve an end, but as a part of myself, or better,' he once said. He had never felt so completely at home in a racing car, and the momentousness of the occasion was marked by the car's colours: instead of the traditional Italian red sported by the Ascari and Villoresi Maseratis, Juan's was painted in the Argentine racing hues of yellow and blue.

Juan flew his country's colours to great effect, to the delight of the nearly 300,000 partisan spectators who watched him.

Though Ascari dominated throughout and won, Juan challenged Villoresi for second place for many laps, only to have his determined pursuit delayed by a pit stop to replace a burst rear tyre. Juan eventually finished fourth, but his countryman Oscar Galvez filled the void admirably with a stirring performance that brought his Alfa Romeo home third, hard on the heels of Ascari and Villoresi.

In the next Temporada event, once more at the Palermo track but this time called the Premio Jean Pierre Wimille in honour of the fallen hero, Galvez and Fangio distinguished themselves again: Juan drove his old Volpi-Chev to victory in a preliminary race for Argentine-built single-seaters, and Galvez triumphed in the main event. The Galvez Alfa Romeo and the Fangio Maserati had been left in front after the leading Italian drivers dropped out with mechanical problems; the Argentinian battle for supremacy was ultimately settled in favour of Galvez when Fangio lost his car in a slide and lightly sideswiped a tree. The damage was restricted to scraped paintwork and he went on to finish second to Galvez, but for Juan the brush with the tree hit home. It was a worrying reminder of the fate suffered by Wimille and the perils of pushing beyond the capabilities of himself or his car.

Neither of the Argentine stars featured in the next race, the Premio Ciudad de Rosario, which was run in wet conditions. Juan was for this race driving one of team entrant Amedée Gordini's small cars, which were better suited to the tight track, but Juan's Gordini was hit by another car on the first corner and he had to watch the race from the pits. He saw his team-mate for the day, Benedicto Campos, acquit himself well, though his Gordini could not keep up with the first two finishers, Farina's Ferrari and Parnell's Maserati.

The final race of the 1949 Temporada series took place on 27 February only a few miles away from Juan's home town. Thus it was that at least one tenth of the estimated 300,000 spectators at the Premio Ciudad de Mar del Plata were from Balcarce. Their hero, with one last chance to beat the Europeans at their own game, was again aboard one of the ACA's blue and yellow Maseratis, but the team's weekend got off to the worst possible start when another of its drivers, Adriano Malusardi, crashed heavily in practice and was killed. There was more tragedy during the race when a Uruguayan driver lost control on one of the street circuit's fast corners and careered into the crowd, killing one spectator and injuring fifteen others. Juan led in Mar del Plata from start to finish. In the early laps he had to fight off a determined Ascari, who was then overtaken by Villoresi who fought equally hard to unsettle the race leader whose every lap around the 2.5-mile course was accompanied by increasingly frenzied euphoria from the assembled multitude. In the cockpit of his Maserati, Juan remained calm, concentrating hard on controlling the pace without over-extending himself or the car, but for the last third of the race he could hardly hear himself think – not the crowd this time, but a deafening din caused by a split in the exhaust pipe running alongside the cockpit. Meanwhile, their vigorous pursuit of Fangio was more than the cars of Villoresi, Ascari and Farina could take and they all retired, leaving Bangkok-born Bira – Prince Birabongse Bhanuban of Siam – to finish a distant second to the now fully fledged Argentinian hero. For Juan, this first win in a Grand Prix car was a moving experience he remembered for ever: 'When I finished my lap of honour and shut the Maserati's engine off while coasting into the pits, I felt entirely transfigured, different somehow. It awakened in me one of the most intense pleasures of my life.'

Following his Temporada triumph, Juan won again, at the wheel of his Volpi-Chevrolet in the Premio Fraile Muerto. This race, through the streets of the town of Bell Ville, was also marred by a tragedy that detracted from Juan's victory. A mechanical failure caused one of the cars to spear off the track and scythe into the densely packed crowd. The driver escaped with broken bones and severe cuts, but six people were killed and a dozen injured.

A few days later, while he was on a business trip selling trucks in Patagonia, Juan was summoned back to ACA headquarters in Buenos Aires where he was informed that he had been chosen to lead an Argentine team that would over the next four months contest several major Grands Prix in Europe. Since Oscar Galvez had been taken ill and was unable to travel, Juan's team-mate would be the promising Benedicto Campos. At the Equipo Argentino's disposal would be a pair of Grand Prix Maseratis and, for races for the smaller-engined category, two Simca-Gordinis. Thus, at 37, an age when most professional drivers performing on the international stage were either retired or were in the twilight of their careers, Juan Manuel Fangio was handed another opportunity to begin his. Still, as always, his publicly stated ambitions were conservative, and as he boarded the plane in Buenos Aires he told well-wishers that he would consider the European foray a success if he managed to win just one race.

Chapter Seven

Dream Debut in Europe

'When I left for Europe, even if I was happy and pleased with myself, I couldn't forget that the move put me under obligation to the government for backing me, and to the people who supported me.'

THE ACA TEAM CALLED ITSELF the 'Equipo Achille Varzi' in honour of the late driver who had befriended Juan, and whose father Menotti Varzi had been deeply impressed by Juan's sympathy and kindness when Achille was killed in 1948. As a mark of his gratitude, Menotti Varzi generously offered Juan and the six other members of the team the use of his home in Galliate near Milan as their living quarters, and also arranged for them to use a nearby building as a garage and workshop. It was here that the team brought its equipment from the port of Genoa, where the four cars and crates of spares had been shipped from Argentina. For transport, the team had two trucks, a Kaiser-Fraser which Campos drove and a Dodge for Juan, whose duties encompassed many aspects of running the team, though the team manager was the veteran Italian mechanic Amadeo Bignami, whose background included working with the likes of Nuvolari, Chiron and Varzi.

It was Bignami who recommended that the ACA team play itself in by first competing in the smaller, provincial Grand Prix races as opposed to the major national 'Grand Epreuves' contested by the top drivers that were traditionally staged in France, Italy and West Germany on the famous Reims, Monza and Nürburgring circuits. Bignami also guided the team through the particular intricacies and conventions associated with European race weekends. Juan was infinitely adaptable to new situations, and Bignami offered him valuable advice on how to handle himself in the sophisticated Grand Prix environment, which was far removed from the rough and ready circumstances in which he had flourished back home in South America. Bignami's contribution even extended to making worthwhile suggestions as to how Juan might polish his still relatively crude driving style to better suit the more sensitive Grand Prix cars.

Though it was ostensibly operating under the auspices of the Argentine government, the ACA team was by no means financially secure, as Juan soon found out. Before leaving for Europe, Juan, with the support of friends in Balcarce, had offered to buy his Mar del Plata-winning Maserati, but the ACA told him it wasn't necessary and that the club was buying the cars on account from the European factories. But at the start of the 1949 campaign money even for such elementary operating costs as tyres and lubricants was in short supply, and in his search for further funding and trade support, Juan proved to be most persuasive.

In Milan, he visited the Pirelli tyre company and convinced them that supplying the blue and yellow liveried 'Achille Varzi' team with tyres would be good publicity for Italy's national rubber company. Perhaps it was his down-to-earth honesty that impressed the hard-nosed Pirelli officials, who were accustomed to being solicited by hopeful sponsor-seekers making all sorts of optimistic promises. Juan told Pirelli the truth: that the team couldn't afford to pay for its tyres until it earned income, either from the starting money on offer at the races or possibly from prize money, should the team have some success. Using a similar approach, he made a proposal to Lubra, a small Milan-based oil company run by Francesco Corvella. Juan suggested to Corvella that in exchange for free oil the Achille Varzi team would paint the Lubra name on its trucks, and personnel would wear the Lubra identity on their overalls and caps. (He didn't mention it, but Juan would continue to race in his customary costume, donated to his cause by the Suixtil clothing company: blue trousers, yellow shirt and blue linen helmet.) Corvella accepted the proposal and offered a further incentive, telling Juan that Lubra would give the team 150,000 lira for any race it won, though neither party really expected such a sum would ever change hands.

The first Grand Prix, on 3 April, was at San Remo, on the two-mile Ospedaletti circuit that wound up and down through the hilly streets of the Italian holiday resort on the Mediterranean coast. The previous year Juan had watched Alberto Ascari win this race in a Maserati identical to the one he now had. Ascari was not entered this year, though the list of 22 competitors included such notable names as Bira, Bonetto, Chiron, de Graffenreid, Levegh, Rosier and Sommer. Moments after opening practice it seemed likely that Fangio's name would have to be scratched from the entry list. Certainly that was the opinion of Bignami, who took one look at the Maserati engine's broken big-end bearing and said it would be impossible to fix in time for tomorrow's race. Juan, however, refused to accept Bignami's diagnosis. Though the Italian was well skilled in preparing and maintaining racing machinery, his expertise did not extend to making the kind of improvisational repairs at which Juan, accustomed to surviving in reduced circumstances, was particularly adept. The engine was the one with which Juan had won in Mar del Plata. After that race, Juan remembered, the engine had been taken apart and reassembled before it was put on the ship bound for Genoa. Suspecting that the work had been done incorrectly, Juan took it upon himself to fix it. In a garage at San Remo, he removed the engine's sump and found the crankshaft was scored because the big-end bearing had turned. For two hours he laboriously polished the scored shaft by hand, using an emery cloth to restore the pitted surface to a mirror finish. Several hours later, after having securely fitted a new bearing and made sure everything was ready for final assembly, he left the remaining work to the mechanics and went to bed – at one o'clock on the morning of the race.

Juan used his few hours' rest to full advantage. Though his predilection was for a long, untroubled sleep of up to twelve hours a night, having for years endured serious sleep deprivation during epic road races he had developed the ability to catnap at a moment's notice. Feeling refreshed, he proceeded to drive the repaired Maserati to great effect. In the first heat, mindful of the benefits of being in front on a tight street circuit where packs of cars running in close quarters were invariably exposed to accidents, he powered his way past Prince Bira and won by a big margin. In the second heat, in consideration of the fact that the overall winner would be determined by an aggregate time over the two heats, he drove more conservatively, tucking in behind the leader Bira and staying there to the chequered flag. Juan's victory, at an average of 52.8mph, over the acknowledged stars in the San Remo Grand Prix confirmed that the Achille Varzi team was a force to be reckoned with in Europe, a fact that was further substantiated by his team-mate Benedicto Campos, who finished fourth overall.

If the team had a weakness, it lay on the mechanical side in terms of deficiencies in both equipment and maintenance personnel. Fortunately, Juan's hard-earned skills, plus his sheer physical strength, in this department saved the day again in the next race, at Pau in the foothills of the Pyrenees in south-west France. The Pau Grand Prix was another street race, this time through the spa town's picturesque Parc Beaumont. Run in a single heat over 110 laps on the 1.75-mile circuit, the event presented more of a mechanical challenge than Juan's Maserati was capable of enduring without protest.

From the start, he leapt into the lead and held it comfortably, impressing the 50,000 spectators with the consummate artistry with which he swept around the corners in wonderfully controlled powerslides, changing gears constantly with lightning-fast yet astonishingly smooth shifts that scarcely altered his car's engine note. Soon he had built up a substantial advantage over his fourteen pursuers, but just a few laps from the finish the Maserati's oil pressure gauge dipped towards the danger point. Since the engine's consumption of oil was a known quantity, Juan had prepared for this eventuality by instructing his pit crew to have at the ready a two-litre can of oil. Now that it was required, he made the prearranged hand signal to alert the crew of his intention to come in on the next lap. His race lead was sufficient to keep him in front had the stop been routine, but it wasn't. When Juan came in he kept the engine running because the team did not have an electric starter motor, nor were push-starts allowed, but to Juan's consternation a race official ran up and shouted in his ear that it was illegal to have the engine running when the car was being serviced. Juan immediately complied, and once the oil supply was replenished his mechanics, led by Bignami, frantically began to tug at the engine's starting handle. With their efforts proving to be as ineffectual as they were strenuous, Bignami decided the only solution was to take off the engine cover and install new sparkplugs. When Juan saw that his chief mechanic was about to begin this lengthy task which would surely rob him of the race win, he jumped from the cockpit and took matters into his own hands. He ran to the front of the car, shoved the straining mechanic away from the starting handle, grabbed it with both hands and heaved upwards with all his strength, whereupon the engined fired up immediately.

Back on the streets of Pau, he now transferred his energies to the task of usurping Baron de Graffenreid, who had in the meantime assumed the lead. In short order, Juan caught the Swiss aristocrat, overtook him neatly and went on to a victory that as well as being momentous was also a complete surprise to the brass band hired by the organisers to salute the winner. Though the band had in its repertoire the national anthem of every European driver of note in the race, they didn't have the appropriate music for Argentina. Thus it was that Juan's second successive visit to the top step of the podium in a European Grand Prix was conducted to the tune of an obscure Brazilian military march.

Back in Argentina, more suitable music was being aired. Orchestras were tuning up to play and make records of 'Fangio!', a celebratory song written for the national hero in tango form by the composer Javier Mazzea and first performed in 1941, when Juan captured the country's imagination with his epic road-racing adventures. New lyrics were added to commemorate his 1949 European triumphs; had a radio hit parade then existed, 'Fangio!' would have been number one. The song's tale was told in three verses, the first of which sought to explain El Chueco's significance to Argentinians, the second to express their predictions of victory:

> The flag begins to fall,
> We hear the engines roar,
> Fangio's the name we call.
> We feel excitement grip,
> Your name's on every lip;
> We watch you as you go
> To triumph true and sure,
> An arrow from a bow.

Fangio! You're champion of the road.
With a wheel in hand you're king.
Your courage is your code,
To win's no easy thing.
Fangio! On the European tracks,
Chueco, you'll beat them all.
How can they hold you back?
For you the flag will fall.

While the hopes expressed in the first two verses were borne out in his first two Grands Prix, Juan's victories in the next two were commemorated in a triumphant final stanza:

You let all Europe know
In San Remo and Pau,
Perpignan and Marseilles.
The victor's triumph hail,
You've won the world's acclaim.
That's why we call your name,
And each elated heart,
Astounded at your art,
Cries, 'Fangio, go on!'
The champions' champion!

In the Grand Prix of Roussillon at Perpignan, the champions' champion had beaten Europe's best by winning the first 50-lap heat and finishing second in the final; his team-mate Campos was again classified third overall, as he had been at Pau. Juan's victory in the Grand Prix of Marseilles had been completed behind the wheel of one of the team's Simca-Gordinis, to which Juan had added an aerodynamic technical innovation.

Though the nimble little car was well suited to the short and narrow confines of the seaport city's Parc Borely circuit, its comparative lack of horsepower was a decided disadvantage on the track's half-mile-long straight. During a practice session, Juan's upper body was seriously buffeted about by the wind. He tried to improve the car's streamlining effect by crouching low in the seat and hunching forward over the steering wheel, but this awkward position both interfered with his driving style and fell short of making much headway in terms of reducing the Gordini's wind resistance. At the end of qualifying, Juan suggested to Bignami that the car's aerodynamic shortcomings could be greatly improved by replacing the tiny windscreen mounted on the front of the cockpit with a full-width wraparound screen that could be fashioned from a piece of plexiglass. Since the factory Gordini team was also contesting the race, Juan told Bignami that to preserve whatever advantage the windscreen modification would confer, it should only be unveiled on the day of the race.

The device worked wonders. On the straight, the tiny 1430cc Simca motor clocked 400rpm more than it had before, and Juan was able to control it from his preferred upright, straight-arm posture. The race was divided into two elimination heats from which the top finishers would compete in the Grand Prix final. In the first heat, the Fangio Gordini was narrowly beaten by Philippe Etancelin's Talbot, which had an engine three times larger; in the second heat, Juan's team-mate Campos won from another French star, Maurice Trintignant. In the Grand Prix proper, Juan trounced both Etancelin and Trintignant, and on this occasion the organisers, by now fully aware of Monsieur Fangio's potential, were ready with the Argentine national anthem.

'Fangio has earned himself a reputation for driving as fast as possible from start to finish of a race, sliding all his corners and giving very little quarter – in fact, motor racing all the time,' wrote Rodney Walkerly in *Motor* magazine. 'His braking is finished long before the corner begins, and after that the right foot is hard down through the bend. He is the specialist in cornering on the slide and in the use of wide throttle in all gears at all times.'

Many thousands of voices continued to sing Juan's praises in accompaniment to the now famous 'Fangio!' tango that served as the theme song in broadcasts transmitted live back to Argentina on Radio Belgrano. The broadcasters, who had earlier covered some of Juan's South American road races, were the brothers Manuel 'Corner' Sojit and Luis Elias Sojit, whose loud, histrionic commentary conducted against a background of howling racing cars brought home the thrilling drama in which the country's national hero was now immersed.

The success of the Argentine team was rewarded with increasing amounts of appearance money paid by race or-ganisers. This was sorely needed, since the prize money on offer at each Grand Prix averaged between 20,000 and 30,000 francs per win, which was substantially less than Juan had received for winning post-war races in South America. The 'starting money' was put to good use to pay for the team's travel costs, though as the controller of the purse strings Juan continued to practise strict economy measures. They ate frugally in cheap restaurants, and for most race weekends the Achille Varzi team transporters served as sleeping quarters. Meanwhile, in Italy, where the Lubra-sponsored team was based, the oil supplier now owed Juan 600,000 lira, a substantial amount that Juan at first had difficulty collecting. It took three visits to the Lubra headquarters before Francesco Corvella finally made himself available to present Juan with a cheque neither of them had really expected to see. As was his custom, Juan's winning ways were accompanied by such infectious charm that Corvella became a firm friend.

But no Lubra bonus was collected in the next race, the Grand Prix of Rome, where another friend led Juan astray by suggesting he should compete in an untried Maserati sports car instead of the Gordini, which was much better suited to the short track. On the first lap at the Caracalla circuit Juan nearly crashed when he had difficulty finding the unfamiliarly mounted brake pedal. On the second lap the gearshift knob came off, and within a few laps Juan's hand was cut and bleeding profusely. His forward progress was further hampered by the Maserati's tendency to veer alarmingly sideways in corners because of a handling imbalance. Juan's miserable race ended with a not unwelcome piston failure.

The Rome Grand Prix was dominated by Villoresi and Taruffi in V12-engined Ferrari Formula 2 cars, which Juan decided would be essential investments for his ACA team's future. Since the Scuderia Ferrari team was winning all the major races it was necessary for the Equipo Achille Varzi to be similarly equipped. Juan made this suggestion in a telephone call to the ACA's head of motorsport Francisco Borgonovo in Buenos Aires. Juan explained that the team's well-worn, year-old Grand Prix cars were now badly in need of extensive overhauling that could only be done at the Maserati factory at a cost likely to be not much less than buying new Ferraris. There was a sense of urgency, Juan insisted, because the forthcoming Grand Prix at Italy's famed Autodromo di Monza, on 26 June, was an important Formula 2 event for which the Italian stars in the latest Ferraris were entered.

Juan's assessment of the sorry state of his Maserati was confirmed at the next race, the Belgian Grand Prix at Spa, where a broken piston in qualifying was followed by a broken valve on the second lap of the race. Back in Argentina, the wheels were set in motion for the country's team to make a comeback. A few days before the Grand Prix at Monza, Juan received a telegram from the ACA informing him that the Perón government had authorised the purchase of two new Ferrari Tipo 166

Formula 2 cars, which were now awaiting collection at the Ferrari factory in nearby Maranello. When Juan arrived there, however, he was told that no payment had yet been received and the cars could not be released. During a hurried phone call to the ACA, Juan was informed that Borgonovo and club president Carlos Anesi, who were already in Europe to attend the annual meeting of the International Federation of Motorsport, would go to Maranello and sort out the situation.

When the ACA representatives arrived at Ferrari headquarters they found to their despair that the two brand-new cars, one ready to go but still painted in Italian racing red and the other not yet fully assembled or painted, would not be sprayed as requested in the Argentine colours of yellow and blue, let alone leave the factory until Ferrari received the sum of $11,000 per car. Juan made another phone call to Buenos Aires, this time to a friend who was a government official, who told Juan that there were indeed some misgivings about making an investment of $22,000 that would only ever pay off if a Ferrari won for Argentina. Juan assured his friend that a win was entirely possible, and was in return assured that the money for at least one of the cars would arrive in time for the race. This promise from the Argentine government, together with the persuasive efforts of the ACA's Borgonovo and Anesi, resulted in one red Ferrari being released to Juan.

Three days before the race he drove it from Maranello to the nearby Modena circuit where, after a few laps, a gearbox fault became apparent. Juan drove the car back to Maranello, but the car's inability to properly engage fifth gear could not be rectified in the limited time available.

In qualifying at Monza, despite being unable to use fifth gear and being unfamiliar with the track, Juan managed to circumnavigate the nearly four-mile lap in a time that put him on the second row of the grid. The handicap of having only four gears had been partially alleviated by fitting his Ferrari's rear axle with longer gearing that sent the two-litre engine soaring and screaming on the redline at 7,500rpm down Monza's two long straights. To compensate for any time lost there, Juan attacked the track's famous corners – Lesmo, Vialone, Vedano and the Parabolica – with all the vengeance and vigour his Ferrari's nimble chassis allowed.

When he was not on the track, Juan wandered around, looking over the opposition in the paddock and savouring the atmosphere of Italy's storied circuit. Located in the industrial suburb of Monza twelve miles north of Milan, the Autodromo was surrounded by a heavily wooded park that was first used in 1806 as hunting grounds for royalty and aristocrats. Over the years it had been given over to public use, with the addition of a golf course, a polo ground and a race track, which became Italy's shrine of speed. During World War Two the park and the race facilities were commandeered by the military and eventually used as a storage depot for armoured vehicles by troops fighting on both sides of the conflict. When the Allied forces pulled out at the end of the war the grounds and the race track were left in considerable disarray. The first post-war race had been held only eight months previously, and improvements and modifications were still being made right up to race day in 1949.

Ahead of Juan on the front row of Monza's wide starting grid were the four Ferraris of the official factory team driven by Villoresi, Ascari, Felice Bonetto and Piero Carini. Beside Juan on the second row were the privately entered Ferraris of Franco Cortese and Chico Landi, and a German-entered AFM-BMW driven by the pre-war Auto Union star Hans Stuck. For Juan, to be so well placed in such illustrious company at the historic Autodromo di Monza was a racing dream come true. Similarly affected, and equally anxious for the impending drama to be played out in full, were the millions of his countrymen who that Sunday were glued to Radio Belgrano. Mercifully, they remained unaware of just how close the Grand Prix of Monza came to being a non-event for Argentina.

In the final countdown prior to the start, the cars were pushed from the pit garages into their positions on the grid. But there was an ominous gap on the second row, for Fangio's Ferrari was being held back in the pits. There, a spectating Borgonovo and Anesi were told that the car would not race unless payment was immediately forthcoming. With nothing less than Argentine national honour and prestige at stake, the two ACA officials hastily drafted and personally signed an IOU to the tune of $11,000. It was a huge gamble on their part since the club's finances fell far short of such an amount (in fact, the money – for both cars – was eventually supplied by a wealthy businessman friend of Juan Perón). At Monza, as his Ferrari was finally pushed on to the grid, the disturbing financial facts were withheld from Juan so as not to burden him with added pressure.

As the starter waved his flag with a flourish, the field stormed away in unison down the long straight, Stuck just managing to edge into the lead as the cars disappeared into the forest. In short order, the AFM-BMW was displaced by the Ferraris of Ascari, Villoresi, Fangio, Bonetto and Landi. After another few laps of furious wheel-to-wheel racing, the order was Fangio, Villoresi, Ascari, Bonetto. As Juan sped down the pit straight he glimpsed a message on his pit board showing he had just broken Monza's lap record. He quickly reduced his pace, bearing in mind his strategy of making only one pit stop for fresh tyres and refuelling, and that 312 miles of absolutely flat-out racing in the shimmering heat of the Italian summer would surely be too much to ask of his car's overstressed engine. He let Ascari, Villoresi and Bonetto go by, then tucked in behind the Ferrari factory trio. With the Brazilian Landi closely following Juan, the five-car train thundered around Monza at a fearsome clip.

On the 22nd lap, Villoresi's car gave up the struggle, leaving Bonetto, Ascari and Fangio in front until lap 40 – the halfway point of the race – when all three cars peeled off into the pits for servicing. The Ferrari team's more efficient pit crew performed their duties fastest, and by the time he resumed racing Juan was twelve seconds behind Ascari, though still ahead of Bonetto. To reduce the gap, Juan drove like a man possessed, and on the 51st lap he set by far the fastest lap of the race. As his pit crew informed him that he was now six seconds behind Ascari, a burning sensation in his legs made Juan aware that his relentless pursuit was taxing his car in the extreme. The heat in the cockpit soared, and a glance at the temperature gauge confirmed that the engine was at boiling point. Juan was forced to ease up.

Salvation came on the 69th lap when Ascari pulled into the pits again, handing the lead back to Juan. But his first place became increasingly tenuous. Some of the spokes on the Ferrari's rear wheels began to give way, causing a serious vibration and making hard cornering increasingly risky. Meanwhile, the oil pressure gauge began to drop towards zero whenever Juan negotiated right-hand turns. But another pit stop was out of the question, so Juan modified his pace by limiting the engine revs to 7,000, though he was still averaging over 100mph. Bonetto and Ascari were now closing in at a rate of two seconds a lap, but Juan managed to nurse his ailing car across the finish line first.

It seemed incredible that a man from faraway Balcarce in Argentina could come to the Autodromo di Monza and in his first race in a Ferrari, in a car identical to those driven by the Ferrari stars in their team's home race, could actually win.

'Fangio himself is an extremely quiet chap, short, thickset, extremely powerful, balding, beefy, and speaks with a surprisingly high, small voice, rather reminiscent of Rudolph Caracciola,' *Motor*'s Rodney Walkerly wrote. 'He is unmarried, friendly, modest, and drives like a demon.' In *Motor Sport*, Denis Jenkinson echoed Walkerly's delight: 'To those of us who have been fortunate enough to see this Fangio in action, the fact that he scored several wins in his first appearances in European racing does not come as such a surprise, for he really "motor races" with his car, in a manner that is a joy to behold.'

But though his Monza victory was a major milestone in terms of establishing his name in Europe, to his car supplier Juan Manuel Fangio was just another creditor. To repair the damaged engine, which was so far gone that it refused to fire up after the race, Enzo Ferrari presented Juan with an invoice for 300,000 lira, which was considerably more than the prize money he won at Monza.

There were more bills to pay when the rebuilt Maseratis were collected from Modena, from where they were transported to central France for the next race, at Albi. There, Juan won again after a terrific duel with Farina, whose similar Maserati failed to finish, leaving Bira's Maserati in second place. In fact, Bira was able to compete only because Juan had loaned him the ACA team's only spare engine block after Bira's had cracked in practice. Juan's natural generosity was in this case coupled with a need to have strong opponents to inspire him to keep on improving as a driver, but his gesture of good will provoked an angry outburst from Amadeo Bignami, who strongly disapproved of such close fraternising with rivals and thought it stupid to loan out vital spares.

The team's last Grand Prix of that summer was at Reims, where Juan had made his unheralded European debut the year before, and where this year there were races for both Grand Prix and Formula 2 cars. During practice on the champagne-country circuit, Juan's rebuilt Maserati engine began to falter. He suspected it was running on only three cylinders, but Bignami disagreed. They argued, and when Juan insisted that the engine be taken out and examined it was found that one cylinder was indeed not firing properly because a valve seat had been damaged and pressure was escaping. Bignami said nothing could be done to repair it in the time available and the car could not race, but once again Juan said he would do the job himself. That night, he took the engine into Reims and found a General Motors dealership where he removed the damaged valve seat, reground it, put the engine back together again and arrived back at the track early in the morning with only a few hours to spare before the race began. Though he'd had hardly any sleep, his repair work was first rate; Juan was leading comfortably in the race when he was forced to park the Maserati after the accelerator cable broke. In the Formula 2 race, with Ascari and Villoresi representing the Ferrari team, Juan built up a lead of some 30 seconds when his Ferrari's gear lever snapped off and he had to stop. Ascari went on to win the race, and Juan later found out that the fault was common to all the Ferraris, though it had only been fixed on the official team cars.

Despite the twin failures at Reims, Juan's four wins in the Maserati, another in the Gordini, and especially his sensational Ferrari victory at Monza marked him out as the rising single-seater star of 1949. Ever level-headed and modest, Juan felt that the time had come to leave Europe. 'When one runs the risk of losing a sense of proportion,' he said, 'it's time to go home and sleep in the same bed in which one dreamt while still a nobody, and to eat the simple, healthy dishes of one's childhood.' But the widespread recognition and praise from the media and public in Europe paled in comparison to the reception that awaited Juan in his native land.

On 25 August, he boarded a Constellation at Orly airport in Paris and slept all the way across the south Atlantic to Buenos

Aires. It was early evening when the plane landed at Ezeiza airport and taxied to the terminal. As Juan descended the stairway to the tarmac, thousands of flashbulbs popped and the tremendous crowd that had assembled to greet him chanted his name. 'Fangio! Fangio! Fangio!' they exclaimed. A military band played a rousing version of 'Fangio!', and the dramatic tango beat was accompanied by hundreds of rhythmically waved banners and placards that proclaimed WELCOME HOME CHAMPION. Government officials whisked the conquering hero through the clutching fans to a waiting limousine which became part of a triumphant motorcade that set off with horns blaring on a victory parade through the streets of Buenos Aires to Casa Rosada, the palatial residence of the Peróns. Both the president and his wife Evita waved formalities aside and kissed and hugged the nation's most celebrated citizen, before taking him inside to a state reception and banquet. Among the honoured guests paying tribute were the Galvez brothers and Domingo Marimón.

When Juan finally managed to extricate himself from the Buenos Aires homecoming, he drove an Alfa Romeo road car back to Balcarce, where his arrival was met with scarcely less enthusiasm. He drove slowly through the assembled throng, many of them standing on rooftops or perched on top of buses to get a better view, acknowledging their 'El Chueco!' chants and shouted tributes with bashful waves and an embarrassed smile. By the time he got to the family home he was fighting back tears, and when Papa and Mama Fangio rushed out to embrace their returning son he wept openly.

This return to his roots gave Juan a renewed sense of well-being. Despite all his success, there had been an aura of unreality about it that he found unsettling. And there was always a chance that success could go to a man's head and transform his character for the worse. The best way to prevent this from happening, Juan decided, was to immerse himself straight back in his old life. 'Once back in my garage, with my hands covered in grease and oil, I felt relieved,' he recalled. 'I had risked letting the glory go to my head, but I was still really myself.'

Over the next couple of months, Juan helped his partners run the Balcarce garage and sold trucks on the side. And though he was now a committed single-seater racer, the lure of tackling another marathon road race in his trusty old Chevrolet coupé was too great to resist, and he entered the Gran Premio de la Republica. Run over three weeks in November, the event's twelve stages covered nearly 7,000 miles of the wildest roads in Argentina. Some of his friends thought it unwise for Juan to take what would be a backward step akin, they said, to a jockey switching from a thoroughbred racehorse to a mule. But for Juan his mode of transport mattered less than the nostalgic need to return to his racing roots and indulge again in the risky yet romantic extremes that could only be found in adventures on the open road.

To start the race, he was given the number two position between the Galvez brothers, Oscar starting first and Juan third. Throughout the event the trio traded stage wins, with Fangio victorious in the second, seventh and ninth. He might have won more had he not been delayed by a typical long-distance misadventure. During a refuelling stop at a remote crossroad junction he was given a drum of petrol that proved to be tainted with traces of water. He emptied the contaminated batch from the Chev's fuel tank, but the damage was done, and the water droplets lingering in the fuel line periodically clogged up the carburettor. Frequent stops to drain the system and change the fuel filter failed to cure the misfiring engine. By the time Juan traced the continuing malfunction to a broken coil, too much time had been lost for him to win overall, though he still split the Galvez brothers in the final standings.

Juan Galvez won, but it was Oscar who suggested to their friend Fangio that perhaps he was now too far out of touch with this specialised category of racing in which he had formerly excelled. Juan agreed, admitting that he was badly out of practice and no longer felt quite as much at home on dirt roads. From then on, while the Galvez brothers continued to dominate South American road racing for several years, Juan would thereafter only ever race occasionally in sports cars, mostly in single-seaters.

He furthered his education in the latter discipline with the resumption of another series of Argentine Temporada races, which began in December 1949 and continued into January the following year. Juan contested the four races in one of the ACA club's Ferraris, with the Italians Ascari, Villoresi and Farina, driving similar cars, forming the main opposition. In the first race, the Premio Juan Domingo Perón on the Palermo circuit in Buenos Aires, Ascari led Fangio and Villoresi, whose private battle for second place lost them valuable time and enabled Ascari to go on to an untroubled win. Anxious to make a mark in the race for his cheering home crowd, Juan set a new lap record. In his zeal to lower it again, he sped through a patch of freshly dropped oil and spun wildly, though he managed to recover and finish second, ahead of Villoresi.

In the second race, again on the Palermo circuit but this time named the Gran Premio Maria Eva Duarte de Perón, the lead was again disputed by Ascari, Villoresi and Fangio. Juan led from the start, and Ascari's challenge ended with a spin into the straw bales that lined the circuit. Villoresi took up the chase, and in his effort to stay ahead Juan suffered a similar fate to Ascari. However, Juan's Ferrari was able to continue after a pit stop to replace a broken wheel, and he eventually finished fourth.

In the Gran Premio Ciudad Mar del Plata, the Italian stars vowed to put the Argentine upstart in his place and set the fastest practice times. But Juan beat them off the startline and a battle royal commenced, Farina joining his countrymen in their pursuit of Fangio. When Farina's engine failed, Villoresi chose to overtake Juan on the inside of a corner, but lost control and spun sideways into the middle of the track where Juan was unable to avoid hitting him. It was an extremely dangerous incident, though fortunately neither driver was hurt. Their Ferraris, however, were smashed beyond repair, and Ascari won the race unopposed.

In the last Temporada race, the Premio Ciudad de Rosario, Juan learnt yet more valuable lessons the hard way. Again leading from the start, he soon built up a lead of over a minute over Villoresi, and by the time Ascari had dropped out with an overheating engine Juan had begun lapping slower cars. One of them was a Maserati driven by the Italian Felice Bonetto, who was so busy concentrating on his own race that he failed to notice Juan's Ferrari as it began an overtaking manoeuvre on the outside of a fast corner on the narrow street circuit. When the Maserati swerved directly into his path in the confined quarters, Juan had no choice but to drive straight off the track. His Ferrari jumped the kerb, ploughed through a pile of straw bales and crashed head-on into a metal lamp-post. Villoresi won the race, and though Juan was completely unhurt, the painful experience of throwing away a certain win through an act of imprudence stayed with him. Granted, there had been no flag marshals to warn Bonetto to give way, but the responsibility to exercise patience lay with the overtaker, especially when he had by far the faster car. When you have this advantage, Juan understood, you must never be in too much of a hurry to get past opponents. Furthermore, and most importantly, he realised the fundamental truth contained in the old racing adage: to finish first, you must first finish.

Though his Temporada misadventures should have been explained away as just racing accidents, the fiercely partisan

Argentine media, to Juan's consternation, construed them as examples of an Italian conspiracy intended to undermine his growing reputation, if not deliberately to place roadblocks in his way. News of this controversial and quite wrong theory spread to Italy, where the media retaliated furiously, condemning the silly South Americans for questioning the honour and sportsmanship of the great Italian drivers. The atmosphere became increasingly tense, and even threatened to escalate into an international incident that might hinder Juan's chances of furthering his career in Europe. Ascari and Villoresi took Juan aside and told him as much. Juan apologised profusely to the rivals he admired and respected. When Ascari and Villoresi suggested he make a public statement to quell the growing controversy, Juan quickly agreed. He spoke on Radio Belgrano, telling the Sojit brothers that the Argentine media must stop making unfounded and untrue statements and cease insulting the integrity of his rivals.

Later, both Alberto Ascari and Luigi Villoresi confessed to Juan that they had at first been surprised and concerned at how immediately competitive he had been in a discipline they had considered a private domain. While impressed by his obvious talent, they were also soon won over by his personal warmth and humble charm. They had a meal together, and the trio became fast friends, often meeting with other drivers for boisterous get-togethers at a café in Milan. Juan, fluent in the language of his parents, was treated as an honorary Italian, and was welcomed into the exclusive fraternity of Grand Prix drivers, a profession that now took over his life.

Part II: Maestro

1950–58: The Old Man Becomes a Legend

Chapter Eight

1950: First Formula 1 Season (Alfa Romeo)

'*I felt like a singer suddenly invited to perform at La Scala di Milano, or the Metropolitan in New York, or the Colón in Buenos Aires. It was the happiest moment of my life.*'

IN 1950, THE BIG NEWS in international motorsport was that single-seater competition at the highest level would henceforth be formally organised into an annual series of Grand Prix races for the World Championship of Drivers. While a world championship had first taken place in 1925 (it was won by Alfa Romeo), it was for national makes of Grand Prix cars rather than drivers. The new series, though it would still very much showcase national automotive prestige, put more of an emphasis on the men rather than the machines.

The governing body of motorsport, the Fédération Internationale de l'Automobile (FIA), based in Paris, established a mechanical formula for the cars limiting engine capacities to 1.5 litres supercharged or 4.5 litres unsupercharged. The Formula 1 cars, as they were known, would in 1950 compete in seven international Grands Prix, each one in a different country at a road-racing venue with a tradition of staging major motorsport events. Though the series was naturally heavily biased towards Europe, where cars were invented and where motorsport had begun in the late nineteenth century, the FIA made a token gesture to the New World by including the USA's famed Indianapolis 500 in the championship. But this 500-mile race, held on an oval track and contested by purpose-built cars using special engines, was destined to remain very much an insular American affair, with only the occasional crossover between the two disciplines.

The inaugural World Championship race was scheduled to be held at the British circuit of Silverstone in an event called the Grand Prix of Europe. This would be followed by the Monaco Grand Prix, run through the streets of Monte Carlo; the Indianapolis 500 (uncontested by non-American drivers); the Swiss Grand Prix at Bremgarten; the Belgian Grand Prix at Spa-Francorchamps; the French Grand Prix at Reims; and the Italian Grand Prix at Monza. At each race points would be awarded to the drivers: eight for first place, six for second, four for third, three for fourth and two for fifth, with one point given to the driver who set the fastest race lap. At the end of the season the scores would be added up and the overall winner would be officially declared the World Drivers' Champion.

In 1950, Europe was still recovering from the devastation of war, so the first entrants in the new championship would have to use updated pre-war machinery that conformed to Formula 1 requirements. In France, Talbot and Gordini cars were available, while in Italy Maserati and Alfa Romeo had suitable cars. Ferrari was preparing cars for the new series, but they were as yet an unknown quantity – unlike the team's driving strength, which featured three drivers with excellent track records: Alberto Ascari, Luigi Villoresi and Raymond Sommer. Alfa Romeo, following the fatal accidents that claimed the lives of its top drivers Varzi (1948) and Wimille (1949) and the recent death from cancer of Count Trossi, was now in search of suitable candidates for cars the Italian manufacturer felt sure were capable of winning the new championship. Indeed, though the 1.5-litre supercharged Alfettas were first designed in 1937, they had been virtually unbeatable whenever they appeared in post-war competition. The Alfa Romeo directors decided to enter a team of three cars that preferably should be driven by Italians. The best available were Giuseppe Farina and the pre-war star Luigi Fagioli, both of whom were promptly signed to contracts. For its third driver, Alfa decided to pursue Juan Manuel Fangio, whose ancestry after all was Italian, and whose Italian-based racing team was named after the great Achille Varzi. Moreover, and most importantly, this Fangio in his recent performances had demonstrated that he was capable of acquitting himself well against the world's best drivers. Besides, the publicity-conscious Alfa Romeo hierarchy decided, a line-up of Farina, Fagioli and Fangio – the 'Three Fs' – had a nice ring to it.

In February 1950, as he was preparing to head back to Europe with the ACA's Achille Varzi team, Juan received a telegram from Alfa Romeo headquarters in Milan requesting his services for the forthcoming World Championship series of Grand Prix races. Under the terms of the proposed arrangement, Juan would be free to compete in other events in which there was no official Alfa Romeo team entry. Without a moment's hesitation, Juan sent a telegram back to Alfa Romeo accepting the offer to drive for one of the most famous teams in racing, in a car whose thoroughbred lines he had first admired at Reims in 1948. There, he had watched Wimille win in the Alfetta bearing Alfa Romeo's lucky four-leaf clover insignia. In the paddock at Reims, Juan had been fascinated by the car's little 1500cc eight-cylinder engine; how could such a comparatively tiny device produce so much horsepower? Now, he had heard, with a two-stage supercharger it was developing 334bhp, and he couldn't wait to get behind the wheel of the Alfa Romeo Tipo 158, as the 1950 Formula 1 car was called.

Before the Alfetta opportunity came along, Juan had raced two other Italian cars for the ACA's Achille Varzi team. He came third with the Formula 2 Ferrari in a 125-mile race run in torrential rain in Marseilles, behind the identical but much better-tuned factory cars of Villoresi and Ascari, and at Pau, where he had won in the Maserati in 1949, he did so again, defeating Villoresi and Ascari convincingly. In the Marseilles race, Farina crashed and broke his shoulder, meaning that he could not drive at San Remo, a non-championship race in which Alfa had chosen to make its 1950 debut with a two-car entry for the veteran Italian and the new Argentine recruit. The two cars were duly brought to San Remo, but in the absence of the reliable veteran, the Alfa team's management was reluctant to place its complete trust in Juan, who hadn't even signed a contract yet, let alone driven an Alfetta, and whose presence in the team had already caused a backlash in the Italian press. Fearing adverse publicity should Fangio falter, Alfa Romeo seriously considered withdrawing from the race and returning to Milan. As word of this possibility reached the organisers, who had attracted a huge crowd by basing all their pre-race publicity on the return to competition of Italy's all-conquering Alfetta cars, there were threats of lawsuits for lost revenue, cars being impounded, potential rioting among disgruntled spectators, and so on. Finally, albeit reluctantly on Alfa Romeo's part, Juan was allowed to venture out on a few practice laps, during which it began to rain, a state of affairs that was also forecast for the rest of the weekend. It did not bode at all well for a newcomer in an unfamiliar car.

In the pit lane at San Remo, Juan presented his increasingly nervous new bosses with a proposition that put his neck on the line and his car in the race. Juan told them they had nothing to lose in the San Remo Grand Prix. A loss would be attributed to the incompetent Fangio; a victory, by a virtual debutant in an obviously unbeatable car, would bring glory to Alfa Romeo.

During qualifying on the sinuous and intermittently wet Ospedaletti circuit, the Fangio Alfetta traded fastest times with Ascari and Villoresi, who were driving new Ferraris with 1.5-litre supercharged engines. 'Those first laps were just about the worst in my life,' Juan said later, 'for my whole future depended on the outcome.' In the end, the Alfetta qualified on the front row between the two Ferraris, and on Sunday, 16 April the Grand Prix of San Remo commenced, on a rainswept track on which only the most sure-footed would remain mobile for the 190 miles of dangerous driving that lay ahead.

In his anxiety at the start, Juan applied too much throttle and wasted several precious seconds in futile wheelspin; a flood of cars left him behind in their spray. Momentarily, he was plunged into despair, fearful that this, one of the worst starts of his life, would result in an embarrassingly short tenure as a professional Formula 1 driver. But his racing future depended on overcoming such emotions, as well as the elements, and Juan began to take control of himself and his car. Systematically, concentrating hard on driving with delicacy and precision, he began to make progress, picking off cars one by one and gradually reducing the distance between himself and the race-leading Ferraris. Before long, the Alfetta appeared in the misty wake of the Villoresi car, and a few laps later it splashed past it. On the thirteenth of the 90 laps, as it was negotiating a hairpin bend, the Alfetta dived into the blinding spray behind the Ascari Ferrari, and by the time they emerged from the sodden gloom the Alfetta was in front. Twenty laps later, Ascari's ambitious pursuit of Juan proved beyond the limits of adhesion available on the circuit's soaked surface, and his Ferrari spun off, leaving Villoresi to chase in vain after the frontrunning Alfetta. In the end, Juan's winning margin was over a minute and his Alfetta had averaged over 60mph in a race that completely won over his team. The joyful Alfa Romeo mechanics hoisted Juan on to their shoulders and carried him to the victory podium.

Back at the San Remo hotel where they were staying, the Alfa team principals eagerly presented their new star with a contract that contained all the terms of his employment except for the vital matter of money. Ceremoniously, they proffered a gold pen for his signature and somewhat apprehensively asked him how much he wanted. As he solemnly inscribed his name on the document that entitled him to drive the best Grand Prix car in the world, he refrained from uttering aloud what was on his mind: that this was one of the greatest opportunities of his racing life and he would gladly drive for nothing. Instead, Juan looked up at his new employers and quietly said that they could fill in the blank space with whatever amount they thought suitable. 'They didn't know what to think,' he recalled. 'I had given them a sort of blank cheque. What they didn't understand was that this was one of the best moments of my life.'

A week later, Juan's first official job as an employee of Alfa Romeo was to represent the company in Italy's classic 1,000-mile road race, the Mille Miglia. Following his brilliant debut in San Remo, Juan had been hastily added to the team's sports car roster, leaving him with very little time to familiarise himself with the experimental two-seater six-cylinder 2500cc Alfa Romeo Sport and no time at all to learn the famous route, firmly etched in the minds of every Italian with an ounce of sporting blood (that is to say, most of the nation). It went from the city of Brescia in the north southward to Rome and back via excursions on to both the Adriatic and Mediterranean coasts and into the mountainous regions in between. Passing through many historic cities, the route might have served as a history and geography lesson had Juan been on a tour of the land of his forefathers, but the Mille Miglia was a serious race in which he was expected to lead the country's most famous racing team in an assault on a battlefield with which he was worryingly unfamiliar against opponents who knew it by heart. To help Juan find his way, Alfa Romeo assigned a senior mechanic, Augusto Zanardi, to ride with him.

Their Alfa Romeo Sport was a hardtop model, inside which the engine noise reverberated like a drum. Conversation, had it been possible, would have had to be made through teeth sent chattering by the hastily assembled car's undeveloped and rock-hard suspension. As a means of communication, Zanardi devised a system of banging his fist on the dashboard within sight of Juan's juddering vision. One blow of his fist meant a dangerous corner lay ahead; a two-fister meant rather more danger; and three blows from Zanardi signified extreme danger ahead. Though he wondered if his passenger's warning system might benefit from being reversed, so that a single blow signified the biggest hazard, Juan soon found out that Zanardi might as well have constantly thumped the dashboard for 1,000 miles.

Unlike the South American open road races which mostly traversed remote areas where local traffic and spectators varied from scarce to non-existent, Italy's Mille Miglia, which was first run in 1926, took place on ordinary public roads that were not closed to civilian traffic, even when the competitors were hurtling through cities, towns and villages. In urban areas, there were also dense crowds of hyper-enthusiastic onlookers who expressed their passion for the tremendous spectacle of speed by leaning out in front of the careering cars, sometimes even slapping them as they shot past within inches of their feet. Though the roads were paved, they were also often severely potholed, especially in the less populated mountain regions where they were bordered by low stone walls that afforded little protection from the rocky ravines below.

At the start in Brescia, it seemed to Juan that half the cars in Italy had entered the race, which was open to proper sports racing cars, touring coupés, family sedans and nearly every category of roadworthy machine. In fact, there were almost 400 entries, among which the Fangio-Zanardi Alfa Romeo Competizione coupé was assigned the number 730, signifying its starting time of 7.30 a.m. The cars were flagged off at one-minute intervals from the starting ramp on the outskirts of Brescia. For Juan, the many hours that followed – through Verona, Vicenza, Padua and Ferrara to Ravenna, then down the Adriatic coast to Rimini and past Ancona to Pescara before heading inland through the Abruzzi mountains – passed in a blur. Though the Abruzzi region was where the Fangios had originated, Juan's ancestry was the furthest thing from his mind, which was fully occupied with trying to maintain control over his speeding Alfa as it climbed up the mountain curves towards L'Aquila in a blinding rainstorm – weather with which the Alfa was seriously ill equipped to do battle, because the wipers didn't work. Nor were the by now well-worn brakes doing their job adequately. Several wild slides ensued, and on one of them, a particularly vicious side-to-side tank-slapper, Juan accompanied his frantic yet successful corrective steering movements and quick-shifting gear changes with a high-pitched yell that made the startled Zanardi wonder if his precious life was in the hands of 'a wild Indian from the pampas'. On another occasion, the Alfa bounded over a sudden bump at 112mph and crash-landed heavily, bringing Zanardi's head into sharp contact with the roof. Juan slowed briefly and shook his groggy passenger back to consciousness.

As the Alfa sped on through the persistent rain towards Rome, the route ahead became doubly difficult to see as the increasingly heavy breathing of its occupants caused the inside of the wiperless windscreen to steam over. They almost missed the checkpoint in Rome, hardly saw Civitavecchia on the Ligurian coast, and were mostly unaware of Siena, Livorno, Pisa and Florence. By the time they had climbed back through the Tuscan hills and down into Bologna on the Lombardy plain, nightfall, as well as heavy fog, made anything more than a snail's pace nigh on suicidal.

Summoning up one of the old survival techniques that had served him so well in several South American road races, Juan slotted in behind another car, an open-cockpit Frazer Nash whose occupants had the benefit of being able to see where they were going. With the Frazer Nash leading the way, the Alfa passed through Modena, Reggio, Parma, Piacenza and Cremona and finally arrived back where it had started, at the finish line in Brescia. When the timekeepers had tallied the results, the winner of the 1950 Mille Miglia was declared as the Marzotto-Crosara Ferrari Berlinetta. In second place was another of the Ferrari team's Berlinettas. In third, having covered the 1,000 miles in a time of fourteen hours, two minutes and five seconds, was the Fangio-Zanardi Alfa Romeo.

GRAND PRIX OF EUROPE

To accommodate his new situation with Alfa Romeo, which would require visits to company headquarters in Milan and attendance at test sessions at the nearby Monza circuit, Juan moved from the Varzi house in Galliate to the Albergo Colombia, a small, unpretentious but well-kept hotel located on a quiet backstreet near Milan's bustling central station. In a city renowned for its chic and trendy areas it was a less fashionable neighbourhood than a professional racing driver might have been expected to reside in, but Juan's needs were modest and he felt comfortable in a down-to-earth environment that soon felt like home. With his gentle, modest manner he charmed everyone he met, befriending the hotel staff, the proprietors of shops and cafés, and street vendors, remembering their names and enquiring after their families. He ate his meals at a lively family-run taverna around the corner from the hotel, and in the evenings he often visited Tinarelli's, a small automotive workshop not dissimilar to the Fangio premises in Balcarce that served as a clubhouse where racing-minded people met. Soon the rustic former mechanic was the talk of Tinarelli's, indeed the talk of all Italy and the racing world at large.

For personal use Juan was given a red and black Alfa Romeo coupé in which he shuttled back and forth between Milan and the ACA's base in Galliate. The Argentine contingent for 1950 included two new drivers as team-mates for Juan, Alfredo Pian and José Froilán González. Neither of them featured in a non-championship race at Monza, where Juan's fight for the lead with Ascari ended with engine failure in the ACA's Ferrari. A week later, Juan was again behind the wheel of the Alfetta to contest an historic event: the first race of the World Championship.

Given the significance of the Grand Prix of Europe, the British venue of Silverstone, about 70 miles north-west of London, seemed somewhat nondescript compared to the better-known European tracks, which tended to have more character as well as a longer tradition of racing. During the war, Silverstone's flat, featureless terrain had served as an RAF bomber base, and from the airfield's windswept concrete runways a road course had been fashioned on which Formula 1 cars would perform. The entry list was for the most part also rather rag-tag, consisting mainly of privately entered and well-used Maseratis and Talbots, as well as several British-built ERA and Alta cars driven by amateurs. In light of this, the official Alfa Romeo team, its driving strength of Farina, Fagioli and Fangio augmented by a fourth car piloted by the Englishman Reg Parnell, was expected to dominate.

Before the start, on Sunday, 13 May, the twenty drivers were presented to the British royal family, whose sporting interests were mostly confined to horsepower of a non-motorised variety but whose presence at the race signified its importance to the country. King George VI and his smiling queen, together with their young daughters Princesses Elizabeth and Margaret, showed a keen interest in the drivers, and the King exchanged a few words with most of them. When Fangio's turn came, the King asked a question to which Juan responded with a 'no speak English' answer that led to an embarrassing pause in the proceedings. The awkward situation was skilfully retrieved by Juan when he told his interpreter to tell the King that he didn't need to speak in order to drive fast. The amusing remark raised a right royal laugh.

For once, even the fickle British weather rose to the occasion, and the Grand Prix took place in pleasant spring sunshine. As a race, however, it was more of a demonstration run for the Alfettas, the Three Fs taking it in turns to lead, followed by Parnell. With eight laps to go, the frontrunning foursome was reduced to a trio when an oil pipe broke on the second-placed Fangio car and it retired in a cloud of smoke. Thus it was that Farina, Fagioli and Parnell were the first drivers to stand on an official F1 World Championship podium.

GRAND PRIX DE MONACO

Juan's second chance to make an impression on the new championship came the next weekend in the famous race through the streets of the fairytale principality of Monaco. Clinging to the precipitous cliffs of the Alpes Maritime and overlooking the blue Mediterranean, the tiny country's splendid architecture was crammed into crowded confines that afforded even its privileged citizens precious little room to manoeuvre. Yet as a glamorous and exotic backdrop for a motor race it was a theatre second to none, and had been since 1929.

Before that first Monaco race, many safety-conscious observers questioned the wisdom of setting loose high-powered racing cars on tight, twisting thoroughfares where even horses, let alone horseless carriages driven at a sedate pace, needed to be ridden with caution. 'It goes without saying,' stated the *Nice Matin* newspaper in 1929, 'that the track is made up entirely of bends, steep uphill climbs and fast downhill descents. Any respectable traffic system would have covered the track with danger signs left, right and centre.' Very little had changed in the intervening 21 years, except that the cars were now much faster, and on the evening before his first appearance there Juan conducted some private research into previous races. The fifteen drivers entered in the 1950 Grand Prix were invited to a reception at the Monaco Automobile Club's headquarters, where Juan entertained himself by examining photograph albums of past events, many of which featured accidents. For the 1936 race, Juan found a photo showing a tangle of wrecked cars, among them two Mercedes-Benzes, a Maserati and an Alfa Romeo driven by his new team-mate, Farina. Studying the shot in detail, Juan came to the conclusion that the crash had probably occurred after one of the cars spun across the track and stalled in the middle of a sharp corner. Because the closely following drivers had been unable to see over the stone walls that lined the track, they had ploughed into the stationary vehicle. Perhaps, Juan thought, they had been too preoccupied to take note of the flags that must have been waved by track marshals. Anyway, he concluded, it would be important to be prepared for such emergencies, and he filed the information away in a memory bank in which he had already deposited many cautionary notes about Monaco's myriad hazards.

Though it was one of the shortest of all circuits – 1.976 miles in its 1950 configuration – it was filled with complications out of all proportion to its length. With no straight worthy of the name, the entire lap was a continuous struggle against centrifugal forces around a profusion of corners, many of them acute and several of them accompanied by an abrupt loss or gain of elevation. Bounded by stone kerbs and balustrades, its undulating surface treacherously disfigured by painted traffic markings and manhole covers, the course was in some places barely wide enough to accommodate a single car, whose occupant must maintain concentration of the highest order to drive with the inch-perfect precision necessary to avoid making even the slightest mistake. An extreme demand was also placed on manual dexterity, since the steering wheel, brakes, clutch, accelerator and gear lever were in constant use. With at least twenty gear changes per lap there would be some 2,000 of them over the 100 laps of the race, which would last, for those that survived, over three hours.

One of those who did not make the race was Juan's compatriot Alfredo Pian, who was driving one of the Achille Varzi team's Maseratis, a Formula 2 car that was among several of this type invited to compete because there wasn't yet enough Formula 1 machinery to fill the grid. During the final practice session, Pian lost control and crashed heavily on the entry to the notoriously difficult Casino Square. Pian was pulled from his wrecked car with a painfully broken leg.

But Argentina was still represented prominently in the race, since pole position was claimed by Juan. Beside him on the starting grid was his Alfa Romeo team-mate Giuseppe Farina, while on the outside of the front row was the second Achille Varzi entry, the Maserati driven by Jose Froilán González, whose unexpected pace was the talk of the town. Behind these three, the impressive entry list boasted the new Formula 1 team fielded by Enzo Ferrari, whose choice of Monaco for his cars' World Championship debut added considerable lustre to the event, and whose drivers (Villoresi, Ascari and Sommer) would, the organisers hoped, provide stiff competition for the much-favoured Three Fs. Also taking the start was the closest Monaco had to a home team, the Gordinis driven by Maurice Trintignant and Robert Manzon, while France was also represented by the Talbots of Rosier, Etancelin and Claes. Though he was driving an Italian car, the great Louis Chiron also sported a French flag on his Maserati.

At the start, wary of Farina's reputation for recklessness, especially in the early laps, Juan fought strenuously to preserve the advantage afforded by his pole position. Farina battled back, but he was also occupied with defending his position against Villoresi, who had sensationally powered his Ferrari forward from the third row of the grid. By the time the wildly jostling pack rounded the Ste Devote corner, Juan's closest pursuer as they charged up the hill was Villoresi, who had managed to elbow aside Farina's Alfetta and was also in front of Fagioli in the third of the F-driven cars. In a crescendo of noise that reverberated off the walls of the buildings, the fiercely fighting field tore up the hill and roared through Casino Square, rocketed down the hill to Mirabeau, careered around the station hairpin, blasted through the darkness of the long tunnel and shot out into the bright sunlight along the harbour front.

But as Fangio and Villoresi pounded past the Bureau de Tabac, chaos erupted behind them. At the Tabac corner, Farina's Alfetta came unstuck on the slick of water thrown up by the waves crashing against the harbour wall. Farina's frantic corrections fell far short of what was necessary to salvage the situation, and his wildly oscillating car struck the kerb and rebounded sideways, directly in front of oncoming traffic. Confronted with this sudden emergency, Fagioli threw his car into an avoidance manoeuvre that failed. As the two Alfettas smashed together, the closely following Maserati of González speared into the wreckage with enough force to part the entwined Alfettas and emerge on the other side. Also managing to squeeze through the aperture created by the González battering ram were Chiron, Sommer and Ascari. When Rosier arrived on the scene, he braked suddenly, whereupon his Talbot was rear-ended by Manzon's Gordini, thus setting off a chain reaction of spins and crashes that within seconds left the track littered with nine crippled cars, several of them with ruptured fuel tanks.

As Juan sped through the harbour chicane, he caught a glimpse of yellow flags being waved in the distance. 'I could detect agitation among the spectators,' he recalled. 'They were not looking at me leading the race, but were looking the other way.' In a flash, Juan remembered the photo of the 1936 accident scene and immediately applied the brakes while raising his hand to warn his pursuers of likely danger ahead.

At the crash site – where, miraculously, no one had been hurt – the route was still blocked by a confusion of sidelined cars that frantic track marshals and course workers were having difficulty clearing aside. Juan took matters into his own hands. Manoeuvring his Alfetta alongside one of the trapped cars, he reached out and managed to push it aside far enough to create a gap through which he could ease his car. Villoresi, after some toing and froing, followed Fangio's cue, as did Ascari and the few others who remained in the Monaco Grand Prix. None of them came close to catching Juan, who finished a lap ahead of Ascari; Villoresi had had to retire with a seized axle, leaving Chiron's Maserati to claim third, two laps behind the leader, who finished three laps ahead of fourth-placed Sommer in the third Ferrari. Only three other cars survived the gruelling contest which lasted three hours and thirteen minutes. Juan's fastest race lap of 64mph, which was only a fraction slower than his pole position time, gave him a total of nine championship points, tying him with Farina.

Yet Juan's first World Championship victory was made less enjoyable by his concern for his injured friend González, whose escape from the multiple crash at Tabac had been followed by a fiery disaster. When González scraped between the two crashed Alfettas, his Maserati's fuel filler cap, located just behind the driver's head, had become dislodged. A few moments later, as González was braking for a corner, the sloshing fuel had sprayed out into the cockpit and was ignited by the backfiring engine. González, momentarily engulfed in flames, had leapt out of the car while it was still moving and rolled over and over on the tarmac. Spectators had rushed to his aid, pulling him off the track and tearing off his smouldering shirt. González, suffering from serious burns to his arms and back, had been taken to the hospital, where his compatriot Pian was also being treated for his badly broken leg. Juan, though he was due to race the next weekend at Monza, spent half the week attending to the welfare of his injured fellow Argentinians. Two days after his Monaco win he removed the seats from his Alfa Romeo road car to make room for a stretcher and drove Pian to a hospital in Bologna that specialised in treating orthopaedic injuries. Juan then returned to Monaco, where he loaded González into his improvised ambulance and transported him back to Italy, to a burns clinic in Novara.

Having expended so much energy on caring for his country-men, Juan was perhaps ill prepared to carry on the crippled Achille Varzi team's fight at Monza. However, it was the engine in Juan's Formula 2 Ferrari that failed to go the distance, forcing him into retirement on the twelfth lap when he was running fourth.

GROSSER PREIS DER SCHWEIZ

The next weekend, another engine malfunction, this time in his Formula 1 Alfa Romeo, left Juan pointless in the third round of the World Championship at the Bremgarten circuit in Switzerland. During qualifying, Juan was easily the best of the Three Fs, putting his car on pole by a comfortable margin. He also led the early laps, but then a burnt valve intervened and he was forced to pull out, leaving his team-mates Farina and Fagioli to run away with the race. Together with his point for fastest lap, Farina improved his championship total to eighteen points, twice as many as his nearest rival, Fangio. Their next confrontation would come two weeks later in Belgium, though on the intervening weekend Juan's peripatetic schedule took him on a detour into France, to Angoulême, for the non-championship Grand Prix des Remparts.

The tiny Angoulême circuit, less than a mile long, made up for its shortcomings by twisting through the narrow streets of the ancient walled town in what amounted to a miniature Monaco Grand Prix. With the 130-lap race starting in mid-afternoon when the temperature stood at 40°C in the shade, this would also be a Grand Prix of endurance for both man and machine. For this race, Juan's Maserati was fitted with a sports car engine and a gearbox that proved faulty at the start, when it jumped out of first gear. Before he was able to force it into action, Juan was overtaken by several cars, among them a Ferrari driven by González, who had recovered remarkably fast from his Monaco burns and was driving as hard as ever, though not as hard as his friend Fangio.

After twenty furious laps, which he later admitted he had driven like an absolute madman ('I thought the heat would kill me'), Juan had carved his way back up through the field and into the lead. Exhausted from the tension and effort of pushing himself so hard in the extreme heat, Juan felt sure he would never be able to finish. His heart sank when he saw the message on his pit board that there were still over 100 laps to go. Nearly suffocating in the cockpit, he reached forward and lowered the

Maserati's windscreen, though the searing heat that flew into his face was only a slight relief. He pressed on, and in the final laps his discomfort was eased when a thoughtful spectator threw a refreshing bucketful of water into the cockpit of what proved to be the winning car.

Juan staggered up on to the podium, where he was joined by González, who had finished a plucky third. After the ceremony they were invited into a nearby house where they were offered champagne and fresh fruit. Juan received his spoils of victory on the floor, where he lay white-faced and hardly able to speak.

GROTE PRIJS VAN BELGIE

For the Belgian Grand Prix in mid-June, the championship contenders were required to drive 35 laps around the roller-coaster network of roads connecting the holiday town of Spa with the farming villages of Malmédy and Stavelot. For this historic occasion, the circuit had been improved and 1,400 trees had been sacrificed to create an extra six feet of racing width, but plenty of pine forest remained, as did the stone fences, houses and farm buildings that bordered the Spa circuit's 8.8-mile length. For the brave drivers, the 307-mile race journey at speeds averaging up to 120mph around almost all the ultra-fast track's turns would take nearly three difficult and treacherous hours.

The Alfa team's Three Fs dominated qualifying, Farina and Fangio clocking equal fastest times and Fagioli a few seconds adrift. Since Farina set his time first, he was awarded pole position, with his team-mates joining him on the front row. From the outset, this trio fought for first place, though Sommer's well-driven Talbot became the frontrunner for five laps when the thirsty Alfettas stopped for fuel. Farina led for seven laps and Fagioli for twelve; but the laps on which Fangio held the lead included the one that really mattered, and he took the chequered flag to win the Belgian Grand Prix. Fagioli was second and Farina, having experienced falling oil pressure, fell back to fourth, though he set the fastest race lap. Thus, with two championship races remaining, Farina was in front with 22 points, followed by Fagioli with 18 and Fangio with 17.

But Juan had little time to ponder the possibility of winning the first ever world driving title since his intensive schedule of racing every weekend for most of the summer next took him to Le Mans for France's famed 24-hour sports car race, where he would share the driving duties with González. Their car, a little Gordini Berlinette coupé with a 1490cc Simca engine, was barely big enough for Juan's burly team-mate to fit in the cockpit, nor was the underpowered and overstressed machine a likely candidate for victory in the marathon endurance race on the superfast Le Mans circuit. But Juan had been invited into the three-car team by Amedée Gordini, to whom he felt indebted for giving him a ride two years earlier in one of his Grand Prix cars at Reims.

For Le Mans, the Gordini headquarters was a small hotel near the circuit, where the Argentinians played boules in the garden with Gordini and his team's other drivers, who included Manzon, Trintignant and Simon. At four o'clock on the Saturday afternoon, 67 drivers prepared themselves for the traditional start by lining up in a long row on the opposite side of the track from their cars, which were angle-parked in front of the pits. When the starting flag was lowered, the drivers ran pell-mell across the track to their machines. Fangio, taking the first stint in the Gordini, was among the first to arrive, but as the rest of the cars roared away to begin the 24-hour battle, the Fangio Gordini remained stationary. The problem, a cracked distributor head, took several laps to trace and replace, by which time the Gordini was buried far back in the running order. Taking turns behind the wheel, the Argentinians flogged the little car manfully. 'We drove the poor thing so hard it could not stand the strain,' Juan recalled. The car circulated gamely until dusk, when a series of stops began in the Gordini pit, where a grease-covered Fangio expertly wielded spanners to help the mechanics try to repair a broken valve spring. Eventually, after puttering around for a while in the dark, the Gordini came in for a final time and was pushed into retirement behind the pits.

GRAND PRIX DE L'ACF

From Le Mans, Juan travelled north to champagne country for the Grand Prix de L'Automobile Club de France at Reims. The three Alfettas again started from the front row, with Fangio on pole by over two seconds from Farina, who was a further two seconds faster than Fagioli. In the race, the Three Fs put on a demonstration run, Farina leading the formation for the first sixteen of the 64 laps before having to make a pit stop to repair a seized fuel pump, a problem that recurred and eventually forced him to retire. Fangio, who also set the fastest race lap, led for the final 48 laps, with Fagioli finishing second.

On the podium, as the Argentine flag was raised and the band played the country's national anthem, Juan was handed a note by Farina showing the points situation: Fangio 26, Fagioli 24, Farina 22. Though they'd had no opposition for the honour of becoming the first World Drivers' Champion, a title that would go to one of them in the final championship race in Italy at the beginning of September, the Alfa Romeo team-mates were friendly rivals. In fact, all three were very mature men with lengthy driving careers behind them.

Luigi Fagioli was the oldest and the most experienced, having been born in 1898 in a village in the Abruzzi region, where Juan's family had come from. The 'Abruzzi Robber', as he was called, had first raced in 1926, and in the 1930s had become a top driver for the Maserati and Mercedes-Benz Grand Prix teams. In those days his fierce individualism sometimes put him at odds with his teams, especially during his tenure at Mercedes, where he refused to subordinate himself to the favoured Rudolph Caracciola and on one occasion retired a healthy car rather than accept orders to hand it over to the team leader. Fagioli's expressions of displeasure included throwing tools around in the pits; once, it was reported, he even threatened a team-mate with a knife. But with Alfa Romeo in 1950 the Abruzzi Robber had mellowed as a person and was a steady, if unspectacular, performer noted for his ability to finish races. He would go on racing until the age of 54, dying in hospital three weeks after being seriously injured in a sports car crash at Monaco in 1952.

Fagioli's countryman, Dottore Giuseppe 'Nino' Farina, who was born into an aristocratic family in Turin in 1906 and genuinely held a doctorate (in political economy), was lucky still to be alive after an accident-marred racing career that had begun in 1932. Known as the 'Gentleman of Turin', he was the nephew of Pinin Farina, the noted Italian coachbuilder and car designer, and was married to an elegant and stylish woman who ran an exclusive fashion emporium in Turin. Farina the daredevil driver had learnt much of his trade from the legendary Tazio Nuvolari, who was his team-mate at Alfa Romeo before the war. Like the passionately competitive Nuvolari, Farina had a tremendous fighting spirit, but, especially in his youth, his courage often exceeded his skill. His emergence from more than his share of big crashes was mainly due to good fortune, though a road-car accident would finally claim his life in 1966.

What Juan most admired about Farina was his aesthetically pleasing form in the cockpit, a stylish technique that had been pioneered by the late Jean Pierre Wimille and which Juan had adopted for himself. Sitting bolt upright and well back in the seat, Farina grasped the steering wheel with both arms fully outstretched and guided his car with calm, sparing movements and deft applications of the throttle, even around the fastest corners, where he excelled at maintaining a fully fledged four-wheel drift.

To keep this experienced Alfetta trio in fighting trim prior to the championship-deciding race at Monza, the team entered four non-championship events. At the Grand Prix of Bari on 9 July, Fangio and Farina swapped the lead until the penultimate lap when Fangio's car faltered owing to a fuel shortage and Farina won. In third place, behind Fangio's Alfetta, was a much less powerful British racing green HWM driven by a twenty-year old Englishman named Stirling Moss, who had studied Fangio's masterful cornering technique in practice and profited from it in the race. Moss had noted that while other well-driven cars, especially Ascari's Ferrari, consistently slid sideways to within an inch of the bales of straw lining the outside of a corner, Fangio's Alfetta actually brushed the stalks of straw, and did so lap after lap. This absolute precision, Moss thought, was surely the mark of a great driver. In the race, following pit stops by the Alfettas for fuel, Moss had close-up views of both Farina and Fangio as they passed him. While Farina scowled furiously at the temerity of an HWM with about 250 less horsepower daring to impede his progress, Fangio looked over at Moss and grinned encouragingly.

There was little cause for amusement for Juan in his next two races, neither of which his ACA Maserati finished. Juan's exit from the Albi Grand Prix in France on 16 July was spectacular in the extreme. Having finished second in the first heat, he was leading the final heat when on the last lap, while speeding down a straight at 100mph, his Maserati's engine burst into flames. With a ruptured line spraying fuel over the red-hot exhaust pipes, the wind-driven inferno engulfed the cockpit and licked dangerously towards the fuel tank behind Juan's back. To keep the flames at bay, Juan immediately slowed down, whereupon the conflagration shot skyward. Peering through the thick black smoke, Juan noticed the finish line was only a few hundred yards away and tried to make a dash for it, but when he floored the accelerator burning fuel spurted into the lower cockpit, setting his trousers alight. Juan reached down and managed to beat out the flames, stomped hard on the brake pedal, stood up and threw himself out of the still moving car. His slightly singed arms and legs required no medical attention, but the contents of several fire extinguishers were needed to put out the fire in his car.

The next weekend, at the Zandvoort circuit in Holland, while Juan's Maserati was being forced out when its ignition system stopped firing, it was his team-mate's turn to have his car catch fire. Fortunately, the González Maserati was in the pits at the time and the inferno, caused by fuel spilled on to the hot exhaust pipe, was quickly extinguished. González resumed racing and eventually finished seventh in his fire-blackened car.

From the Dutch Grand Prix, Juan travelled to Switzerland where he joined the Alfa Romeo team to contest the non-championship Grand Prix of the Nations at Geneva. There, the Alfetta drivers found potential threats to their dominance in the form of Alberto Ascari and Luigi Villoresi, whose Ferraris were powered by new 4.5-litre engines that had been developed in secret by Enzo Ferrari's team. Proof of their competitiveness came during qualifying, when Ascari and Villoresi set times that put them on the front row of the grid beside Juan's Alfa Romeo. Juan went on to win, but for three quarters of the race he was pestered by Ascari, whose Ferrari then broke its rear axle, forcing a retirement. Almost simultaneously, Villoresi's Ferrari was involved in a tragic accident. Travelling at 140mph, it slid wide on a corner, hit a kerbstone, hurtled over the straw bales, slewed into a group of spectators, then careered back on to the track, where Villoresi was thrown out, unconscious, directly in front of Farina's on coming Alfetta. To avoid him, Farina threw his car sideways and crashed heavily into the bales. He was uninjured, but in the spectator enclosure three people were dead, and those who had been badly hurt were taken away in ambulances along with Villoresi, who had suffered serious head injuries. 'Gigi' Villoresi, whose brother Emilio was killed when his Alfa Romeo crashed at Monza in 1939, was hospitalised for many weeks, though he recovered and eight months later was racing again.

A fortnight after that ill-fated Swiss event, after which Farina was given time off, Fangio and Fagioli represented Alfa Romeo in the Grand Prix of Pescara, one of the great Italian races, which took place on one of the longest circuits in Europe. Composed of public roads between the Adriatic towns of Pescara and Ancona, the sixteen-mile route included two long straights. Each year the organisers offered a 200,000 lira prize to the driver who achieved the fastest speed over a timed kilometre on the 5.25-mile-long Montesilvano straight. Juan won the money, recording an average speed of 192.84mph; he also won the 250-mile race, even though it had been previously agreed that Fagioli, who'd been born near Ancona, should be victorious in his home race. Encouraged by the 250,000 spectators, Fagioli was in fact leading until the very last lap when his Alfetta's front suspension collapsed and the car juddered to a halt. Juan pulled up alongside and urged him to try to make it to the finish line. Besides wishing to honour their pre-race agreement, Juan felt that because he had been the unluckiest of the Three Fs in the races so far, Fagioli should be given every chance to win. They set off again, with Juan tucked in behind, waving encouragement, but their progress was painfully slow, the leading Alfetta's right front wheel rubbing against the bodywork. As they neared the finish line, Fagioli became greatly animated, shouting and pointing behind to the fast-approaching Talbot driven by Louis Rosier and waving Fangio onwards. Juan accelerated away and won. The gallant Fagioli was passed by Rosier just 500 feet from the finish line.

GRAN PREMIO D'ITALIA

At the end of August, after yet another Alfetta runaway in the International Trophy race at Silverstone (Fangio finished second to Farina), the team returned to Italy to prepare for the championship showdown. Though the Three Fs were separated by only a few points, the Argentine driver's record was more impressive. Juan had won three of the five championship Grands Prix as well as five non-championship races for Alfa Romeo, and even the highly partisan Italian newspapers decreed that, statistically at least, Fangio must be favoured over Farina for the title.

Leading the 25-car entry at Monza were not three but five Alfa Romeos, Piero Taruffi and Consalvo Sanesi backing up the three championship contenders. Ferrari, also determined to make a strong showing in what was also its home race, entered one of its new cars for Ascari and another for Dorino Serafini, who replaced the injured Villoresi. The seven Italian cars duly qualified at the front, Juan securing pole with a time of 1m 59.6s, though Ascari was just two tenths of a second slower. Third and fourth on the grid were the Alfettas of Farina and Sanesi, while Fagioli's Alfetta, Serafini's Ferrari, Taruffi's Alfetta and Sommer's Talbot rounded out the top eight, half of whom were destined not to last all 80 laps of the 313-mile race.

Juan made the prudent decision not to press home his pole position advantage, choosing instead to measure his progress by keeping tabs on his team-mates and championship rivals. From the start, it was Farina who showed the greater pace, so Juan slotted in behind him and awaited developments. Very quickly one appeared in Juan's rear-view mirror in the form of Ascari's flying Ferrari. In his efforts to keep it at bay, Juan set the fastest lap of the race, completing the 3.915-mile journey in a fuel-laden car in a remarkable two minutes flat. Then, choosing not to stress his Alfetta unnecessarily, he moved over, let the Ferrari past and assumed third place, remaining about 500 yards behind what rapidly became a fierce fight for the lead between the two fired-up Italians.

For the first quarter of the race, Farina and Ascari swapped places several times, but on lap 22 Ascari's Ferrari coasted into the pits with a failed engine. Since the rules permitted teams to change drivers, Ferrari called in Serafini, whose car Ascari commandeered. Two laps later, Alfa Romeo was forced to make a similar move for Juan. 'I was about to make my effort when a tyre burst,' Juan recalled. 'After a pit stop, steam began filling the cockpit.' The mechanics discovered that the radiator had been holed by a stone, so Taruffi, who was now running second to Farina, was called in, and Juan took over his Alfetta and set off in pursuit of the race leader, who was also being chased by the remounted Ascari. But before Juan could close in on the fight at the front his newly acquired Alfetta developed a misfire and he again veered off into the pits, where a broken valve spelt the end of his race, and his championship challenge. On the last lap, the 100,000 fans at Monza cheered home the seven survivors who were led across the finish line by the Alfetta of Farina. Juan's point for fastest lap left him three points short of the 30 that confirmed Dr Giuseppe Farina as the first ever World Drivers' Champion.

Further statistics showed that of the total of 1,520 miles covered in the six championship races, Farina had led for 775.7 miles, Fangio for 662.8 miles and Fagioli for 30.6 miles. In the final analysis, it had to be said that against such illustrious rivals as the stylish Gentleman from Turin and the wily Abruzzi

Robber, the Boy from Balcarce had performed like a champion. Before he left Italy for Argentina, even the Pope paid tribute to Juan when he visited the papal residence at Castelgandolfo along with other members of the ACA's Achille Varzi team. Certainly he was once again received like a conquering hero when he returned home. On 4 October, Juan was met at Buenos Aires airport by government dignitaries and paraded through the streets en route to a series of state-sponsored receptions where he was congratulated by the Peróns. In Balcarce, more parades and functions were followed by joyful reunions with family, friends and partners at the garage.

A month later, Juan began racing, and winning, again. Driving an ACA Ferrari, he won a race through the park of the Argentine city of Paraná, then drove the same car to victory in the Gran Premio Presidente Palma at Pedro de Valdivia in northern Chile. His last race of 1950 was another edition of the Millas Argentinas, this time a 500-mile event on dirt roads at Rafaela in the state of Santa Fe. Proving that a season of racing on paved roads in Europe had not erased the old skills that had served him so well on less sophisticated terrain, and again demonstrating his ability to adapt to any kind of machine, Juan hopped into a modified Talbot Lago Grand Prix car and easily beat all-comers. His appetite and aptitude for furthering his business interests had not dimmed either, and with his Balcarce partners he formed a branch of Fangio & Co. in Buenos Aires, and set up a Mercedes-Benz dealership and a YPF service station at a prominent location in the city centre.

But never far from his mind was the Formula 1 World Championship that had been such a roaring success, and he eagerly awaited the resumption of competition, especially since the Alfa Romeos adorned with the famed four-leaf clover were expected to face a serious challenge mounted by a full team of Ferraris sporting prancing horses.

Chapter Nine

1951: First World Championship (Alfa Romeo)

'*whenever he came home, he brought us his trophies, presents and money. I told him we didn't need the money, but he wouldn't listen.*'

TRIBUTE TO FANGIO

F OR THE 1951 CAMPAIGN, the new alfetta, designated tipo 159 and now featuring a supercharged straight-eight engine producing over 400bhp, was a development of the 158 model that had served the Three Fs so well. All three drivers were re-signed by Alfa, but the ageing Fagioli was scheduled mainly to act as a reserve driver; reigning world champion Farina and runner-up Fangio would be joined by a new team-mate, Felice Bonetto, and Alfa's chief test driver Consalvo Sanesi was also expected to race occasionally.

Up against them was the Ferrari Type 375 featuring a new 4.5-litre unsupercharged V12 engine that produced slightly less than 400bhp but consumed much less fuel than the hard-working 1.5-litre Alfa Romeo motor (the Tipo 159, which weighed 1,500lb/680kg, got about three miles to the gallon, while the 1,180lb/535kg Type 375 got nearly seven). Other than the fuel consumption factor, which would require the Alfettas to make more pit stops, the two Italian teams seemed evenly matched, from both the mechanical and driving strength points of view: Ferrari's line-up included Ascari, Taruffi and Villoresi, and it was rumoured that Enzo Ferrari was also considering the promising González as a candidate.

Aside from the two official factory teams, the Maserati brothers were also preparing cars to be run by private entrants, as were the French manufacturers Gordini and Talbot Lago and the English company BRM. And early in 1951 there was tremendous excitement when news broke that Mercedes-Benz was planning to return to racing for the first time since 1939.

During the war, the previously all-conquering fleet of German cars had been scattered far and wide throughout Europe, some of them having been confiscated by the Red Army and transported back to Russia. Now, with an ever-improving market for Mercedes road cars, the company directors decided to publicise the three-pointed star marque by returning to the sporting arena in which it had had so much success, under the leadership of the racing team's legendary manager Alfred Neubauer. The portly Neubauer (he weighed 270lb, or just over nineteen stones) was entrusted with the task of locating and preparing suitable examples of the silver-coloured pre-war Type W163 cars, whose supercharged twelve-cylinder three-litre engines produced a massive 600bhp.

Though the ultimate objective was for Neubauer to lead the team into the new World Championship series, Mercedes chose to test the waters first in the 1951 Temporada races in Argentina where the newly opened, Fangio-operated Mercedes dealership in Buenos Aires would be the chief beneficiary of the famous team's return. But the Argentine hero had mixed feelings about the presence of the hugely powerful Silver Arrows cars in the two Temporada races, which would take place on the Circuito Costanera Norte, a new course fashioned out of several major thoroughfares in central Buenos Aires. In fact, since he was scheduled to race an ACA two-litre Ferrari in his home races, Juan decided to do something to curb the expected might of Mercedes. When shown a plan of the proposed circuit by the ACA's Francisco Borgonovo, Juan suggested that the lengthy straight – along which the Mercedes would surely run away from the underpowered opposition – should be shortened considerably. A tighter track configuration, Juan advised, would hobble the heavier German cars and tip the balance of power in favour of the more nimble Ferraris. Borgonovo agreed, and the Fangio-inspired modifications were duly incorporated into a new layout.

Shortly after the circuit revisions were made official, Juan was summoned to a meeting with Neubauer, who invited him to lead the Mercedes driver line-up, which included the German stars Hermann Lang and Karl Kling. Juan felt he couldn't turn down such an important opportunity, so he agreed. However, the honour of driving for the illustrious team was undermined by a sense of guilt over his having conspired against it, and a fear that fate might conspire to punish him for it. Both Temporada races, the Premio Ciudad de Buenos Aires and the Premio Eva Perón, were won convincingly by an ACA Ferrari driven by José Froilán González, results that confirmed González as a rising star but also completely overshadowed the much-vaunted Mercedes team's return to racing. Indeed, the debut was seen as a débâcle in the newly created Federal Republic of Germany and prompted Mercedes to postpone its plans to enter Formula 1, even though in each of the Buenos Aires events the Silver Arrows cars finished second and third, Lang and Fangio in the first race, Kling and Lang in the second race, from which the chastened Fangio retired with a mechanical failure. 'Sometimes,' Juan reflected, 'when you do something you ought not to have done, you get punished for it. God needs no whip to punish, as the saying goes. That's what happened to me.'

Just a matter of weeks before his 40th birthday, Juan returned to Europe for a season that began with three non-championship races in which he drove three different cars, with negative results that made him begin to wonder if 1951 was going to be jinxed. On 5 May, in the BRDC International Trophy race at Silverstone, the Fangio Alfa Romeo Tipo 159 beat the Farina-driven version to win the first heat, but the final was abandoned because of a sudden downpour. In the Grand Prix of Monza, Juan's ACA Ferrari retired with mechanical failure, a fate that also befell his Gordini in the Grand Prix of Paris on 20 May. After being unlucky for a third time, Juan admitted that while he was not particularly superstitious, there were occasions when he had needed to work hard to suppress thoughts that supernatural forces might be conspiring against him. An opportunity to eliminate them entirely from his mind came at the first championship race of the season.

GROSSER PREIS DER SCHWEIZ

The weekend of the Grand Prix of Switzerland at the Bremgarten circuit in Berne began in fine weather, which Juan used to best effect, putting his Alfetta on pole with a time that was nearly two seconds faster than his world champion team-mate Farina and over three seconds better than the third-placed Ferrari of Villoresi. Leaving nothing to chance, that evening Juan went on a reconnaissance mission in order to memorise every detail of the tricky Bremgarten layout. With two friends as passengers, he set out on several laps in his road car. Suddenly, a black cat darted out from some bushes and ran directly in front of the car, and Juan had no chance to avoid squashing it. Showing no sympathy for the unlucky animal, his friends teased Juan: not only had a black cat crossed his path, but Juan had killed it, so he was bound to have bad luck in the race.

Juan made light of their superstitious predictions, but that night he had trouble sleeping. He recalled that on the thirteenth lap of the 1950 Swiss race, which he was leading at the time, an engine valve had broken at the very spot where he killed the cat. Moreover, in 1949 at Silverstone, a valve had also broken on the thirteenth lap of a race he might have won. Worse than that, Juan remembered, his mentor Achille Varzi was killed in 1948 in an Alfa Romeo in a wet race at the Bremgarten circuit, and the forecast did not rule out rain.

When he awoke from his troubled sleep the next morning, the dangerous-even-when-dry circuit was awash with teeming rain that was expected to last all day. As if to obliterate his fears, or at least leave them as far behind as possible, Juan sped away into the teeth of the storm, immediately establishing a lead that was never threatened. 'Juan Manuel Fangio established himself as a true rain master,' Gregor Grant wrote in *Autosport* after the race. 'His fearless passage through the circuit's inumerable fast bends gained him the sincere admiration of all, elevating him still higher in the ranks of Grand Prix drivers.' The appallingly wet conditions, which at one point were so bad that the organisers considered stopping the race, did claim several victims, though mercifully the worst injury was the broken leg suffered by a French driver.

For Juan, the handsome trophy he received for winning the first championship race of the year was slightly less significant than the fact that the victory supplanted in his mind's eye the haunting spectre of the corpse of a black cat. His driving skills had soundly beaten superstition into submission. 'This win was very important for me, not just because I had done my best in the race, but also because I had resisted the temptation to let myself be dragged down by superstition,' he said. 'If fate is unkind to you after you happen to run over a black cat, you remain a slave to superstition for the rest of your life.'

With black cats out of the way, Juan now had to deal with the reality of an oncoming herd of black horses – as depicted on the Ferrari badges. While Taruffi's Ferrari had only managed to be second best in Switzerland, this was mainly due to Juan's superior performance behind the wheel of an Alfetta that no longer enjoyed mechanical supremacy. Juan also had misgivings about his crew's ability to handle stressful situations during pit stops, when the Alfettas needed to be serviced quickly. In addition to these factors, he remained mindful of the championship threat posed by his team-mate Farina, who was third in Switzerland and whose hopes of retaining his driving title were given a big boost in Belgium.

GROTE PRIJS VAN BELGIE

During qualifying for the Belgian Grand Prix in mid-June, Juan mastered the mighty Spa-Francorchamps circuit with a scintillating pole-position lap that was a full three seconds faster than Farina. But behind the brace of Alfettas on the starting grid lurked the Ferrari phalanx of Villoresi, Ascari and Taruffi. At the start, Juan at first left the others to sort themselves out, and Villoresi and Farina took turns to lead; then, in consideration of the fact that he would soon have to stop for refuelling, Juan proceeded to take the lead and extend it by means of a series of breathtakingly quick laps around one of the fastest tracks in the world. On the tenth tour, when his car's fuel load was suitably reduced, Juan launched the lightened Alfetta into an all-out attack that resulted in a new lap record that was an astonishing seven seconds quicker than his pole-setting time.

But this sensational 120.509mph lap amounted to an exercise in futility, since it was followed by a disastrously slow pit stop that turned a handsome lead into a two-lap deficit. The fourteen-minute delay, on lap sixteen, was caused by a rear wheel that became jammed on its hub. Refuelling had gone smoothly, but to replace the worn tyre the Alfa mechanics had to take off the entire hub assembly, fit a new tyre, then replace the hub assembly. In the pits, onlookers were amazed that while the frantic Alfa crew fell over themselves in a chaos of shouts and flying spanners, the car's driver was a picture of serenity. 'People wondered how I could stay calm as I saw my chances of a win slipping away,' Juan said, 'but it was not me the chances were slipping away from. I had done everything as it should be done, and had made no mistakes. I believe that someone might get nervous, or at least uneasy, when he has made a mistake. But that was not the case here.'

Farina made no mistake either, nor did his pit stops go wrong, and the good doctor went on to win the Belgian Grand Prix, though he was chased all the way by Ascari and Villoresi, whose Ferraris in turn finished a full two laps ahead of the fourth-placed Talbot Lago of Louis Rosier.

Juan, who eventually finished ninth in Belgium, then accompanied Rosier to Le Mans, where they shared a 4.5-litre Talbot Lago converted to sports car configuration. The Frenchman drove the first shift and handed the Talbot over to Juan when it was in third place, six minutes behind the leading Jaguar C-Type driven by Peter Whitehead and Peter Walker. During the night it rained constantly, and on the wet track the Argentine driver, who was fast becoming recognised as a rainmaster, made great inroads into the Jaguar's advantage. Juan's best lap of 4m 54.3s at an average of 102.5mph was the quickest recorded that year. When he handed the Talbot back to Rosier, it was in second place, just 90 seconds behind the leading car. With Rosier also driving well, the Talbot seemed on course for victory, but then an oil leak developed and the car had to be retired.

GRAND PRIX DE L'ACF

The third round of the World Championship, the Grand Prix de L'ACF at Reims, was this year also designated the Grand Prix of Europe. The anticipated Alfa Romeo versus Ferrari battle duly took shape in qualifying, with polesitter Juan joined on the front row by Farina and Ascari; on the second row of the grid (in a 3–2–3 arrangement), the Ferrari of Villoresi stood alongside the Alfetta of Sanesi, and behind them was the threesome of González, in his first official race with Ferrari, Fagioli in the third Alfetta and, representing the rather dim French hopes, Louis Chiron in a blue Talbot Lago.

From the outset, the race was a wheel-to-wheel duel in the sun between Juan and Ascari. Side by side they roared down Reims' long straights; neck and neck they slid sideways around the corners; back and forth they went, trading first and second places all the while and leaving behind them a toiling confusion of red cars that confirmed an evenly matched Alfetta–Ferrari free-for-all of epic proportions. So furious was the pace in the stifling heat, so extreme was the stress on components, it seemed certain the nearly three-and-a-half-hour-long 370-mile conflict would be settled by mechanical intervention.

And so it was. Both the Fangio Alfetta (broken fuel pump) and the Ascari Ferrari (broken gearbox) failed to go the full 77-lap distance, but in both instances the combatants resumed racing in cars handed over by their respective team-mates. On the 28th lap, Juan took over when Fagioli brought his fourth-placed Alfetta into the pits for fuel and fresh tyres, and on the 34th lap Ascari relieved González of the Ferrari he had quite brilliantly brought up to second place. From then on, with Farina's chances of winning having vanished after a shambolic Alfa pit stop, Ascari and Juan continued to fight furiously for first place.

Gradually, despite his thirsty Alfa's disadvantage of requiring more frequent fill-ups in the pits, Juan eased ahead. But Ascari hung on, and on one occasion nearly usurped the lead when Juan momentarily left the road to avoid the stalled Talbot of his Le Mans team-mate Rosier. In the end, after the hardest-fought World Championship race yet, the twosome flashed across the finish line in the order of Fangio–Ascari, with Villoresi's Ferrari a full three laps behind and Parnell's Ferrari and Farina's Alfa a further lap in arrears. Juan was now leading the championship standings with 15 points, one more than Farina, while the up-and-coming Ascari had nine points.

Juan's first thoughts after the race were for Fagioli, in whose car he had won. They went out to dinner and toasted each other, but Fagioli's show of camaraderie was short-lived, and resentment set in. A few days later, the proud 53-year-old veteran announced to Alfa that he would never drive for them again, and in fact the race in France was his last in a Formula 1 car. Juan sympathised with Fagioli's point of view and felt that the system of car-swapping was unjust. Thus it was that Juan commiserated with his compatriot González, who had been forced to sacrifice his very well-driven Ferrari for the Ascari cause.

Two weeks later, in mid-July, the Argentine friends were driving around the Silverstone circuit in Juan's Alfa Romeo road car. As Juan pointed out the landmarks they would encounter in the forthcoming British Grand Prix, he predicted that if he had the chance he would help his amigo get his revenge in the race. As it turned out, González needed no help at all.

BRITISH GRAND PRIX

The González weekend in England got off to a flying start when he planted his Ferrari quite firmly on pole, setting a time that was a full second faster than his friend Juan. Joining them on the front row were their respective team-mates, Farina and Ascari, while the presence on the second row of Villoresi's Ferrari and the Alfettas of Sanesi and Bonetto promised another battle royal between the Italian cars. Few prognosticators considered the polesitter, in only his second appearance for Ferrari, to be a serious threat for overall honours, but that was to sell José Froilán González far too short.

Born in 1922 in Arrecifes, about 75 miles outside Buenos Aires, González was eleven years younger than Juan and just as short and stocky; indeed, his tendency towards corpulence was at the root of two of his many nicknames. Because of a somewhat oversized cranium perched on a short neck, González was known in Argentina as 'El Cabezón', or Fathead. But unlike his bow-legged countryman El Chueco, El Cabezón did not drive as much with his head, but was noted instead for relying on a heavy right foot, which was why 'Lead Foot' became another of his appellations. In his homeland, where he distinguished himself as a dirt-track daredevil with a propensity for starting explosively then lashing himself into a car-flogging frenzy, he was also called 'The Whip'. In England, his bullish physique and occasional bull-in-a-china-shop approach to racing earned him the moniker 'The Wild Bull of the Pampas'. From the way he seemed to grab the car by the scruff of the neck and wrestle with it in a series of strangleholds as if to throttle it into submission, the Europeans decided he resembled the ferocious mountain lion of the Americas and nicknamed him 'The Puma'.

Everyone, however, agreed that González had explosive talent, though he needed to manage it with his mind. His new boss Enzo Ferrari, who fancied himself as a talent-spotter who could polish a diamond-in-the-rough, noted that while the likes of Fangio and Ascari could be relied upon to go round and round like clockwork, González alternated between marking time and unleashing furious bursts of speed. The latter was used to attack adversaries from behind. Once he had accomplished an overtaking manoeuvre, Ferrari felt, González tended to slacken off and allow himself to be overtaken. Ferrari could never understand why he was so extraordinarily inconsistent and sometimes wondered, given the amount of mental and physical exhaustion he seemed to suffer, why González raced at all.

Ferrari's new recruit was very nervous and tense in the moments before the start at Silverstone, walking to and fro around his car on the grid. Muttering to himself in Spanish, and with his brow furrowed in deep concentration, it seemed as if González was in a trance. He ignored attempts at conversation made by worried Ferrari mechanics who tried in vain to calm him down. With five minutes to go, he ran off in search of the Silverstone toilets. Since he couldn't speak English, he had no idea what the track announcers were saying on the loud-speakers. At the last minute, he rushed back from relieving himself and heaved his hefty body into the cramped cockpit.

The Wild Bull of the Pampas then proceeded to whip his prancing horse into the forefront as never before. Demonstrating all the good and bad qualities attributed to him – though the former far more than the latter – El Cabezón lead-footed his way to a sensational victory over Juan in a private battle *Autosport*'s Gregor Grant considered 'the greatest race ever seen at Silverstone'. While Juan raced with his usual style and grace, González attacked the track with ferocious abandon, sometimes shortening his route by using his Ferrari as a battering ram to scatter aside straw bales, and once even an oil drum. Round and round he thundered, barrelling down the straights, bellowing around the corners in spectacular, tyre-smoking, 100mph powerslides, his rotund upper torso bulging out of the cockpit, his beefy arms flailing wildly and his Ferrari's engine note howling ever higher as if in anguished protest against such a merciless flogging. Everyone was transfixed by the astonishing display, even his team-mate Ascari, whose Ferrari had retired with a broken gearbox. When González stopped for fuel on the 61st lap, he shouted an offer of his car to Ascari, who shook his head and gestured that the Argentine phenomenon should continue to pursue the victory he so obviously deserved. Though Juan was handicapped somewhat by his car's extra fuel requirements, he still managed to lead a third of the race's 90 laps, but González was in front for all the others, and after two hours, 42 minutes and 18.2 seconds of supreme effort he took the chequered flag, half a minute ahead of Juan.

His friend did not begrudge him his moment of triumph. On the podium, where they were joined by Villoresi, González became very emotional when his Argentine amigo hugged and congratulated him. The last time that had happened was when Juan acted as best man at his friend's wedding. 'I was embraced warmly by Fangio,' he recalled. 'That meant a lot to me. Then they played the Argentine national anthem. I had never experienced anything like this before. When I saw my country's flag being hoisted, it was just too much for me and I cried.'

The González win was historic from several points of view: it was Alfa Romeo's first defeat after 27 straight Grand Prix victories since 1946, it was the first time an unsupercharged car had won a World Championship race, and above all, it was the first World Championship win for Enzo Ferrari, whose earlier successes had come when he ran the pre-war Alfa Romeo team. After the milestone achieved by González, whom he congratulated for his combination of courage and tenacity, Ferrari was moved to tears he confessed were a mixture of joy (at winning with one of his own cars) and sadness (at having beaten his former team).

GROSSER PREIS VON DEUTSCHLAND

In late July, the next stop on the Formula 1 tour took the combatants to the Federal Republic of Germany, where the fifth round of the championship would take place on the mighty Nürburgring. Carved out of ruggedly rolling terrain in the heavily wooded Eiffel mountain region about 40 miles west of Koblenz, the Nürburgring's tortuous, tree-lined, 14.5-mile length punctuated by 176 distinct corners and many lesser curves and kinks represented the ultimate road-racing challenge for brave men in fast cars. Originally built in the 1920s as a test track for the German automotive industry, as well as for racing, it was wonderfully picturesque. Starting near the ramparts of the medieval Castle Nurburg, standing high on a hill, the long and winding road followed the natural contours of the land, darting hither and yon, up hill and down dale, and often disappearing deep into the eerie forest of dark fir trees.

It was indeed a journey into the great unknown, for this roller-coaster ride of a circuit – where speeding cars slewed sideways around the convoluted swoops and swerves, hurtled inches from the trees over a surface often made slick by the nearly ever-present mist and fog, and flew several feet into the air over the blind brows – was a great leap of faith for the drivers. Over its turbulent 35-year history, the treacherous Nürburgring had become notorious for creating as many martyrs as heroes. It was also the scene of epic races and heroic drives, none more so than the 1935 German Grand Prix in which the legendary Tazio Nuvolari took his tiny little Alfa Romeo to an historic victory over the much more powerful Mercedes-Benz and Auto Union machines. Nuvolari's admirable exploits were always a great inspiration for Juan, who also appreciated the fact that at the Nürburgring Nuvolari had shown how a driver could count for more than a car. Though it was called the mother and father of all tracks, to Juan it seemed more like their beautiful daughter, and it was love at first sight. 'I felt attracted to the Nürburgring from the very first moment I saw it,' he said. 'What happened there was like what happens when a friend speaks to you about a woman you don't know, and when you meet her she turns out to be much more attractive than you had imagined. Getting to know the Nürburgring was like getting to know a woman. You can't memorise 176 curves over more than fourteen miles, just as you can't memorise 176 feminine wiles after a short acquaintance.'

Juan was eager to satisfy his curiosity, especially since Ferrari was now on the ascendancy and the team's lead driver, Ascari, had the advantage of circuit knowledge, having won a Formula 2 race at the Nürburgring in 1950. Before practice began, Juan embarked on what proved to be a steep learning curve behind the wheel of his Alfa Romeo road car. On the shorter Grand Prix tracks he was able to conduct his reconnaissance missions in reasonably short order, but working out the lie of the land around the lengthy Nürburgring was a time-consuming process. He decided that the best way to begin to unravel its mysteries was to take it in stages, a mile or so at a time, travelling slowly, acquainting himself with landmarks, finding reference points for braking and shifting, and stopping at potential troublespots to study them in more detail. After the Carousel section, for instance, he noted that the relatively less complex first and second curves could probably be taken flat out, but on the following fast downhill stretch there was a wooden hut that could serve as an alarm bell to warn about the forthcoming series of dangerously difficult, high-speed S bends. For Juan, slow corners were not a problem, since he dealt with them using his mountain-driving technique: go by what you see and take them as they come. At the Nürburgring, he blotted out of his mind the slower parts of the circuit, concentrating instead on developing a deeper understanding of the faster corners, and trying to separate them in his mind so as not to confuse one corner with another.

But time ran out before his store of knowledge was complete; when he had to exchange his road car for his racing Alfetta, his familiarity with the Nürburgring only went as far as about the eighth mile. Just beyond that point, in the opening practice session, he mistook one left-hand bend for another and entered it too fast. Taken by surprise, he tried to scrub off speed by shifting down a gear, but the clutch didn't respond quickly enough and a last-minute stab on the brake pedal failed to avert a slide that sent the Alfetta thumping into an earth bank. Fortunately, the obstacle stopped the car from flying into the trees, but the rear bodywork was crumpled and fuel trickled from beneath the Alfetta. 'I went back to the pits with a split fuel tank and a great sense of shame,' Juan recalled. 'I always hated returning a damaged car to the pits. As I had been a mechanic myself, I felt that somehow it showed lack of respect for the work they had put into my machine.

The Alfa mechanics were able to fix the fuel tank, but the impact had also damaged the clutch and gearbox. First and second gears were now difficult to engage, but despite this handicap Juan qualified his Alfetta third on the grid alongside the Ferraris of González and the polesitting Ascari, and it was this trio that fought fiercely at the front for the three hours, 23 minutes and 3.3 seconds it took to complete the 1951 German Grand Prix.

As they accelerated away from the start. Juan's car remained stuck in first gear, forcing him to take the first two corners that way. By the time he had levered second gear into play, he discovered that the clutch was not working, and from then on he was able to use only third and fourth gears, which could be readily engaged without the clutch but which left him seriously ill equipped to deal with the 3,520 corners that would confront him during 20 laps of racing around a circuit with which he was not yet fully familiar. And yet, while Ascari led for eleven of those laps, Juan was in front for eight, with González leading the other. The three drivers crossed the finish line in that order, but for most of the crowd of several hundred thousand spectators strung out along the Nürburgring's great length, the driver of the day was the phenomenal Fangio, who emerged from his car in a state of battle-weary disarray. 'I was aching in every bone in my body. I wondered how I was still in one piece, and how I wasn't thrown out of the car. With no seat belts, and what with flying up and down and going over bumps, and knocking from left to right in the corners, I ended up pulverised.'

Forced once again to make more pit stops than the fuel-efficient Ferraris, and on one stop stalling his Alfetta because of the inoperative clutch, Juan had overcome the deficit each time by driving, as Gregor Grant noted, 'like a demon, his muscular arms working away at the wheel, his Alfa emitting a stirring yowl as it burst past'. On the twelfth lap, Juan's fuel-laden Alfetta set the fastest race lap by far, stopping the clock in a time of 9m 55.8s, which exactly duplicated the time that had put Ascari's Ferrari on pole. At the finish, though it was only 30 seconds behind Ascari, Juan's second-placed Alfetta was the only non-Ferrari in the top six.

Farina's retirement from the race, with a broken gearbox, meant there were not enough points in the remaining two races for him to hang on to his driving title. With the pendulum of mechanical advantage now surely having swung towards Ferrari, Ascari was considered a more likely champion than Fangio, while González was also a contender with an outside chance. However, Juan still had in his mental repertoire a considerable bag of tricks with which he had outwitted better-equipped rivals in the past.

Then, in late August, Juan was shocked to hear that one of his first racing heroes had been killed back home. Ricardo Risatti crashed fatally in one of the Argentinian open-road races (the Vuelta del Chaco), where before the war Juan had first seen and been inspired by him. What had most appealed to Juan was Risatti's astonishing tenacity, his refusal to be beaten by setbacks. Juan recalled that on a mountain stage of one race, after Risatti's car rolled over, he summoned up seemingly superhuman strength, righted the car himself, made roadside repairs and kept on racing. Though a ruthless competitor, Risatti was also kind and humane. Juan was particularly moved when Risatti, in the middle of another long-distance race he was leading, stopped in his home town and paid a quick visit to his ailing wife's bedside before resuming racing, and going on to win. But his idol was now dead, and Juan mourned his passing.

Juan's next confrontation with his championship rival Ascari was the non-championship Grand Prix of Bari on 2 September, which Juan won by means of a ruse. The circuit in the seaside town included a very long straight that ran along the coast and which firmly favoured the Ferraris. But his Alfetta, Juan thought, could probably gain ground on the twistier parts of the track. In practice, unbeknown to Ascari, Juan experimented with the braking point at the end of the long straight, delaying it as long as he dared until he had established the point of no return on the entry into the sharp 90-degree bend. In the early laps of the race, with Fangio leading and Ascari following closely, the Alfetta braked much earlier than its driver knew was necessary for the corner, and the Ferrari followed suit. Indeed, it came closer and closer until, on the fateful lap, as they approached the tight corner at 180mph, it seemed the Alfetta was not going to brake at all. By the time it did, in a cloud of tyre smoke, it was too late for the Ferrari, which spun off in an even greater cloud of dust while the Alfetta safely scrabbled around the corner. And so Juan won at Bari, but in the final laps his gearbox had become contrary, and by the finish it had seized itself in fourth. With Farina's Alfetta having again retired with a mechanical problem, the team seemed not best prepared for the forthcoming Italian Grand Prix.

GRAN PREMIO D'ITALIA

Monza was a fiasco for Alfa Romeo and another runaway for the opposition, Ascari and González leading a four-cars-among-the-top-five finish for Ferrari; only the third-placed Alfetta shared by Bonetto and Farina prevented a total whitewash. The four-leaf clover contingent's race was an unlucky tale of mechanical woe. Farina's engine failed first, and he was given Bonetto's car; Juan's later engine failure left him carless, since guest driver de Graffenreid's Alfetta had lasted only two laps. A post-mortem conducted at the Alfa Romeo factory suggested that the Monza misfortunes were not just a run of bad luck. Instead, the findings – an incorrect fuel filter in Juan's car, a damaged fuel tank in Farina's, and a failed supercharger in de Graffenreid's – pointed to possible sabotage, and several people were fired.

GRAN PREMIO DE ESPAÑA

By now, with only one race remaining, the championship fight had reached fever pitch and the stakes were exceedingly high. Italian honour and prestige were on the line for Alfa Romeo and Ferrari, yet the championship was far from an all-Italian affair since the threesome in contention for the driving title included two Argentinians. The standings showed Juan Manuel Fangio leading Ascari and González, but for the showdown in Spain, the odds, if not the gods, seemed to favour the Italian driver with the illustrious racing pedigree.

Alberto Ascari was the son of the great Antonio Ascari, whose Alfa Romeo dealership and success as an amateur racer had led to his recruitment as a driver for the Alfa Romeo Grand Prix team in the 1920s. Antonio proved to be outstandingly good, winning thirteen times in 32 starts, only to crash fatally while dominating the French Grand Prix on 26 July 1925. Alberto, then just six years old, was devastated and thereafter became very superstitious, since the date of his father's death was twice the unlucky number thirteen. Still, Alberto felt compelled to go racing, and at seventeen he overcame his mother's objections and began to follow in his father's wheel tracks, at first competing in motorcycles, then turning to four wheels in a Ferrari in the 1940 Mille Miglia. This drive was personally arranged by Enzo Ferrari, who had been a great friend of Antonio Ascari. During the war, Alberto teamed up with Luigi Villoresi and formed a trucking business, hauling fuel for the Italian Army during the desert campaign in North Africa. After the war, they formed their own race team, and under the tutelage of Villoresi, Ascari honed his skills and racecraft. As a driver, Ascari was both hard-charging and analytical, and always fiercely determined and incredibly brave. Yet the legacy of his father's death made him chronically apprehensive about racing, the dangers of which made him prone to bouts of insomnia and stomach ulcers. Despite being quiet and undemonstrative, and (like González) having an untypically pudgy physique for a racing driver, he was the idol of the tifosi, the passionate Italian fans, who nicknamed him 'Ciccio', or Chubby.

On 28 October, more than 300,000 spectators lined the streets of Barcelona, where the 3.925-mile-long Pedralbes circuit was fashioned from five major thoroughfares. Among the massive crowd of Formula 1 fans who had come from all over Europe was a large contingent of tifosi, who naturally favoured

Ascari. But since Juan had an Italian heritage, and González had Spanish forefathers, and both drivers came from a Spanish-speaking country, there was no shortage of support for the Argentinians.

The friendship between them, and the possibility of his inadvertently revealing it to González, prompted Alfa Romeo to withhold from Juan the fact that he would have to stop for fuel during the race. This was contrary to Ferrari's belief, since the Alfettas were for this final race fitted on each side of the bodywork with dummy fuel tanks so that Ferrari would think Alfa Romeo had solved its problem of having thirstier cars. The subterfuge worked wonderfully well: in the pits before the race, Ferrari's understanding that its rivals would race non-stop prompted a change to smaller-diameter wheels, which would provide more get-up-and-go but which also meant Ferrari would run the risk of greater tyre wear on smaller, faster-spinning wheels forced to work overtime on cars carrying heavier fuel loads.

This 'camouflage' trick was only revealed to Juan shortly before the start, as was another secret weapon. At his feet in the cockpit was an air duct that could be opened or closed, though the purpose of the device was not for Juan to cool his heels, but to help show them to his rivals. When the duct was opened, it would feed air directly into the engine's twin superchargers, thus providing a surge of extra power. Juan was instructed not to open the duct until the dust had cleared after the opening laps.

The grid for the championship showdown could not have been more perfectly poised, with Ascari, Juan and González having qualified in that order, in front of seventeen other cars. At the start, the assembled multitude watched enthralled as the mechanical monsters thundered off on a rampage through Barcelona like a herd of enraged bulls responding to a red flag.

Horns were locked in the opening laps of the unruly stampede and several cars spun off, yet one of the brave matadors, who was both clever and courageous, kept his wits about him and played a waiting game.

As was his custom, having adopted them years ago as methods of keeping his mind in gear and his emotions in check, Juan was humming quietly to himself and methodically chewing a stick of gum. When González swerved briefly off course, Juan slotted in behind Ascari. By the second lap, small shards of rubber, shredded from the Ferrari's hard-working tyres, began to fly into his face. Smiling to himself, Juan kept the pressure on, filling the Ferrari's mirrors with his presence, thereby adding an extra burden to Ascari's already busy mind. On the third lap, when he opened the air duct, which force-fed a blast of air into the superchargers, Juan felt as though he'd been given a massive kick in the seat of his pants. Halfway around the Pedralbes circuit, the Alfetta powered past the Ferrari and Juan settled into an unbeatable rhythm that saw him circulate comfortably alone in front for the remaining 67 laps of the race. The González Ferrari finished second, though nearly a minute behind, with Farina's Alfetta third and Ascari's Ferrari fourth.

'There were tremendous scenes of excitement on the podium as the winner of the Spanish Grand Prix and the 1951 world champion was given a rapturous reception,' Gregor Grant reported in *Autosport*. However, the object of the crowd's adulation was unable fully to appreciate the moment since he was suffering from a blinding headache. Juan, who was unaware that the problem stemmed from his serious accident in Peru in 1948, thought the pain had been caused by his head being buffeted in the wind for nearly three hours. Despite his throbbing temples, that night Juan enjoyed himself at a victory dinner hosted by his team in one of Barcelona's seaside restaurants. There, he was informed that the occasion was also a form of farewell, since Alfa Romeo had decided to withdraw from championship racing while it was on top and would not compete in 1952. Though Juan was surprised, and of course realised that his Formula 1 future was now in jeopardy, he graciously paid tribute to his employers and his team-mates: 'I realised that it was thanks to Alfa Romeo and their cars that I had the chance to win various races, and above all the World Championship. Just as importantly, it was thanks to Alfa that I got to know a group of people I can never forget. I have seldom met others for whom I have felt greater affection and appreciation.'

The newly crowned title-holder then went back to Italy to participate in a prearranged celebration with his main rival. Before the race in Barcelona, Juan had made a bet with Ascari that whoever won would pay for a big party, and whoever lost would choose the venue and invite the guests. Ascari chose one of the finest restaurants in Milan, where about 50 people gathered, including an Argentine contingent headed by González. Though it was an expensive evening for Juan (it cost him 30,000 pesos, including the fee of a troupe of Spanish singers he hired for the occasion), he felt it was well worth it. He laughed and joked with Ascari, whose sense of humour he appreciated. 'Alberto was a tough man to beat,' Juan acknowledged, 'but if he had a chance to make jokes about anybody or anything, he would.'

Having succeeded Dr Giuseppe Farina as champion, Juan paid tribute to the Italian as a worthy rival and credited him for being the role model for the straight-arm driving style that had served Juan so well. When it came to discussing Farina's predilection for driving like a madman, Juan preferred to use religious terms: 'We all say that Farina is protected by the Madonna, but even the holy Madonna's patience has a limit, and he should consider that she can't be at his disposal all the time.' Among the gifts presented to Juan that raucous evening was a splendid silver platter inscribed in flowing script with a message in Italian: 'A little souvenir for a great champion'. It was from Luigi Villoresi, who made a short speech as he handed it to Juan. 'Fangio,' he said, 'I always tell the truth. I'm not pleased that you've won the championship. I would like to have won it myself, or failing that, one of the Ferrari boys. But you've deserved it, and that's why I'm giving you this.'

Back in Argentina, the results of the 1951 season only formally recognised what his proud countrymen had known for several years: that El Chueco, the (40-year-old) Boy from Balcarce, was El Campeone del Mundo – champion of all the world. After the customary state reception in Buenos Aires, he was fêted and fawned over by President Perón, his wife Evita and assorted dignitaries with even more fervour than usual. So that the populace could see and salute their hero, he was paraded through the streets on the back of a truck.

As soon as he could diplomatically extract himself from the well-wishing, Juan headed back to Balcarce for the welcome he most cherished. On the way, he thought about Mama and Papa Fangio, who had sacrificed so much for their family and whose lives were still full of the hard work they had always known. They were illiterate, and though their now famous son raced around the world, they didn't even have passports. Juan remembered how his father had told him he was not unhappy to leave school before he had learnt to read or write because he was ashamed of coming from a poor family who could not afford to buy him the proper clothes worn by other children. Juan knew that among his parents' greatest gifts to their children was the example they set: the sense of responsibility, the ambition to improve and the strong work ethic – qualities Juan felt were at the root of his success. He recalled how as a boy he had studied at school by day and worked on cars at night, then how as an adult he had worked as a mechanic by day and prepared his cars at night. 'Before becoming a driver,' he once stated, 'a young man with racing ambitions should become a mechanic. The chap who wants to be champion must cover himself with grease and oil from head to foot. He must work with his hands and his heart and he must drive the same way.' Juan knew that none of the top European drivers had come from such a humble, hard-working background, and because of this they had gone further faster. But none of them was faster now, and though it had taken him longer to get there, Juan believed his championship was just reward for hard labour as well as hard driving.

After winning the championship, Juan had telephoned Papa and Mama, offering to bring back from Europe anything their hearts desired. Loreto had asked for a Bianchi racing bicycle, which Juan had duly purchased; Herminia had asked only that her son return home safely, which he was now able to do, though in a few months' time his mother's worst nightmare would come very close to being fulfilled.

Chapter Ten

1952: A Nearly Fatal Accident

'When I came round, I began to remember the things that had
led up to the accident. I said to myself, "How easy it is to die!"
I had gone from life to a kind of death in no time at all,
without feeling a thing.'

THE WITHDRAWAL OF Alfa Romeo and the absence of any
real challengers to Ferrari meant the 1952 World Championship series was destined to lack the tension and excitement
of the previous season. In light of this, the governing body of
motorsport, the FIA, announced a new Formula 1 for 2.5-litre
unsupercharged engines. However, because it would take time
for the manufacturers to develop suitable cars, the new formula
would not come into effect until 1954. In the interim, the FIA
decreed that for 1952 and 1953 Formula 2 cars with two-litre
engines would in effect be elevated to Formula 1 status. This
decision was made because two-litre machinery was either
already available or under preparation on several fronts. In
Italy, where Ferrari already had a fleet of two-litre, four-
cylinder-engined cars, Maserati was developing a six-cylinder,
two-litre engine, though it would not be ready until mid-season.
The new formula would also provide a forum for France's
Gordini cars, while England would be represented by machinery
from Connaught, Cooper, ERA, HWM and BRM.

As the reigning world drivers' champion, Juan had no shortage of offers to lead teams in the new formula, and there were also opportunities for him to compete in other categories. Early in 1952, Juan made an agreement with Maserati owner Count Omer Orsi to drive one of his cars when it became available for the World Championship series. He also maintained his allegiance to Alfa Romeo by signing a contract to lead his old team in sports car races. To round out his European season, Juan accepted an offer to drive a British-built BRM in Formula Libre, a free formula series for cars that included ex-Formula 1 machinery, and he also agreed to make a guest appearance in a Cooper-Bristol.

Juan began his racing year as usual, competing in South America for the ACA team. In the first three months of 1952 he drove his Ferrari Tipo 166C to victory in six of the seven races he contested. He won twice in Brazil, and would have won a third time had his car not failed him, twice in Argentina and twice in Uruguay. Following these impressive displays of his superiority, Juan headed off to Europe where he was met with a series of misfortunes, one of which came precariously close to being fatal.

In England in April, Juan's misfiring Bristol-engined Cooper finished sixth in the Richmond Trophy race at the Goodwood circuit. The event was won by González in a modified Ferrari, and second was the Cooper-Bristol of the flamboyant young Englishman Mike Hawthorn, who was destined to become a major rival of Juan's in the future.

In Italy in May, Fangio and the Alfa mechanic Augusto Zanardi renewed their partnership in another round of the Mille Miglia, this time in an Alfa Romeo GT car whose 1900cc engine worked much better than its brakes. Very soon after the 1,000-mile journey began, the Alfa's brake pedal went to the floor and whole stretches of road had to be covered with only the handbrake providing any semblance of stopping power. At one checkpoint, the Alfa team mechanics looked the car over and pronounced the brakes to be in perfect working order, a diagnosis that proved to be completely wrong. In Florence, Juan took matters into his own hands and found that the brake master cylinder was mounted too close to the exhaust pipe and on the road was being overheated to the point of total malfunction. Juan procured a piece of asbestos and wired it around the exhaust pipe to isolate the brake cylinder from the heat. From then on the brakes worked perfectly, but too much time had been lost for him to figure prominently in the results, and the Fangio-Zanardi car was classified 22nd overall.

Juan's next misadventures took place back in England, where he and González were invited by British Racing Motors to test the BRM at the company headquarters near Bourne. The BRM, featuring a complex supercharged sixteen-cylinder engine, was intended to represent the best of British engineering in competition against the European machinery that had dominated single-seater racing for many years. BRM had made periodic appearances in Grand Prix races since 1950, but a variety of problems meant it had failed to make much of an impression. British hopes now rested on the 1952 model, which the Argentine drivers were asked to evaluate. The test took place on a circuit laid out on an old airfield, Folkingham, on the runways of which the BRM behaved rather like an aircraft intent on taking off. Juan found that when the supercharger was activated, the car blasted down the straights 'like a wild beast' at a fearsome rate of knots, its tiny 1.5-litre engine shrieking like a banshee at 12,000rpm as it kicked up a storm of nearly 600bhp. To keep the sixteen cylinders fully on song in the corners required continual work on the gear lever, since there was scarcely any power below 7,000rpm. When terminal velocity was reached, Juan discovered that the car's drum brakes were inadequate, and he spun off in a corner, slightly damaging an exhaust pipe on a runway light. (BRM later replaced the drum brakes with aircraft-style disc brakes, which were much more effective and became the norm for racing cars.) By the end of his first BRM experience, Juan's ears were ringing from the engine's din, and there was such intense heat in the cockpit that he thought his legs were on fire. He suggested that air vents be fitted to ventilate the cockpit. The car was certainly a handful to drive, but Juan enjoyed the challenge of taming the wild beast and looked forward to racing it.

Before they left England, Juan and González stayed overnight in London, where they went to the cinema. Since neither of them could understand much English (and they spoke the language even less), they chose a Western film which they assumed would have more action than words. Unfortunately, they were wrong; the film was full of dialogue. Juan whispered to his friend that they should leave and look for another cinema. As they were heading up the aisle there was a resounding crash of broken glass followed by screams of alarm from the audience. The lights came on to reveal that a huge crystal chandelier had fallen from the ceiling directly on to the two seats recently vacated by the Argentinians. Along with the other shocked patrons, several of whom were slightly injured by flying debris, Juan and González made a hasty exit. They went back to their hotel thanking their lucky stars and wondering whether racing was really any more dangerous than civilian pursuits. Indeed it was not, as Juan was about to find out.

At Albi in France on the first day of June, Juan's first BRM drive started with him breaking the lap record and ended with the car breaking a water pump that put him out of the race. González's BRM went on to set the fastest lap in the race, which was won by Louis Rosier in a Ferrari. From France, the BRMs were shipped to Northern Ireland for the Ulster Trophy race at

Dundrod, near Belfast. For this race, Juan's BRM team-mate was the up-and-coming Englishman Stirling Moss, who was to become his great rival and friend and who on this occasion quickly agreed with Juan's negative assessment of the BRMs. Neither of them finished the race (which was won by Taruffi's ThinWall Ferrari Special), nor were they unhappy about their early exits, which were caused by mechanical failures rather than the accidents that threatened at every turn. The BRM V16 Mk1 was completely unsuited to the twisting Dundrod track, where the supercharger kicked the car into skids, even on the straights.

As soon as he retired from the race, Juan went looking for the Siamese Prince Bira, who had promised him a ride in his private plane on a flight to Italy, where Juan was scheduled to make his debut with Maserati in a race at Monza the following day. But at Dundrod, Bira was nowhere to be found. Having crashed his OSCA through a hedge several laps before Juan's BRM had given up the ghost, the prince had left without him. With less than 24 hours to make it back to Monza, Juan joined up with Louis Rosier, who had also retired early from the race and was heading for Belfast airport to fly to London and catch a flight to Paris. When they got to London, Juan found there were no suitable connections to Milan, so he decided to accompany Rosier to Paris. In Paris, where they had landed at Le Bourget airport in a severe storm, Juan found that all flights to Italy were cancelled because of the bad weather. Increasingly desperate, he sought to continue his journey on an overnight sleeper train, but all of them had already departed. It was now nearly midnight, and though both of them were exhausted, the Frenchman generously offered to drive Juan in his Renault road car to Lyon, where it might be possible to get a morning flight to Italy. After driving all night in the teeming rain, they arrived at Lyon airport just as dawn was breaking, only to find that the

Left Juan Manuel Fangio (*centre*), with sisters Celia and Herminia and brother Jose. Proud of his humble origins in Argentina, he believed his rise to undreamed of international fame and fortune owed much to the support of his loving family and close friends.
© Museo Fangio

Juan at 11, dressed up for st Communion and already med by a passion to rk on the automotive tures that would take over e and make him a legend.
seo Fangio

Above In his primitive, self-prepared Chev coupe Juan's heroic exploits in epic So
American road races put his home town of Balcarce on the map. These incredibly a
marathon events made European competition seem like child's play. © Museo Fangi

Below Already middle-aged, Juan quickly adapted to the much more sophisticated
world of Grand Prix racing. At Monaco in 1950 he cleverly drove his Alfa Romeo
through a multiple pileup to score his first championship victory. © Sporting Picture

In 1952 he was
to survive a dreadful
nt at Monza. The
eath experience,
left him with a
nently stiff neck, had
ound effect on his
e, though it didn't
im down.
ty Images

The quest to beat
eat Fangio, which
ne the goal of every
ng star, produced
sensational duels.
53 at Reims Mike
horn (number 16
i) made a name for
lf by narrowly
ting the Maserati
n by the 'Maestro'.
Photographic

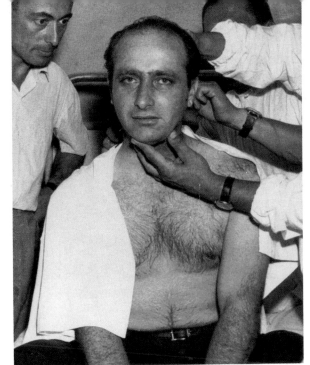

Above Universally ad[mired]
and respected by his [peers,]
Juan developed espec[ially]
close friendships with [the]
youngsters Peter Coll[ins]
(*left*) and Stirling Mo[ss]
(*centre*), who said he [loved]
the 'Old Man' like a [second]
father. © Getty Images

Left Everyone thoug[ht]
the vivacious 'Beba' w[as]
Mrs Fangio, though t[hey]
weren't married. Thei[r]
tempestuous 20-year
relationship ended wh[en]
she said if he didn't li[ke]
being with her he sho[uld]
leave. He did, though [he]
never lacked female
companionship.
© Getty Images

t The combination of
...o and Mercedes was
...lly unbeatable,
...cing two more world
...pionships for Juan.
...partnership ended
... Mercedes withdrew
... racing after the 1955
...ans disaster, in which
... narrowly escaped
... involved.
...tty Images

w A trio of title
...rs. In the first eight
... of the World Drivers'
...npionship Alberto
...i (*left*) won it twice
...Giuseppe Farina
...*t*) once. The five
...· driving titles went to
... Manuel Fangio.
...tty Images

Left Though Juan's relationship with Enzo Ferrari was uneasy, his single season in motor racing's most famous [team] resulted in yet another world championship.
© LAT Photographic

Below Princess Grace [and] Prince Rainier of Mon[aco] presented the 1957 winner's trophy to the man whose natural ch[arm] won over nearly every[one] he met. Juan moved e[asily] in all circles of society, [but] was most comfortable [in] the company of the common people he fe[lt he] most represented.
© Sporting Pictures

e His Homeric victory in the 1957 German Grand Prix at the notorious
urgring is still considered by many to be the greatest drive of all time. Here, late
e race, Fangio's much-delayed Maserati closes in on the faster Ferraris of Collins
nd Hawthorn (8). © LAT Photographic

v On the Nurburgring podium Collins (*left*) and Hawthorn (*right*) celebrated the
Man's tremendous feat. Juan said he had never pushed himself so hard before and
 never do so again. It proved to be his last world championship victory.
T Photographic

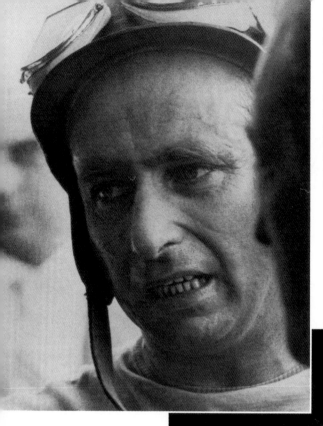

Left At 47, the strain
racing life in which ov
30 of his peers were k
had taken their toll. J
no longer felt able to
up to his own exactin
standards, and after
excelling in over 200
he retired, leaving bel
a winning record that
never be beaten.
© Getty Images

Right Juan Manuel
Fangio in 1988 and aged
77. Even 30 years after his
retirement his personal
magnetism – the quiet
dignity, the essential
warmth and humanity –
made him a commanding
presence. His
extraordinary life ended in
1995, but his legend lives
on. © Sporting Pictures

continuing inclement weather meant flights were unlikely for several hours, perhaps the whole day.

In an airport café, Rosier and Juan discussed the dilemma over café au lait and croissants, which would prove to be Juan's only nourishment in two days. With nearly eight hours before the mid-afternoon start of the non-championship Grand Prix of Monza, they decided it might still be possible for Juan to make it by driving over the Alps via the Mont Cénis pass in Rosier's Renault; Rosier would take a taxi to his home at Clermont-Ferrand near Lyon, where his car could be returned to him at a later date. So they bid each other a fond farewell and Juan embarked on a high-speed alpine journey reminiscent of the Andean escapades with which his racing career had begun. He drove like a man possessed, slapping his face hard to stay awake and sliding the Renault around the corkscrewing mountain roads as he'd once done with his old Chevrolet. By the time it screeched to a halt in Monza on Sunday afternoon, 8 June, just half an hour before the race was due to start, the Renault's tyres were worn down to their fabric lining and its driver was utterly exhausted.

Leaping out of the Renault, Juan hit the ground running, took a quick shower and changed into his faded yellow shirt and blue trousers, the familiar costume that continued to distinguish him from the other drivers, nearly all of whom wore well-tailored blue cotton overalls. But his favourite blue linen cap was not now part of his regalia; from his small travel satchel he produced a shiny new crash helmet, modelled after those used by polo players and made mandatory by the FIA for the 1952 season – no longer was the wearing of one a sign of fear. Pulling on the light brown helmet, and gulping down a handful of aspirins in an effort to ward off a splitting headache brought on, he assumed, by having to concentrate so hard for so long during his dash through the mountains, he ran for the starting grid where the mechanics had his Maserati ready on the last row.

Having not practised for the race, he was theoretically not allowed to take part, nor was he obligated to do so since he had not yet signed a contract with Maserati and this was not a championship race. But Juan, who was above all a man of his word, had promised Maserati owner Count Orsi that he would drive in the team's debut. The Monza race organisers were also counting on the appearance of the reigning world champion, and much of their pre-race advertising had been based on it. The other drivers, all 28 of them, welcomed Juan; they had all agreed that he should be allowed to start, albeit from the back of the grid. Perhaps some of them felt even the great Fangio would not be much of a threat in a car he had never driven, let alone seen, before. Yet Juan was full of confidence. Monza was a circuit he knew particularly well, and on many occasions in the past heavy doses of race-induced adrenalin had drowned out extreme fatigue and he had raced well.

In front of him now was a confusion of smoking and flame-spitting exhaust pipes. With an ear-splitting roar, the field surged forward. From the start, Juan began an all-out attack that saw him overtake six cars on the first lap, several of them in a breathtaking manoeuvre around the outside of the 125mph Curva Grande. His confidence thus boosted, he embarked on an even faster second lap that took him past nine more cars. Then he arrived at the twin Lesmo corners, which were usually taken in second and third gears. Later, Juan thought he might have tried to take the second Lesmo in fourth. In any case, the Maserati was travelling faster than his judgement could accommodate. The right-front wheel clipped a low kerb on the inside of the corner and the light impact set in motion a sideways skid. Still confident that his quick reflexes would come to his rescue, Juan delayed correcting the slide and allowed the car to drift wider. His intention was to regain control on the outside of the corner where there was more room to manoeuvre, but his exhausted reflexes were not up to the task and the car went beyond the point of no return. Slamming into a row of straw bales made rock hard after years of exposure to the elements, the Maserati A6GCM proceeded to run amok.

What followed was for Juan a momentary blur of flying straw and dust followed by a sequence of sensations that seemed to unfold in slow motion. There were glimpses of sky-blue, tarmac-black and forest-green, images that turned lazily over and over like a slowly revolving kaleidoscope. There was the odd feeling of his body being gripped by alternately demented and playful centrifugal forces that for a surprisingly long time tossed him around like a toy, then casually catapulted him high into the blue and green void. He recalled hearing the sound of a howling engine fading into the distance and feeling on his body the cooling comfort of a fresh breeze, in which he was almost gently soaring. But in his final moments of consciousness he realised the serene blue of the sky was gone and only the dark green of onrushing trees remained in his vision. The last thing he remembered was the smell of the fresh grass and damp earth on which his contorted body lay. He felt no pain. Then came oblivion.

The ferocity of the accident and its seemingly interminable duration shocked the group of marshals and members of the Carabinieri standing at their post among the trees at Lesmo. The old-timers among them gasped in horror, remembering the terrible day at the 1933 Grand Prix of Monza when Campari, Borzacchini and Czaykowsky were all killed in massive crashes at Lesmo. The onlookers had stood transfixed as the red Maserati flew high into the air and flipped over and over like a leaf in the wind. On those occasions when it was completely inverted, the car's yellow-shirted occupant could be seen gripping the steering wheel firmly, as if he was still in control of the wildly gyrating projectile. Then, in the midst of one of those terrifying somersaults, the driver soared skyward, alone, in an arc before plummeting like a stone to a hard grassy knoll where he landed with a sickening thud, convulsed once and lay still.

When the track workers rushed to Juan's aid they found him shoeless (his footwear was later recovered from the cockpit of the totally destroyed Maserati), and his crash helmet was scraped on its peak and along the left side. Carefully, they carried his inert body to a waiting ambulance which took him to the Monza track infirmary. From there, he was transported to Monza's Hospital Maggiore, where his injuries were diagnosed as severe concussion with some cerebral haemorrhaging, several fractures of the cervical vertebrae, spinal contusions and a broken thumb. X-rays also revealed lesions in the bones and traces of nerve damage in his neck that were a legacy of his crash in Peru in 1948. Undoubtedly, that injury had been the source of his headaches, which never occurred again after his lengthy stay in the Monza hospital.

For the first few hours, Juan wavered in and out of consciousness. At one point he awoke and saw two vaguely familiar faces bending over his bed, regarding him anxiously. One of them was carrying a laurel wreath, and for a desperate moment Juan wondered if it had funereal implications. Then he recognised the Ferrari drivers Giuseppe Farina and Andre Simon. They had finished first and second in the Grand Prix of Monza, and Farina had brought the wreath as a tribute to their fallen comrade. They were shocked by his appearance. The once strong, virile body was lying inert, and the half-closed eyelids flickered faintly on his deathly pale face. 'Farina, Simon,' came the barely audible whisper, and the chastened pair slowly backed out of the room.

Juan was kept heavily sedated for several days, during which time only the hospital staff and those closest to him were allowed near his bedside. On the second day of his confinement, he partially awoke to find his hand being held by a beautiful nurse. At least he assumed she was a nursing sister because she was wearing the nun's habit which all the hospital nurses wore. In fact, it was one of his Italian girlfriends, who in her desperation to see her beloved had persuaded the sympathetic nuns to allow her into his room. As she sat there on one side of his bed, another woman came in – Andreina 'Beba' Berruet Espinosa, known to everyone as Mrs Fangio, though they were never married. Juan was notoriously discreet about his romantic life, though his long-term, frequently tempestuous relationship with the feisty Beba – she of the flashing dark eyes and dazzling smile – was well known. Beba, who was as volatile as she was vivacious, as jealous as she was protective, grabbed Juan's other hand and held it firmly in her grasp. Though she warily accepted the presence of the woman in the nun's habit, Beba reacted violently to the next visitors, two pretty young girls carrying a big bouquet of flowers. In fact they were Juan's nieces from the Italian branch of the Fangios, but Beba didn't know this, neither did she stop to enquire, and angrily ushered the girls out of the room, across which she hurled the bouquet.

For six days, Juan was kept completely immobile in bed on his back, his broken neck and spine in traction, his thoughts veering from the black to the bright. 'When I was lying there in hospital,' he recalled, 'thinking that I was wasting that year, the good year for me as I was world champion and was bound to earn a lot of money, I became very nervous and had high fevers because I was so worried. Then I said to myself, "Why worry? You've gained your life. You're alive." ' His neck, shoulders and upper torso were then encased in plaster. The cast was removed over two months later in a light-hearted ceremony attended by González and Bonetto, another driver whose hospital visits were much appreciated by Juan. There followed a lengthy programme of physiotherapy; Juan's much-needed psychological treatment was self-administered, but he had to contend with some unwanted news.

On 20 June, just twelve days after his accident, Juan had been informed of the death of 54-year-old Luigi Fagioli. After crashing heavily during a sports car race in Monaco, the Abruzzi Robber had been taken to hospital in a coma suffering from a broken arm and leg. Four days later, Fagioli regained consciousness and seemed out of danger, but a fortnight after that he suffered a complete failure of the nervous system and died. When another driver died – and over 30 of them did during his time in Europe – Juan tried to reassure himself that his accident had happened as the result of a mistake. He was fully aware that his crash at Lesmo had happened for the same reason as the 1948 crash that claimed the life of his friend Daniel Urrutia: in each case, the common factor was driver fatigue. He resolved never again to drive when he was tired (a vow he kept even when driving on everyday roads), nor would he allow himself ever again to dwell on the likelihood of crashing. Like most drivers, though he feared dying in circumstances that were beyond his control, Juan felt certain that, provided he could keep his negative emotions in check, he could remain master of his own destiny. 'When you feel sure of yourself and have confidence in your car,' he said, 'you don't think about the possibility of an accident. I believe that if somebody thinks he is going to have an accident it is better for him not to race at all.'

By 7 September, Juan was well enough to leave the hospital for a few hours. He went immediately to the Monza Autodromo where he waved the flag to start the Italian Grand Prix, the final championship race of the season. It was won by Ferrari's Alberto Ascari, whose sixth victory in seven races made him the runaway 1952 world champion. Juan then went north to Viareggio, on Lake Como, where for several weeks he was treated by a doctor who specialised in rehabilitating victims of neck and spinal injuries.

Towards the end of the year, Juan flew back to Buenos Aires. His arrival coincided with the death of Evita Perón, and though all of Argentina mourned her death, thanks were also given for the safe return of the country's wounded racing hero. In Balcarce, his parents welcomed their son with open arms, and over the next few months Herminia fussed over Juan as she had during his teenage illness. For her, he always remained the delicate boy whose dangerous life was a constant worry; Juan's attempts to reassure her by suggesting that Loreto could fall from scaffolding any day and be injured fell on deaf ears. While Loreto hung on to every word during radio broadcasts of Juan's races, Herminia sat in a darkened corner of another room saying prayers over her rosary beads. His nearly fatal injury only proved how right she had been about the dangers, and his recovery fortified her belief in the power of prayer.

During his convalescence, Juan also spent time with his other 'family' – Beba and her son. Beba had first come into Juan's life when she was living in Balcarce with her husband, a potato grower, from whom she was divorced soon after meeting Juan. Shortly after this, on 6 April 1938, Beba gave birth to a son whom she named Oscar Espinosa. Though the identity of Oscar's father remained in doubt – even Juan's family never knew for sure – it was noted that he had Juan's eyes, face and bowed legs. When the time came for 'Cacho' to go to school, Beba took him to Mar del Plata where she left him in the care of her sister. Beba then moved to Buenos Aires, living in a rooming house that became their rendezvous point whenever Juan was in town on business or en route to a race. When he opened his Mercedes-Benz dealership in Buenos Aires, Juan bought a nearby apartment where Beba took up more or less permanent residence.

In 1949, Beba had accompanied Juan for part of his first European season. During their travels, it was rumoured, she developed an intense dislike for the wife of another driver whom Beba came to regard as her rival for Juan's affections; once, she even threatened her with physical violence. According to gossip at the time, Juan punished Beba by leaving her at home during his 1950 European season, but their deep affection for each other was undeniable. Juan benefited from her practicality and her organisational ability – she helped keep his professional life in order – and he was not oblivious to the fact that his attractive female companion was seen by celebrity-watchers as the ideal 'trophy wife' for a famous racing driver. 'A woman can be something conclusive in a man's life,' Juan said of Beba. 'She can make him become great, or she can destroy him. Some women build up a man, others tear him down. In my life, I had beside me a very strong woman.'

As was his custom after each European season, Juan's sojourn in his homeland included staying with Beba in a suite of rooms in a hotel in Mar del Plata, where Cacho Espinosa joined them. Most afternoons Juan joined Cacho and his young friends on the beach for games of football, the sport that had once been El Chueco's passion. Thus, with the help of football, Juan gradually built up the strength in his atrophied muscles, and by the new year only a stiffness in his neck and upper body remained. This condition, which required him to turn his upper torso in whichever direction he wished to turn his head, stayed with him for the rest of his life, a physical reminder of the day on which he'd come closest to dying on the racetrack.

Chapter Eleven

1953: Return to Racing (Maserati)

'A driver needs to win to keep up his spirits. In fact, he must win. Once he gets into a losing streak, all his spirit goes.'

DELIBERATELY PUSHING HARDER than ever to distance himself as far as possible from the Monza catastrophe, in mid-January Juan embarked on what was to prove his busiest ever year of racing. In all, he would compete in two dozen events, eight of them driving for Maserati in World Championship Grands Prix. The first of these required only a short journey, since it took place at the brand-new Autodromo de Buenos Aires. Unfortunately, the Gran Premio de la Republica Argentina turned out to be a difficult day for the local hero on what came to be known as the 'Fangiodrome' – worse still, a deadly one for many of his countrymen.

GRAN PREMIO DE LA REPUBLICA ARGENTINA

The line-up for the 1953 Formula 1 season featured a stronger than ever Ferrari presence, with reigning champion Ascari leading a team that included Italian veterans Farina and Villoresi and the British newcomer, Mike Hawthorn. Given Ferrari's total dominance the previous year, it would be a tall order for the opposition to make inroads, especially as, alongside the usual privateers, only two other teams were officially entered in the series. Gordini had the Frenchmen Jean Behra, Maurice Trintignant and Robert Manzon, the Franco-American Harry Schell and the Argentinian Roberto Mieres; at Maserati, Juan and González had as team-mates their country-man Onofre Marimón (the son of Juan's old friend and road-racing rival Domingo Marimón) and the Italian Felice Bonetto.

With several of their nation's stars among the featured players, the Argentinians turned out in huge numbers for their home Grand Prix. The immense new Autodromo, located 25 miles outside Buenos Aires, boasted public enclosures intended to accommodate 400,000 spectators and five different configur-ations of racetrack. What the otherwise impressive facility did not have were adequate barriers between the crowd and the track.

After seven months of not racing, Juan was impressive in qualifying, setting a time that was beaten only by Ascari, whose team-mates Villoresi and Farina were also on the front row of the grid. Though the seventeen cars were lined up in orderly fashion, the massive crowd, estimated at 350,000, was not, and the drivers at first refused to start. Thousands of people, many of whom had gained entry by cutting holes in the high wire fences surrounding the venue, were clustered five or six deep on the very edge of the track, some of them even standing on the racing surface itself. It was a baking hot afternoon and the crowd became increasingly impatient, shouting their defiance at the police, army personnel and track marshals who tried in vain to move them from the most dangerous vantage points. Fearing a riot, the organisers – and, it was said, General Perón himself – issued the command that started the ill-fated race.

Ascari, Fangio, Farina, Villoresi, González. Round and round went the brave Formula 1 heroes in their fabulously roaring cars, higher and higher soared the emotions of the hot-blooded crowd. The more foolhardy among them edged closer and closer to the action, converging especially at the most critical corners, where some of them ventured beyond the kerbs and stood on the racing line. The drivers, their vision increasingly obscured by the encroaching sea of humanity, shook their fists in anger, but their protestations were seen as a challenge to the manhood of the would-be toreadors. Some of them tore off their shirts and waved them in front of oncoming cars, snatching them away at the last moment. But this was no bull ring, and at exactly the halfway point in the race the inevitable accident happened.

On lap 32, a small boy dashed across the track directly in front of Farina's third-placed Ferrari. Swerving to avoid him, Farina lost control; his car slewed sideways and plunged into the densely packed crowd. Panic-stricken people scattered in all directions; more and more became caught up in the mayhem. The Cooper-Bristol of Englishman Alan Brown struck another child. There were reports that two ambulances had crashed, that a policeman had been either crushed to death or fatally beaten by the hysterical mob. In the end, the official casualty list was announced as ten dead and 30 seriously injured, though these numbers were believed by many observers to be lower than the actual toll.

The race was won by Ascari, whose Ferrari averaged a frightening 78mph on that disastrous January day. His team-mate Villoresi was second, while González steered his Maserati clear of danger to finish third. On the worst day in his country's racing history, Juan retired on lap 36 with transmission failure. Two weeks later, in a non-championship race at the same venue, though in front of a much smaller crowd controlled by armed soldiers following what was now a national scandal, Juan's mechanically troubled Maserati finished ninth.

* * *

Juan had to wait until April for his first podium of 1953, a hard-earned and quite spectacular second place in Italy's annual Mille Migla. As usual, the massive entry list – 573 cars this year – included all manner of vehicles and drivers. Among the celebrity participants was the Italian film director Roberto Rossellini, whose glamorous Swedish actress wife Ingrid Bergman was a focal point of interest among people-watchers at the start/finish line in Brescia. Rossellini was driving a Ferrari just for the fun of it, but Juan was plying his profession on this occasion for Alfa Romeo. The car, a sleek and streamlined Disco Volante Berlinetta that turned out to be more visually attractive than mechanically sound, helped its driver to prove that he had lost none of his former skill, courage and tenacity.

Accompanied by Giulio Sala, an Alfa Romeo mechanic, Juan began the 1,000-mile journey knowing that the main opposition for his 3.6-litre Alfa would be the 4.1-litre Ferraris of the Marzotto brothers, Giannino and Paolo, whose knowledge of the Mille Miglia route was unsurpassed and whose wealthy father Count Marzotto had made sure his sons had an extensive back-up team at the service points in the race. By the time they made the turnaround at Rome, Giannino was running second to Juan, who went on to increase his advantage to two minutes in the mountains between Florence and Bologna. Then, without warning, on a particularly hazardous corner, the Alfa lurched alarmingly off course and only fierce application of its brakes prevented the Disco Volante ('Flying Saucer') from sailing off into space. A quick inspection revealed that the chassis had broken and a steering rod had become detached so that only the right wheel was responding to steering input.

Despite having only half the control he needed, Juan sped off. To compensate for the steering deficiency and to keep the car on course, he resorted to such emergency measures as scraping the Disco Volante's beautiful bodywork against bridge parapets and cliffside rock faces. Since heavy braking made the useless left front wheel splay out even more, he scrubbed off speed by downshifting into lower gears. By the time they got to the service point in Bologna, the crippled Alfa was in a sorry yet still mobile state, holding on to second place behind the Giannino Marzotto Ferrari (which went on to win). Come hell or high water, Juan resolved to keep it there. Fearing that the race organisers, never mind the Alfa mechanics, would not let him continue if they saw the broken steering link, he blasted away from Bologna before they had a chance to investigate beneath the car's bonnet.

After a series of scrapes, near misses and narrow escapes from disaster, the Disco Volante barrelled into Brescia at an improbable rate of knots that defied its crippled condition. Indeed, it had made the journey from Bologna at an astonishing average speed of 100mph. But this was rather faster than the very last corner of the Mille Miglia could be taken in a car with only half its steering, and within a few hundred feet of the chequered flag Juan ploughed head-on into a pile of straw bales. Though not much else was in proper working order, reverse gear was still available, so in a final burst of theatricality the acrobatic Alfa Romeo shot backwards across the finish line, to be classified second overall.

During the following month, May, with the championship series not resuming until June in Holland, Juan busied himself driving an assortment of machinery at a variety of venues on consecutive weekends. At Bordeaux in France, in a Formula 2 Gordini, he finished third; at Naples in Italy, his Formula 1 Maserati was second; in the Targa Florio on Sicily's open roads he finished third in a Maserati sports car (co-driving with Sergio Mantovani); and at Albi in France on the 31st, his Formula 1 BRM failed to finish the final heat.

Since he'd last driven it, the ferociously fast BRM V16 had undergone modifications intended both to improve and tame its massive power. The power was certainly still there, as Juan found out at the start at Albi, when the V16-engined device, its wheels spinning furiously, tore up the tarmac and catapulted him into the lead over Ascari in his Ferrari. On the long back straight, the two cars traded places several times, their wheels in the grass at speeds over 180mph on the tree-lined road. On the third lap, Juan set a lap record that was a full five seconds faster than Ascari could manage. He won the first heat convincingly, and in the second and final heat he rocketed away into the lead again. Yet Juan remained wary of the BRM's enduring reputation for having as many mechanical deficiencies as attributes. To reassure himself that all was well in the braking department, he gave the pedal a tap while travelling at 185mph down the straight. The brake pedal went right to the floor. Fortunately, his safety check had taken place about halfway down the mile-long straight, and by changing down through the gears he was able to slow the car sufficiently and bring it into the pits. There, it was found that a broken wheel bearing had displaced the brake calliper – Juan's race was over. Despite its failings – Juan's BRM team-mate at Albi, Ken Wharton, also came to grief after a tyre failure on the main straight – and partly because of them, Juan always said the BRM was the most fantastic car he ever drove.

GROTE PRIJS VAN NEDERLAND

In World Championship racing, the 1953 Maserati had yet to prove it was a match for the Ferrari, which had seemed far superior in the opening race of the season in Argentina. The Maserati had the edge on power, with its two-litre, six-cylinder engines producing nearly 200bhp while Ferrari's two-litre, four-cylinder engine had about 180bhp, but the more stream-lined Ferrari could match its rival in top speed and its more nimble chassis handled better than the Maserati, whose reliability was also suspect. It seemed likely that to put it on more even terms in a race was going to require more effort from the Maserati driver, and when it came to driving strength, many observers wondered if the 1951 world champion, having missed almost the entire season in 1952, could regain the form needed to dethrone Ascari, whose prowess was now at its peak.

In their second confrontation of the season, the Grand Prix of Holland at Zandvoort on 7 June, Ascari's Ferrari edged out Juan's Maserati to start from pole position. Before the halfway mark in the race, the Maserati retired with a broken axle; Ascari went on to an uncontested second successive championship victory.

GROTE PRIJS VAN BELGIE

For Belgium's championship race three weeks later on the dangerously fast Spa circuit, Juan's pole position time was two seconds faster than that set by Ascari, who became the meat in a Maserati sandwich as González also qualified on the front row. Indeed, the larger Argentinian, whose huge appetite for the highest possible speed probably exceeded that of his less corpulent compatriot, led for the first third of the race. Feasting on Spa's ultra-fast straights, González set a succession of fastest race laps, the last of them, on the eleventh lap, averaging out to just over 115mph. But keeping his big right foot to the floor for so long was more than the Maserati could bear, and on the next lap the accelerator pedal broke off and clattered to the cockpit floor. González coasted to a halt and abandoned his car in a somewhat precarious position at Stavelot corner.

Meanwhile, Juan, whose spirited chase of his friend had overstressed his car's engine, coasted into the pits with smoke pouring out from beneath the Maserati's bonnet. At this point, with Juan leading Ascari by 40 seconds, the Maserati management called in its fourth car, driven in his home race by the Belgian Johnny Claes, and gave it to Juan. Having inherited the Claes car when it was in eighth place, Juan by the penultimate lap had hauled it up into third, behind the Ferraris of Ascari and Villoresi. Ascari was too far in front to be caught, but on the last lap Juan began a concerted attack on Villoresi. As it was rounding the very fast and very long banked corner at Stavelot, the speeding Maserati's trajectory took it perilously close to the parked sister car of González. Juan's last-minute avoidance manoeuvre took his car off the racing line and on to the sand and grit, where it began to zigzag wildly before slamming into a ditch with such force that it pitched Juan out over the windscreen. In light of the potentially lethal circumstances, which included a moment when the flipping Maserati nearly landed on top of him, Juan's injuries were miraculously slight. Against his wishes, he was taken by ambulance to a hospital in nearby Vervier where he was treated for bruises to his face, arms and upper body and kept overnight for observation.

GRAND PRIX DE L'ACF

Two weeks after this lucky escape at Spa – and Juan blamed the accident not on fate but on having been the victim of an uncharacteristic bout of impetuosity that he resolved not to resort to again – Juan became embroiled in an epic battle at Reims. Though it was a fight he ultimately lost, the 1953 French Grand Prix brought forth a worthy new challenger whom Juan thought 'a very nice fellow . . . always in a good mood', and was the first to congratulate.

The triangular course at Reims was not really a stern test of driving skill, but it did lend itself to exciting racing, provided the cars were fairly evenly matched, which the Ferraris and Maseratis on this day were. On the long straights, the Maseratis, which now had improved power, had a slight edge in top speed, while superior braking and better acceleration gave the Ferraris the advantage coming in and out of the circuit's two hairpin bends. Thus it was that Reims became the venue for what came to be called the 'Race of the Century', featuring a scintillating, slipstreaming, see-saw struggle for supremacy between the Ferrari driven by the 24-year-old Englishman Mike Hawthorn and the Maserati of the 42-year-old Argentinian Juan Manuel Fangio. Repeatedly, the Maserati passed the pits inches in front of the Ferrari, only for the positions to be reversed around the track's two tight corners, where late in the race Juan was further disadvantaged by the loss of first gear. Immediately behind this duelling duo, the González Maserati and the Ascari Ferrari furiously traded third and fourth places.

In the breathtaking wheel-to-wheel battle at the front, the freshfaced newcomer and the grizzled veteran took turns breaking the lap record (the fastest fell to Fangio, whose 25th lap in a time of 2m 41.1s averaged out to 115.905mph) and enjoyed themselves every minute of the way. 'We would go screaming down the straights side by side, absolutely flat out, grinning at each other, with both of us crouching down in the cockpit trying to save every ounce of wind resistance,' Hawthorn said later. 'We were only inches apart, and I could clearly see the rev counter in Fangio's cockpit. Once, as we came into Thillois, he braked harder than I expected and I shunted him lightly, putting a dent in his tail. That shook me a bit, but he showed no resentment at all. He just kept on fighting every inch of the way, according to the rules, in the way that has earned him the admiration and respect of everyone in racing.'

On the penultimate lap, they crossed the finish line virtually side by side. Between the hairpins they exchanged places again, and on the last lap the Ferrari flashed past the chequered flag in front by a hair's breadth. A few seconds later, the González versus Ascari battle resolved itself in favour of the Argentinian. But the day belonged to the blond-haired, bow-tied Hawthorn, whose predilection for wearing such neckwear while racing prompted the French to christen him 'Le Papillion' (the Butterfly), and whose victory was the first by a British driver in a World Championship Grand Prix. On the podium, the ecstatic winner's beaming face turned beetroot red with embarrassment when he was warmly embraced by Juan. And when 'God Save the Queen' was played in his honour, he burst into tears and Juan hugged him closer still.

BRITISH GRAND PRIX

Juan's first victory of 1953 came not in a race, but in a hillclimb on a Swiss mountain. In fact, the Vue des Alpes was the shortest event of his career, lasting only the 4m 46.4s it took him to ascend the hill in his Maserati. While it was satisfying to win again, this was only a minor triumph, and Juan fully understood that for a driver accustomed to winning major races against strong opposition the failure to do so for too long a time could undermine morale. What he really needed to do was defeat Alberto Ascari, whose seemingly inexorable march to a second consecutive championship had been interrupted by Hawthorn in France. But in the British Grand Prix at Silverstone, despite a determined effort that kept the crowd on their feet, Juan finished second, a full minute behind Ascari. In a Formula Libre race prior to the main event at Silverstone, Juan's BRM had also been second best, to Farina's ThinWall Special Ferrari.

Doubts were now being expressed about the great Fangio's ability to overcome what was clearly a car advantage held by Ferrari, but his game persistence was still winning him new fans. Among those enthralled by his performance at Silverstone was a thirteen-year-old lad from Scotland whose brother was competing in the Grand Prix. Though Jimmy Stewart's Cooper-Bristol crashed out of the race, his younger brother left Silverstone with a trophy he thereafter regarded as one of his prized possessions, even though he would eventually surpass Juan's number of Grand Prix victories. 'I got autographs from all the big names at Silverstone in 1953: Ascari, Farina, Hawthorn, González, Villoresi, and so on,' Jackie Stewart recalled. 'But the one I was most proud of was Fangio's because he was the driver I most admired.'

GROSSER PREIS VON DEUTSCHLAND

A week after the British Grand Prix, in Belgium, a switch of cars and disciplines brought no end to Ferrari's dominance or Juan's drought. In the 24 Hours of Spa sports car race the Hawthorn-Farina Ferrari won easily, following the early departure of its main competition, the Fangio-Sanesi Alfa Romeo, which crashed during Consalvo Sanesi's first stint.

From Spa, it was just a short hop over the border to the Nürburgring, Juan's favourite circuit, for the resumption of the World Championship. He qualified his Maserati a worthy second on the grid, though his time was nearly four seconds slower than Ascari's. The Maserati got a better start in the race, but about seven miles into the first lap the Ferrari drove past it easily and disappeared into the distance. Seemingly on course for what would be his fourth successive German Grand Prix victory, Ascari was instead interrupted by a rare and extremely dangerous Ferrari failure: a front wheel came off on the high-speed approach to the Tiergarten turn, and Ascari needed all his skill to wrestle his wildly gyrating car to a halt. Sensationally, Ascari then drove his tricycle of a car back to the pits, where the missing wheel was replaced and he resumed racing, albeit a lap down, in a contest that had now boiled down to a fight between Hawthorn, Farina and Juan. After several exchanges of position, the running order resolved itself at the finish line in the order Farina, Fangio, Hawthorn. The drought continued.

GROSSER PREIS DER SCHWEIZ

After outqualifying Ascari by six tenths of a second, Juan started the Swiss Grand Prix on 23 August from his first pole position of the season. But the race, the penultimate championship event of the season, was the same old story: a runaway win for Ferrari, with Ascari trouncing his team-mates Farina and Hawthorn, thus clinching back-to-back world titles. Juan finished a gallant fourth, having taken over Bonetto's car after the engine in his Maserati had blown itself to smithereens.

As if to underline his dominance, Ascari won again the next weekend, this time sharing a Ferrari sports car with Farina in the 1,000 Kilometres of the Nürburgring. In that race Juan, partnered by Bonetto, drove a Lancia (a D24 Sport) for the first time, but the car retired with an electrical problem. In their next race, another sports car event, Juan (back in a Disco Volante) and Bonetto (a Lancia D24) were rivals. Juan won this Grand Prix of Supercortemaggiore at Merano in Italy, and from there journeyed 120 miles south-east to Italy's shrine of speed, his confidence high for the final championship race of 1953.

GRAN PREMIO D'ITALIA

Juan's Italian Grand Prix weekend at Monza got off to a worrying start. During practice, a rear tyre burst as he was braking from 135mph on the entry to the Curva Grande. The Maserati twitched viciously, then broke away into a series of uncontrollable oscillations. The spinning car stopped without hitting anything, but its driver was left both mentally shaken and physically sore. In reacting involuntarily to the frighteningly familiar feeling of being at the mercy of a runaway machine at Monza, Juan had hung on to the steering wheel with such force that his whole body ached that night.

After a troubled sleep, the anticipated thrill of the chase soon restored Juan's equilibrium, and in qualifying he extracted from his Maserati an impressive performance that put it between the Ferraris of polesitter Ascari and Farina, thus making it three world champions in a row. The second row of the grid also comprised a Maserati and two Ferraris, Juan's young protégé Marimón lining up alongside Villoresi and Hawthorn. Behind them were 24 other cars, but it was the first four on the grid that featured in the fabulous race that followed.

From start to finish, Ascari, Farina, Fangio and Marimón fought it out wheel to wheel, occasionally rubber to rubber, thundering around Monza lap after lap in hair-raising high-speed formation, seldom separated by as much as a second. Slipstreaming one another down the straights in a crescendo of noise, they tore into the corners sometimes four abreast, rounding them in unison in magnificent four-wheel drifts that sent smoke spiralling up from the tyres and flames belching from the exhaust pipes. The cars were so evenly matched that the sensational struggle would surely only be settled by the men in the cockpits. Indeed, on the last corner on the last lap it was a slight error by the newly crowned world champion that determined the outcome of the dramatic dash to the chequered flag.

Accelerating out of the Curva Porfido, Ascari was so determined to get to the finish line first that he applied a fraction too much power too soon, and his Ferrari slid broadside directly in front of Farina, who was forced to ease up and put two wheels on the grass. Farina's evasive move was successful by a hair's breadth, but Marimón's Maserati rammed hard into Ascari's Ferrari, putting them both out on the spot. Emerging from the dust cloud and flashing across the finish line first was a lone Maserati, followed a split-second later by a solitary Ferrari. But the passage of these two survivors of the last-lap shunt produced no chequered flag, and it took another lap for the surprised race officials to realise that Juan had beaten Farina to win the Italian Grand Prix.

Juan knew he had won when he arrived in the Maserati pits to find the entire team, including its owner Omer Orsi, weeping copious tears of joy. Amid the wet hugs and kisses, Juan explained that this victory was due to a combination of good fortune, foresight and fortitude. In the last few laps, he had deliberately backed off slightly to play a waiting game. He had anticipated that Ascari and Farina, two Italians driving in front of their home crowd at Monza with victory in sight, would likely engage in a last-ditch, all-out assault for supremacy that in their exhausted condition would make them vulnerable to a mistake. Mindful of his own last-lap attack that had put him in a ditch earlier in the year in Belgium, Juan felt his Monza win was a matter of his having greater presence of mind when it was most needed, and of having the stamina to keep that mind clear when others faltered. As he said, 'It's not so much physical endurance that counts in racing, the important thing is to find time to think of the race during the race.'

Juan's only championship win of 1953 was a personal triumph of considerable magnitude. Far more important than the points he scored – he finished the season second to Ascari and ahead of Farina and Hawthorn – was the point he made to himself. Privately, though his Grand Prix performances had belied it to most observers, he had wondered if the June 1952 accident might have blunted his edge. The Monza victory put such misgivings permanently to rest. In *Autosport*, Gregor Grant put his finger on the importance of the victory: 'The Italian Grand Prix demonstrated the greatness of Fangio. While both Ascari and Farina permitted themselves to be rattled, Juan Manuel serenely went on his way, never allowing the Ferraris a moment's respite and earning a sensational victory on the track where he was so dreadfully injured the year before.' Psychologically, Juan felt stronger than ever.

But it was now mid-September, and the strain of racing so hard so often was taking a physical toll. Juan wished he could go home for some rest and relaxation, but he was obligated to compete in three more events in Europe. A week after winning for Maserati at Monza, he drove the same car to victory at nearby Modena, where he beat his team-mates Bonetto and Marimón (the Ferraris did not compete). The next weekend, driving for BRM in two races at Goodwood in England, he recovered from stalling his car at the start of the first race to finish second to the Ferrari of Hawthorn. In the second event, the Fangio BRM threw a tyre tread, and the Englishman won again.

Back in Milan, packing up in preparation for his return to Argentina, Juan was visited by Felice Bonetto, who had become more than just a Maserati team-mate. During Juan's hospital confinement in 1952, Bonetto had visited him more often than any of his European colleagues. Juan had greatly appreciated this consideration, and the bond between them was now strong. Born in Brescia in 1903, and nicknamed 'Il Pirata' (the Pirate), Bonetto was especially noted for his fierce, sometimes foolhardy drives in the Italian long-distance races the Mille Miglia and the Targa Florio. In the 1952 Targa, Bonetto drove a Lancia sports car to an important victory, and he was now about to lead the Lancia team on an epic venture into Juan's kind of territory.

Bonetto invited Juan to join Lancia in an assault on the Carrera Panamericana, an eight-stage, 1,912-mile race between the Mexican towns of Tuxtla Gutierrez, near the Guatemalan border in the south, and Ciudad Juarez on Mexico's northern frontier with the USA. The first Carrera Panamericana had been run in 1950 to celebrate the completion of the Mexican section of the Pan American highway, and since then it had developed a reputation for being as dangerous as it was spectacular. Having had more than his share of Pan American racing thrills and spills in the Gran Premios of the past, Juan was at first reluctant to agree to Bonetto's proposal. Eventually, however, his friend's persuasive words won him over and Juan was signed by Lancia to drive one of the team's five entries.

The main opposition to Lancia's six-cylinder, three-litre Tipo D24 sports cars was expected to come from several powerful 4.5-litre V12-engined Ferraris, most of which had two drivers to share the heavy workload. But there was strong American representation too. Though open road racing had long ago been banned for safety reasons in the United States, the major American automobile manufacturers used the Carrera Pan-americana as a proving ground for their products, and in 1953 US entries made up a significant portion of the 200-car field.

After attending his parents' 50th wedding anniversary in Balcarce, Juan flew north to Detroit to pick up a Chevrolet, donated by General Motors so that he could reconnoitre the route a week before the race. Accompanied by Felice Bonetto, and also by his old friend and long-distance-racing sparring partner Domingo Marimón, who came along to offer advice, Juan soon found out that the hazards awaiting the competitors in Mexico were at least as formidable as those he had faced in South America. Some of the dangers were unique, among them extremely strong gusts of wind on the plateaus in the Sierra Madre mountains that would in the race blow several cars off the road. Another obstacle among the more remote peaks was of an ornithological nature. Several times during his trial run Juan encountered giant vultures sitting in the middle of the road, apparently oblivious to oncoming cars. With their large wingspans, the birds were accustomed to using the windswept roads as runways to gain momentum in order to heave their huge bulks aloft. Their laborious take-offs were a long time coming, and during the race several cars would be wrecked in collisions with big birds (the previous year a Mercedes-Benz 300SL co-driven by Karl Kling and Hans Klenk hit one at over 120mph, and Klenk was knocked out; the team fitted steel reinforcing rods on the screen and went on to win the 1952 race). Though the vagaries of nature were beyond his control, Juan's extensive pre-race preparations also included laying down personal markers to warn of forthcoming dangers. On the pavement itself, or on roadside rocks, Juan painted blue and white stripes (the colours of the Argentine flag) to act as signposts for hazards that lay ahead.

It was thought that the high winds were responsible for the first fatal accident in the 1953 Carrera Panamericana. Juan started 36th at Tuxtla, and passed several cars during the 392-mile first stage to Oaxaca, where he was classified third overall behind his Lancia team-mates Bonetto, who averaged 94.89mph, and Piero Taruffi. At the finish line, Juan was approached by the sister of the Ferrari driver Stagnoli, who had started before Juan but had not yet appeared. Juan told the anxious woman that he had not seen her brother, but not to worry because his Ferrari had probably broken down. Shortly after their conversation, Juan learnt that the Ferrari had left the road, probably blown by the gale-force wind, overturned and caught fire. Both Stagnoli and his co-driver Scotuzzi died later of severe burns. Also on that first stage, six spectators were killed when an American sedan ploughed into a crowd that had gathered around a previously wrecked car.

Juan's own accident came on the third stage, when oil spilled from a loose filler cap on to a rear wheel and threw his Lancia into a violent skid he was unable to control. The car hit a large boulder, bounced back on to the road and came to rest with a dislocated rear axle and a buckled wheel. Still roadworthy, the

Lancia limped into the stage finish in Mexico City, where a new rear end was fitted.

During the three hours it took for the Lancia mechanics to repair his car, Juan went with Bonetto to look over the next few miles of the fourth stage. From his previous explorations, Juan knew that the series of fast curves on the run into the old Aztec village of Silao was particularly dangerous. He located his previously inscribed blue and white warning markers and pointed them out to his friend, advising Bonetto to approach Silao with circumspection. Juan also suggested that the always aggressive Bonetto should not let his rivalry with their Lancia team-mate Piero Taruffi interfere with his judgement. But the two Italians were running neck and neck for overall race honours, and Bonetto replied that there was no way he was going to give way to Taruffi. Known throughout his career as the 'Silver Fox' (he sported prematurely grey hair), Taruffi was also more popular in Italy than Bonetto, and the Pirate saw this race as a prime opportunity to put the Silver Fox in his place.

The following day, as he was carefully negotiating his way through the first of Silao's fast curves, Juan came across Taruffi's crashed car. In his haste to catch up Bonetto, who had led the stage from the start, Taruffi had gone off the road, bending his Lancia's front wheels and throwing the steering askew. Moments later, Juan came upon a second, more mangled Lancia; Bonetto's car had skidded off a corner, vaulted a three-foot-high stone wall and smashed into an iron lamp-post. There was no one near the wreckage, so Juan assumed that his friend had walked away from the accident, but at the end of the next stage, at Leon, a small boy came up to Juan's car and told him that Felice Bonetto had broken his neck and was dead. 'It came as an awful shock,' Juan recalled. 'It is a most unpleasant experience to be told that a friend has been killed, and then to have to go on racing.' He did in fact consider withdrawing, but was persuaded by Lancia to continue.

Juan scarcely reduced his pace in what remained of the race. Though he never won a stage, his overall average speed of 105.5mph was the fastest, which made Juan the sad winner of the 1953 Carrera Panamericana. As soon as he could, he returned home for a much-needed break from the wonderful highs and appalling lows of motor racing, little knowing that 1954 would bring more of both extremes.

Chapter Twelve

1954: Second World Championship (Maserati/Mercedes-Benz)

'Neubauer was the best team director that existed, and Mercedes was the most complete team.'

FROM 1 JANUARY 1954, the new Formula 1 regulations came into effect, which permitted cars with either of two types of engines, 750cc supercharged or 2.5 litres unsupercharged. Nearly everyone opted for the larger engines, and there were five factory-entered teams, including newcomers Lancia who had lured world champion Ascari and his mentor Villoresi away from Ferrari, and who had also signed Eugenio Castellotti. For Ascari, who had left Ferrari because he felt Enzo Ferrari's financial offer was not of World Championship proportions, signing with Lancia proved to be a poor career move since the team's cars weren't ready until the end of the 1954 season, which left the reigning drivers' champion with only occasional guest drives with Maserati. Meanwhile, Ferrari re-signed Farina, Hawthorn and González, and also contracted Maurice Trintignant, Umberto Maglioli and Robert Manzon to play supporting roles. Italy's other team, Maserati, was again led by Juan (to start with), with Onofre Marimón, Louis Rosier, Prince Bira, Stirling Moss and Sergio Mantovani. The French Gordini team had Behra, Pilette, Bayol and Simon.

However, the main talking point of 1954 was the much anticipated World Championship debut of Mercedes-Benz, though the German team's Silver Arrows cars were not expected to be ready until about a third of the way through the season. Mercedes-Benz had four German drivers under contract – Karl Kling, Hans Hermann, the pre-war champion Hermann Lang and Hans Klenk – but when it began racing, the team would be led by a Mercedes-Benz dealer from Argentina who had driven in that country for Mercedes in the 1951 races, and who had that year gone on to become world champion. Juan had been approached by the Mercedes team manager Alfred Neubauer late the previous year and offered the then quite staggering sum of $2,250 per race. In addition to the attraction of a stipend that was substantially larger than any racing driver had yet earned, Juan was impressed by the mechanical potential of the first new Silver Arrows racing cars to be built in fourteen years. Neubauer explained in loving detail the plans for the new car. The 1954 Mercedes-Benz W196 featured a 2,496cc eight-cylinder engine developing 200bhp and bristling with sophisticated technology, and a 1,600lb chassis with fully enclosed, aerodynamically efficient bodywork. Though he had some reservations about the wheels being enclosed sports car style, as opposed to the open-wheel view afforded by the Formula 1 cars to which he was accustomed, Juan recognised in the sleek and purposeful W196 a car in which he could go places, especially when Neubauer assured him it would not be raced until it was ready to win.

At the Daimler-Benz factories in the Stuttgart suburb of Unterturkheim, where the employees numbered some 35,000 people, the 1,200 technicians in the racing department had for over a year been concentrating on the W196 Formula 1 car. Following the failure of its pre-war cars to impress in Argentina in 1951, the Mercedes team had switched to sports car racing and had achieved considerable success with the gull-wing Mercedes 300SL car, which won both Le Mans and the Carrera Panamericana in 1952. The publicity paid off, and in 1953 the increased sales of its road cars enabled Daimler-Benz to achieve a turnover of $112 million, at least ten per cent of which was ploughed into preparing cars for the 1954 Formula 1 campaign. The plan was not just to win, but to dominate, a state of affairs to which Mercedes had become accustomed in the past.

As had been the case for 30 years, the racing enterprise was presided over by the flamboyant Neubauer, renowned for his leadership qualities and his histrionic antics while carrying them out. This larger than life character was born in 1891 and, according to legend, was already organising and directing local races for horseless carriages at the age of ten. As an officer in the Austro-Hungarian Army, he at first handled horses, then was placed in charge of a battery of motorised armoured vehicles designed by Ferdinand Porsche. When Porsche went to Daimler-Benz in 1923, he took Neubauer with him. The ex-artillery officer soon whipped the race troops into shape, and under his leadership the Mercedes blitzkrieg rolled victoriously through the racing world until the start of the Second World War.

Though a rather forbidding figure, and certainly a strict disciplinarian with a military bearing, a strutting walk, a brusque manner and a commanding voice to boot, Neubauer also had a sense of humour, though more often jokes were made at the expense of his sometimes comic officiousness. Enzo Ferrari loved to make quips about the Mercedes man, whom he'd first met at races in the 1920s when Ferrari was running a team for Alfa Romeo. Though adversaries from the outset, they eventually became good friends. Over the years, Ferrari noted that as the Mercedes racing effort intensified, Neubauer's bulk seemed to grow, 'and he became increasingly more authoritarian and dictatorial. He was to be seen by the pits, casting scornful glances at his rivals and barking out commands in his Wehrmacht officer's voice, while his staff jumped to his orders as though on a parade ground. Very soon, he was a well-known personage in our little world, generally disliked – although this did not worry him in the slightest – yet he was highly esteemed and feared for his efficiency. I thought quite often of Neubauer during the war; indeed, I could not help thinking of him every time a German mechanised column passed in front of my workshops and some officer or other alighted and started shouting orders.

'In 1954,' Ferrari continued, 'Alfred Neubauer turned up once more at the head of a team of sleek silver cars. And he was fatter and more dictatorial than ever. I watched him grow stouter and stouter with increasing concern; he and Mercedes and Germany just seemed to grow as though they were one, pound by pound, success by success, mark by mark. This unhalting progress could not help make me think: if Neubauer doesn't stop putting on weight, it looks as though Germany is getting ready for another war.'

Though no contract was yet signed with Mercedes-Benz, Juan's agreement with Neubauer included the right to continue with Maserati until Mercedes was ready. And in the interim the new Maserati 250F proved to be no slouch of a car, at least in Juan's hands.

GRAN PREMIO DE LA REPUBLICA ARGENTINA

The first round of the championship, at the 'Fangiodrome' in Buenos Aires on 17 January, was won by the local hero, though it was by no means a straightforward affair. When the cars first took to the track, Juan found that the Maserati's new six-cylinder engine, which required long straights to develop its full power, was unable to match the four-cylinder Ferraris in terms of acceleration. Because of this handicap, which led to his being outqualified by Farina and González, Juan hoped that rain, which was forecast to fall during the race, would work in his favour. The rain came on cue, but Juan's goggles misted up and he was forced to take them off, whereupon the rain intensified, falling in huge drops that hit his face hard enough to hurt. He pulled into the pits, where three Maserati mechanics serviced the car and two other crew members helped Juan fit a celluloid visor to his helmet. The latter procedure prompted the Ferrari team to lodge a protest on the grounds that the rules allowed only three people to work on a car during a pit stop.

Ferrari, assuming Fangio's disqualification would be a certainty, was not unduly worried when he resumed racing, especially since he was now almost a lap behind the front-running Ferraris of Farina and González. But, taking full advantage of the appalling conditions in which he was the master, Juan tore around the wet track like a man possessed, passing first González and then Farina to score a sensational victory. Ferrari's protest against him was disallowed on the grounds that it was not the driver but the team that should be punished for such an infraction, and Ferrari had not protested against Maserati's actions.

Juan's 1954 championship season therefore got off to a flying start, but before heading back to Europe he made two more appearances in the Americas, both of which ended with mechanical failure. Two weeks after his championship victory his Maserati 250F dropped out of the Buenos Aires Grand Prix with a broken transmission. A trip to Florida for the 12 Hours of Sebring also proved to be a waste of time, his Lancia D24 sports car, shared with Castellotti, lasting only one quarter of the race distance before a broken propeller shaft put it out of action. During that race weekend in Florida, Gianni Lancia offered Juan a substantial amount of Italian lira (rumoured to be 30 million) to forgo his agreement with Mercedes and drive for the new Lancia Formula 1 team, but Juan politely refused, pointing out that Lancia had already signed two of the best drivers in Ascari and Villoresi. Furthermore, Juan said, having given his word to Mercedes, he could never consider backing out of the deal.

GROTE PRIJS VAN BELGIE

In June, Juan celebrated his return to championship racing in Europe with a resounding victory in Belgium. Having at first been outqualified by the Ferraris of González and Farina, Juan at the last minute took over the Maserati of Marimón (who had qualified it fifth on the grid) and got pole position. But at the start of the race their superior acceleration enabled González, Farina and Hawthorn to gain the advantage. With González removed from the equation when his car's engine failed on the opening lap, Juan proceeded to reel in the others, slipstreaming past both Hawthorn and Farina on Spa-Francorchamps' long straights. Farina fought back and regained the lead, preserving his margin by only a matter of inches over the persistently following Maserati, but Juan's strategy of steadily applied pressure soon paid off: a trail of smoke from its exhaust pipes signified the imminent failure of the Ferrari's overworked engine. Yet when Farina was forced into retirement, the Maserati's engine also began to protest, and during the final laps the temperature gauge rose ever higher. After coasting over the finish line to take his second hard-earned victory of the season, Juan rolled the steaming car into the pits where it was found that the sparkplugs had turned blue and were welded firmly on to the red hot engine head. Yet the motor had lasted long enough to serve a record-breaking purpose: Juan's average race speed of 115.060mph and his quickest lap of 119.022mph were the fastest a Formula 1 car had ever gone around Spa.

Juan's last race for Maserati was not a success. For the Grand Prix of Supercortemaggiore, a long-distance sports car race at Monza, he shared the driving duties with Marimón in a Maserati 250S. In practice, Juan's sparring partner at Spa Giuseppe Farina crashed his Ferrari and was taken to hospital in Milan with severe burns. In the race, the Fangio-Marimón Maserati, which Juan had steered into third place at the time, retired with a broken rear axle seven laps from the end. Saying farewell to his Maserati colleagues, Juan headed off to meet his new team and sign a contract in West Germany, from where he would go to France to put the eagerly awaited new car to the racing test.

GRAND PRIX DE L'ACF

Among the drivers under Neubauer's command at Mercedes in 1954 was Karl Kling, then a grey-haired 43-year-old veteran of many years' service to the Mercedes cause (he didn't retire from the company until 1970, when he was competitions manager). Beginning with an apprenticeship as a mechanic in 1927, Kling had worked his way up to a test-driving role, and in 1950 was finally rewarded with a contract to race for the team. His most notable victory was in a Mercedes 300SL, with Klenk as co-driver, in the 1952 Carrera Panamericana, after which he was voted German Sportsman of the Year. Physically strong, and rather aloof and reserved as a person, in the cockpit he was transformed into a fearless fighter whose strenuous efforts sometimes verged on recklessness. As patriotic as he was ambitious, Kling had his sights set firmly on becoming the first German world champion, an objective that would put him at odds with his new Argentine team-mate, who was already leading the title race by a substantial margin having won the first two races of the year in a Maserati.

Though he never warmed to the crusty Kling, whom he thought was too full of himself, Juan found his other team-mate, Hans Hermann, more agreeable company. Hermann's youthful looks had led to the nickname 'Sonny Boy Hans', but Juan worried about his lack of experience. The 26-year-old had only started racing in 1952 and had competed in just a handful of events in a standard Porsche road car. Despite this, he had Neubauer's trust, and in the coming season Hermann would race more often than the team's other two drivers, Lang and Klenk.

As the day of the Grand Prix of the Automobile Club of France, 4 July 1954, dawned historians noted that it was 40 years to the day since the event, then held at Lyons, was dominated by a Mercedes juggernaut, with Christian Lautenschlager leading the team to a crushing one-two-three victory in what proved to be the last major European race before the outbreak of the First World War. The possibility of the 1954 event at Reims marking the dawn of another era of Mercedes monopoly seemed quite likely. As if to celebrate this historic occasion, the 50 bottles of champagne offered by the organisers to the first driver to exceed 125mph around the Reims circuit was won by Juan, who put his Mercedes on pole. Second on the grid, and a second slower, was Kling, who was in turn a second faster than the third fastest qualifier, Ascari, who was making a guest appearance in a Maserati.

At the start, Ascari's effort to keep up was more than his Maserati could tolerate and the car coasted to a halt with transmission failure at the end of the first lap. From then on it only remained to be seen if the unproven Mercedes machines would last the full 61 laps around Reims. Evidence of their fragility came on lap seventeen when Hermann, who had qualified seventh and then set the fastest race lap (121.455mph), retired with a broken engine. But there was no stopping either Juan, who led for 48 laps, or the determined Kling, who clung on grimly throughout, slightly spinning once and taking the lead on no fewer than thirteen occasions. After lapping the entire field at least once, the Mercedes cars crossed the finish line in triumphant team formation, Juan in front by a foot. The achievement was documented in *Autosport* by Gregor Grant. 'The re-entry of Mercedes-Benz into Grand Prix racing was timed to perfection,' he wrote. 'With Italian supremacy at its highest, the Germans arrived with unraced machines and proceeded to pulverise the opposition. The presence of Neubauer on the circuit, stopwatches in hand, brought back memories of the past. However, Juan Manuel Fangio was the inspiration. The great Argentinian took on the role of Caracciola in the pre-war days, and it was his generalship that made victory possible.'

In Juan's estimation, '75 per cent of the credit went to the car and the group whose work backed it up', but his modesty, if not his underestimation of the importance of the part he played behind the wheel, belied the fact that Juan had also contributed to the non-driving aspect of the Mercedes-Benz effort. His car's technical innovations, especially the desmodromic valves and the first ever fuel injection in a Formula 1 engine, appealed to Juan's mechanically inclined mind, and he understood every aspect of its complicated inner workings. As a driver, however, he found the low-slung, aerodynamically advanced chassis had its drawbacks. While the streamlined, all-enveloping bodywork reduced drag and led to more speed on the straights, it also meant there was less air resistance, so that the brakes had to be used more. Because they were mounted inside the bodywork near the engine, the front brakes especially heated up quickly and were prone to fading fast. Also, Juan found, the internally mounted brakes made the lighter-weighted wheels prone to wobbling at high speeds, making the car worryingly unstable. Eventually, he persuaded the Mercedes technicians to mount the brakes on the wheel hubs, and the situation improved. Juan also never really came to grips with the streamlined version of the W196, finding that his inability to see the front wheels interfered with his predilection for placing them with inch-perfect precision when cornering. Again, he was able to convince the team of the need to dispense with the streamlined bodywork on circuits where handling was paramount – but not before the handicap hindered his progress in the next race.

BRITISH GRAND PRIX

At Silverstone, the perimeters of the former airfield's eight corners were marked out by oil drums. Juan repeatedly clipped them with the front of his car. While his search for the fine line by way of bumping into the barrels netted him pole position, the battering left the Mercedes looking distinctly the worse for wear, and Neubauer looking grimmer than ever. Juan explained to his bothered boss that the pursuit of a quick time was like shooting at a target: in order to hit it, the driver had to be able to aim properly, which in this case he was unable to do because of the offending bodywork.

Having made his point, Juan then turned his attentions to the rivals he would face in the race. Alongside him on the front row were the Ferrari-mounted González and Hawthorn. Next to them, in an impressive showing in his privately entered Maserati, was the up-and-coming British driver Stirling Moss. The presence of two homegrown talents at the front of the grid provoked great enthusiasm among the 90,000 spectators at Silverstone. For the first few laps, while the two Argentinians fought over the lead, the local heroes Hawthorn and Moss became embroiled in a spirited battle for third. Their struggle was eventually resolved in favour of the Moss Maserati, which pulled out a substantial lead. A few laps later, Moss overtook Juan for second and the crowd went wild with excitement. But then, with just ten laps to go, the Maserati's rear axle failed and Moss had to retire. By this time, with González alone in front, followed by his Ferrari team-mate Hawthorn and Marimón's Maserati, the Fangio Mercedes was struggling to stay in fourth place. In addition to having barrel-battered front bodywork and badly fading brakes, the gearbox, which Juan had been using more and more to help slow the car, began to play up. For the last third of the race the car was jumping out of gear in the corners, where several times it broke loose in wild slides. Even on the straights, where it wobbled alarmingly, the car was a handful. Nonetheless, Juan managed to finish fourth, albeit a lap behind; Kling was a further two laps down, in seventh place. Everyone agreed that the German team's fourth place at Silverstone owed more to its Argentinian driver than the W196, and thus it was that Mercedes returned to West Germany with much work to do before its home race.

GROSSER PREIS VON EUROPA

Though it was designated the European Grand Prix, the German round of the World Championship on the first day of August was the most important of the year, indeed for many years, for Mercedes. To tackle the Nürburgring, the most difficult of all Grand Prix circuits, the chassis were made lighter, engine power was increased and two of the cars were fitted with open-wheel bodywork. These were given to Juan and Kling, while Hermann and Lang drove the streamlined models.

The worth of the modifications to his car was immediately demonstrated by Juan, who after only a couple of trial runs hurtled his W196 around the desperately dangerous 14.5-mile course in an astonishing time of nine minutes and 50 seconds.

Next fastest, after equally brave efforts, were Hawthorn in his Ferrari and Moss in a Maserati. Following his excellent performance at Silverstone, Moss had been promoted by Maserati from privateer to team driver. When Moss set by far the fastest Maserati time at the Nürburgring, it did not sit well with Onofre Marimón, who, following Juan's move to Mercedes, had been made the Maserati team leader. In the final moments of qualifying on Saturday, Marimón set off in search of a better time.

When 'Pinocho' Marimón first came to Europe, Juan had promised his father Domingo that he would personally look after him. It was the least he could do for the son of the friend Juan said he loved like a brother. On the Friday night at the Nürburgring, Juan could see that his young protégé had become agitated by the presence of the very fast newcomer Moss. Juan told Pinocho to stay calm, to try his best but not to take too many risks in qualifying, during which Juan would lead him around for a couple of laps to show him the best lines. Juan had done this, and was in the pits when the dreadful accident occurred.

As word of trouble out on the track filtered back from the far side of the circuit, there was great consternation in the Maserati pits. A quick count of their cars confirmed Juan's growing fears: Pinocho's Maserati was missing. In the distance, the lonely wailing of an ambulance siren broke the eerie silence that had enveloped the misty Eifel mountains. Juan ran to the nearby circuit hotel to pick up González, who had returned there after finishing qualifying. Together, the shaken Argentine comrades drove out to the scene of the crash. Beyond the very fast downhill descent to the Wehrseifen corner they found black skid marks on the road, then a car-sized hole in a thick hedge. Behind it, lying below in a dark ravine, were the crumpled remains of the Maserati. Juan and González scrambled down to the wreckage and tried to reconstruct poor Pinocho's last moments. They knew that the right-hand corner above them could only be taken safely in third gear; the Maserati was stuck in fourth. Despite the desperate braking attempt, the runaway car had speared straight through the hedge, uprooted a tree, then tumbled down the hill, crushing to death its young driver.

The sudden tragedy that had snuffed out the life of a well-liked young man in his prime affected even the most hardened drivers, none more so than Pinocho's grief-stricken countrymen. As they prepared for the start, Juan spoke to nobody, his mouth set with grim determination. González was less able to contain his emotions, and as they stood together he broke down and sobbed like a child. Juan, now also with tears in his eyes, embraced him and whispered words of encouragement. They must race for Pinocho, Juan said, and for Domingo, who would surely want them to carry on for Argentina. 'It was very difficult to drive afterwards,' Juan reflected later, 'but that was our profession. It was a very, very sad day, an unhappy time to be remembered for ever with great sadness.'

Hoping for a home victory, over 300,000 spectators were crowded around the Nürburgring, where the Fangio-driven Mercedes was on pole. But for the first half of the opening lap, the 310-mile race was led by the faster-starting Ferrari of González. Rivals once more in the heat of battle, the grieving friends set a furious pace, leaving their eighteen pursuers behind. At the far side of the circuit, as they roared flat out and side by side beneath the Antonuisbuche bridge, the Mercedes crept ahead and edged into the lead. González hung on grimly, and for the next several laps the duel kept the crowd transfixed. Then the Ferrari began to fall back, and on the sixteenth lap, with the Mercedes in front by several minutes, it coasted slowly into the pits. González climbed out and turned his back on the car. His distress over Marimón's death, exacerbated by the considerable fatigue brought on by his chasing Juan, had become too much, and the thoroughly disillusioned González said he could no longer continue. Ferrari signalled Hawthorn, who was running seventh at the time, to come in and take over the González car. Towards the end of the race, which went on for nearly four hours, Hawthorn's Ferrari began to close the gap to the leading car, but at the finish the Ferrari was still the best part of two minutes behind the winning Mercedes, whose anguished driver was having trouble seeing through his tears.

That day at the Nürburgring, the only other threat to a Fangio victory had come from his brave team-mate Kling, whose thrilling charge through the field was the highlight of the day for the partisan German fans. Having not set a qualifying time as a result of a wheel falling off his car during practice, Kling had started at the back of the grid. But he had logged many thousands of testing miles around the Nürburgring, and he used his circuit knowledge to great effect, passing car after car including, on lap fifteen, the leader, who was deliberately taking it easy to conserve his equipment. Once overtaken, however, Juan speeded up again, and while the prospect of a fight to the finish by the Mercedes-mounted men delighted the crowd, it provoked outrage in the pits. With surprising agility, Neubauer heaved his bulk over the pit wall, and as the duelling duo passed by, their big boss pointed furiously at his stopwatch and made thumping gestures with his fist, as if to drum the 'go slow' message into their heads. When Juan gestured back that he was only following the pace set by Kling, Neubauer began shaking both fists at the disobedient German driver. Unbeknown to Neubauer, Kling's car was already experiencing mechanical trouble, suffering from both a leaking fuel tank and a broken axle mounting. Kling knew he would have to make an extra pit stop, but still he was determined to make his mark in his home Grand Prix. Before the pit stop, he set the fastest lap of the race. He eventually finished fourth, but Neubauer was not impressed, and he reprimanded Kling for a foolhardy effort that could have jeopardised both team cars. When it came to winning, Neubauer cared not for the nationality of his drivers, only for Mercedes.

On the podium, where the Argentine national anthem was played in honour of the winning driver, then 'Deutschland Uber Alles' for the winning team, the victor stood with his head bowed. For Juan, this great day in the history of Mercedes-Benz was the saddest victory of his career.

GROSSER PREIS DER SCHWEIZ

'There is no doubt whatsoever that Juan Manuel Fangio is the greatest driver in the world today,' Gregor Grant announced in *Autosport* when Juan won again three weeks later. 'His victory in the Swiss Grand Prix was achieved with consummate ease, and his Mercedes-Benz led from the fall of the flag to the finish of the 66-lap race. On the Bremgarten circuit's succession of fast bends that require a maximum of driving skill, he lapped the entire field, with the exception of his countryman José Froilán González, whose Ferrari took second place.' On the podium, Juan hauled González up on to the top step and insisted they share the enormous, ribbon-festooned laurel wreath together. As their national anthem was played, they solemnly mouthed the words together in remembrance of Pinocho Marimón.

With this, his fifth win out of six championship races, 'Fantastic Fangio' as he was now being called now had against his name a points total nearly twice that of González, who in turn had a substantial lead over his Ferrari team-mates Trintignant and Hawthorn. It was still mathematically possible for one of them to overhaul Juan, though such thinking flew in the face of reality. It only remained to be seen, after successive wins for the open car, if the previously troublesome streamlined Mercedes was up to the standards of its driver.

GRAN PREMIO D'ITALIA

At Monza at the beginning of September the W196 streamliner was used to take advantage of the circuit's longer straights. Juan duly put it on pole. Next to the Mercedes on the front row of the grid was a Ferrari driven by his old sparring partner Alberto Ascari, whose promised ride for the new Lancia Formula 1 team was looking as though it might never materialise. Ascari's deep desire to appear in his home race coincided with Enzo Ferrari's equally fervent wish to have his reigning champion take on the might of Mercedes at Italy's shrine of speed. Joining Juan and Ascari on the front row, and sharing the limelight for the first time with stars of such stature, was Stirling Moss. In only his second outing as an official team driver, Moss had clocked a time that was only a tenth of a second slower than the great Ascari.

Mindful of the nearly three hours of racing that lay ahead in a car whose brakes were extremely unlikely to last that long, Juan obeyed a prudent philosophy of only going as fast as was necessary to win. Not subscribing to such a conservative theory of resource management were Ascari and Moss, who sped past the Mercedes and tore off around Monza as if there was no tomorrow. In fact there wouldn't even be a today for either of their thoroughly thrashed cars. The first to retire from the hammer-and-tongs battle was Ascari, whose flogged Ferrari engine blew itself to smithereens. The Maserati lasted longer, propelling Moss into an ever-increasing lead over Juan, whose pursuit in a by now almost brakeless Mercedes was further hampered by a loss of power due to a stone that had lodged in an engine valve. Then the frontrunning Maserati began to lose oil, and with just twelve laps remaining Moss had to coast into the pits with a split oil tank. The lost oil was replenished, but it proved to be too little too late, and in the Porfido curves just prior to the finish line the Maserati's engine seized solid. Putting the stranded machine into neutral, Moss proceeded to push it over the finish line and was eventually classified tenth. As the plucky Englishman directed his Maserati slowly past the Mercedes pit, Neubauer gave him a sympathetic pat on the back, then turned to congratulate his canny Argentine driver, whose fourth Mercedes victory of the year confirmed him as the 1954 world champion.

Following the podium ceremonies, the victor sought out the gallant Moss and embraced him warmly. Though somewhat embarrassed at the Latin show of affection, Moss was thrilled when Juan told him he was the moral victor and that he had clearly arrived.

The victory was Juan's last of the season. He finished fourth in a Lancia D24 sports car, shared with Castellotti, in the Tourist Trophy race at Dundrod in Northern Ireland, but for Juan the result was secondary to the relief he felt that his friend González had survived a potentially disastrous accident in practice. The González Ferrari had spun out of control on a fast corner and ricocheted viciously between earth banks on either side of the road. On the second impact the nose of the car dug in and threw González out on to the track, where he lay motionless for a moment before slowly sitting up, shaking his head and removing his helmet. Fortunately, before another car arrived track marshals rushed to his aid and carried the dazed driver to safety. The injuries – he was treated for shock, a sore shoulder and leg abrasions – were comparatively slight considering what might have happened, but for González the 1954 season was over.

This left only his compatriot to fly the Argentine flag in the two remaining races, though the first of them, the Grand Prix of Berlin on 19 September, did not count for the championship. Still, the race on the superfast Avus circuit on the outskirts of the city gave Mercedes another chance to parade its might in front of an appreciative home crowd. The chances of a rout by the Silver Arrows cars were greatly improved when the Italian opposition failed to appear. Both Ferrari and Maserati withdrew their cars, claiming the need to concentrate on preparing for the final championship race of the year, in Spain. Consisting of two very long straights joined at either end by two corners, one of them banked, the autobahn-like 5.15-mile Avus track was the fastest in Europe. To officially commemorate the race as a celebration of speed, the organisers offered a beautiful handcrafted steering wheel to the driver who set the fastest lap. When Juan saw the prize he decided he wanted to add it to his collection of trophies. As a tune-up for the main event, he broke the Avus practice lap record with an average speed of 140.5mph; in the race, his fastest lap average of 139.1mph was good enough to win the steering wheel. He might also have collected the race winner's trophy had Neubauer not gently suggested that a win for the home team by a German driver would be warmly received by the Daimler-Benz hierarchy. In truth, Juan needed no prompting, since he felt that Kling had done a good job and deserved the reward. The race was indeed merely a Mercedes demonstration run, and in the end less than a second separated Kling, Juan and Hermann as they crossed the finish line in that order.

GRAN PREMIO DE ESPAÑA

At the Spanish Grand Prix, the final race of the season, Juan's appearance on the podium was due to a combination of luck and pluck, with the emphasis on the latter. After trying out both types of cars in practice on the Pedralbes street circuit in Barcelona, Mercedes opted to use the open versions. Juan extracted from his car a time that put him second on the grid, next to a familiar opponent who was driving an unfamiliar car.

In their belated debut, the brand-new Lancias under the guidance of Ascari and Villoresi had proved exceedingly quick, and Ascari had put his on pole. But in the race the untested cars proved as fragile as they were fast, Villoresi retiring on the first lap and Ascari on the ninth, when he was leading.

With the Lancias gone, the race then became a Ferrari versus Mercedes contest. The battle was eventually settled in favour of the former, Hawthorn winning from Luigi Musso. In third place was the oil-drenched survivor of an off-day for Mercedes. Having run second to Hawthorn for most of the latter part of the race, Juan's waiting game had been waylaid by an overheating engine. The problem, which originated in a fuel mixture that was too lean for the very hot conditions, was worsened when flying scraps of paper lodged in the radiator intakes. With ten laps to go a main oil pipe broke and the Mercedes began to lay down a heavy smokescreen around the circuit. Meanwhile, in the cockpit, Juan's face and arms were being sprayed by boiling hot oil. Despite his growing discomfort, not to mention the serious problem of having oil-smeared goggles, Juan battled gamely on. By the time his Mercedes smoked across the finish line he was drenched in the lubricant and suffering from a painful scalding to his face, arms and upper body that required medical treatment.

Juan's tally over the eight-race season thus reached a mammoth 42 points, which left González (25), Hawthorn (24), Trintignant (17), Kling (12) and Hermann (8) flailing in his wake. Yet these statistics fell short of telling the full story of the champion's dominance in 1954. He had just become, for instance, the only driver since the championship series had begun in 1950 to finish every race in a season and to score points in all the races. Moreover, he failed to make it to the podium on only one occasion, when he finished fourth in the British Grand Prix. Aside from that and his third place in Spain, he won all the other races, driving two different makes of cars. Further underlining his value to the German team, for whom he scored more than double the combined points of his team-mates, was the fact that the combined totals of the drivers who scored points for Ferrari and Maserati was higher than those scored by Mercedes-Benz. Had there been a team championship (and there would be in later years), it would have been won by an Italian company.

Needless to say, the signature of Juan Manuel Fangio was quickly and indelibly inked on a Mercedes-Benz contract for 1955.

Chapter Thirteen

1955: Third World Championship (Mercedes-Benz)

'*The human body is like a car. With time, the wear and tear on a car does not depend on the age of the vehicle, but the treatment it has received.*'

To PREPARE FOR HIS sixth Formula 1 season, in which he would face an ever-growing number of ever more youthful opponents, Juan subjected himself to a more strenuous training programme than usual. In an era when most of his peers believed the physical effort of driving racing cars was enough to keep their bodies in fighting trim, Juan's regimen made him a pioneer on the fitness front. In fact, though his naturally heavy-set physique suggested otherwise, his insistence on keeping it honed would pay off dramatically in the first race of 1955.

With the season scheduled to start, as usual, in Buenos Aires, he spent the two weeks prior to his home race preparing himself for the sweltering heat that was expected. In Mar del Plata, as was his wont, Juan stayed in a hotel suite with his companion Beba. With Beba presiding over the domestic arrangements, Juan's daily routine varied only slightly from the way he lived in Europe, though in Argentina he joined Beba's son Cacho and his friends in particularly vigorous games of beach football. They played every day for three or four hours under the glare of the afternoon sun, and to the other, much younger footballers it seemed El Chueco's 43-year-old legs were as strong as ever. Blessed with a naturally slow metabolism, as evidenced by his resting heart rate of 44 beats per minute (as opposed to the norm of 72bpm), Juan had the endurance capacity of a man half his age, and he worked hard to preserve it.

But though he could spring into action instantaneously and then perform vigorously for hours on end, he came to understand that this capability owed much to his facility for being able to, whenever possible, do the exact opposite: switch off completely so as to recharge his batteries. He preferred no fewer than twelve hours of undisturbed sleep every night. His ritual was to climb into bed with some light reading material – newspaper sports pages, adventure magazines, sometimes even comic books. He had enjoyed reading as a pastime since boyhood, when perusal of the printed page opened up all kinds of possibilities in his childish imagination. In maturity, he came to regard reading as a means of relaxation and a form of escapism to take his mind off the realities of a high-profile life that was itself being written about around the world. Invariably, within two minutes of starting to read he would fall fast asleep, lying on his back with his arms resting on the pillow above his head. This posture, he believed, was conducive to deeper, more healthy breathing because it expanded his lungs. He slept like a log, nothing could rouse him, and half a day later he would wake up fully refreshed, senses alert and rested, reflexes ready to go.

Through strictly applied self-discipline, he developed the ability to manage his mind and adjust it to circumstances; he could shut it down at a moment's notice, or concentrate hard for hours. The night before a race, when jitters might be expected to interfere with sleep, Juan dispensed with his reading ritual and, rather than count sheep, visualised the racetrack's corners. Lying back on the pillow with his hands behind his neck and his eyes half closed, he would imagine his way around the circuit, taking it corner by corner, until he had completed in his mind's eye the perfect lap. Having reached this happy conclusion, he would sleep dreamless into the morning. Similarly, on race days, after having a light lunch about four hours before the start, he would lie down and quietly turn over in his mind a range of circumstances that might arise in the race and plan ways to deal with them most effectively.

His food intake was similarly regimented and measured, his meals comparatively frugal. He was no gourmet, preferring plain food simply prepared, consuming it on the basis that it should provide energy like fuel for a car. Breakfast was a slice or two of bread with butter and jam washed down by tea taken with milk, no sugar. For lunch, he had a small piece of grilled steak, some fresh fruit and mineral water. His preferred evening meal began with a bowl of soup, was followed by some lean meat with a few vegetables, and ended with a bit of cheese and fruit. Following this, he religiously took a short walk to improve his digestion. He might occasionally have a glass of red wine, but he seldom touched stronger drink. Whenever his prize winnings took the form of alcoholic beverages, as was often the case at races in France, especially at Reims where he won more than his share of champagne, he gave away most of the bottled booty to his engineers and mechanics. The one foodstuff Juan could not have done without was chewing gum. He maintained that the methodical action of chewing helped keep him relaxed and concentrated, and it also acted like a shock absorber to cushion his jaw against the continual buffeting in the race car. Depending on the rigours of a race, he got more or less mileage from the gum. In a hectic race he might go through several sticks, effecting the changeover during pit stops. After an easy race it was not unusual for him to carefully rewrap a partially chewed wad and place it in his kitbag for use in the next race.

He only smoked the occasional cigarette, and then mostly on festive occasions. Beba, however, smoked like a chimney, having developed the habit as a means of steadying her nerves while Juan raced. Though their relationship was still often rocky, especially when Beba noticed his roving eye at work, Juan preferred her companionship to the pitfalls of a succession of shorter-term affairs. According to his somewhat misogynistic philosophy, a man's love life had three stages. When young, he played the field with all sorts of women of all ages, a carefree time that cost him nothing in either emotional or material terms. The second stage, when he had become more discerning and particular, involved seeking out special women and sometimes having to pay for their favours by promising emotional commitment, perhaps even buying their affection by presenting them with gifts. If a man had not gone through the first two stages he was more susceptible to the dangers of the third stage: an older man falling for a younger woman. In this case, Juan believed, he left himself open to being taken advantage of by an insincere thrill-seeker or gold-digger who, having had her way, might then suddenly reject him. In spite of this seemingly hard-hearted attitude towards romance, Juan at this time believed that Beba loved him and that he, in turn, loved her. Nearly everyone regarded them as man and wife anyway, and in Mar del Plata that was the way they lived.

For Juan, it was the ideal preparation for a season that was monopolised by Mercedes-Benz, in both Formula 1, by means of more highly developed W196 cars, and the Sportscar World Championship series, where the team used 300SLR cars derived from the Grand Prix machines. To tackle the expected might of Mercedes, the three Italian teams chose to outnumber them, at least in terms of manpower: between them, Ferrari, Maserati and Lancia had fifteen drivers. Mercedes, while staying with the triumvirate of Juan, Kling and Hermann, had also signed a fourth driver.

'Mercedes wanted Stirling Moss in their team for 1955,' Juan said, 'so they came to me first to ask my opinion. I told them he was the best driver they could take. For me, it would have been better to have a mediocre driver beside me. Instead, I chose the best driver because of the team.' In fact, Moss had approached Alfred Neubauer in 1954 with a view to getting a Mercedes ride. Neubauer had advised him to get more experience and had then been deeply impressed by Moss's performances for Maserati. Before the 1955 season began, Neubauer put his new recruit to the ultimate test by comparing him to the team's number one driver on the world's most difficult track. In the private practice session at the Nürburgring, Juan went out first and after three laps set a target time. Moss, who had some previous experience around the 14.5-mile jigsaw puzzle of a track, took several laps to play himself in and then clocked a time impressively quicker than Juan's. At this point, with the British newcomer having in his first drive in a Mercedes beaten Juan, the crafty Neubauer declared that it was time for a lunch break. Noticing that his Argentine driver lacked an appetite, Neubauer asked Juan if he would like to do a few more laps. Indeed he would. Juan went out again to salvage his wounded pride and within three laps had beaten Moss's time. When he returned to the pits, the three mechanics assigned to Juan's car presented him with a bouquet of wild flowers they had picked from the Nürburgring's grass verges. Surprised at this display of sentiment from the normally reserved and supposedly unemotional Germans, Juan thereafter considered the flowers to be one of the best prizes he ever received.

Everyone involved in the exercise had made his point. Moss had proved himself entirely capable of holding his own against the champion, who now knew that his estimation of the Englishman's potential was valid, as did Neubauer, who would benefit from having the two drivers push each other, as well as back each other up, thereby strengthening the team. But the chief beneficiary was Moss, for whom the opportunity of following in the wheel tracks of the best driver in the world would be invaluable in terms of developing a driving prowess that would eventually establish him as the great Fangio's successor. Beyond this, the personal relationship between Moss and the Maestro, as Moss began calling the man who was eighteen years his senior, became the closest either of them had in all their years of racing. What started as a teacher-pupil association developed into something of a father-son relationship.

Stirling Moss had been introduced to motorsport by his parents. Alfred Moss, a well-to-do dentist, raced in British club events and twice competed in the USA's famed Indianapolis 500, where he finished fifteenth in 1924, while Aileen Moss drove a Morgan in club racing. The couple was also active in showjumping. Following their lead, Moss rode in over 100 events and became quite a skilled horseman. In 1948, with the help of prize money earned from showjumping successes, he bought a 500cc Formula 3 Cooper and won eleven races. In 1950, the first World Championship season, at the age of twenty he drove an HWM Formula 2 car in several Grands Prix. In the Naples Grand Prix of that year, he crashed, breaking his knee and knocking out his front teeth. A few days later he disobeyed doctors' orders, discharged himself from hospital and went back to England to compete in a race at Brands Hatch. In 1951 he was asked to drive for BRM, and was also given a place in the Jaguar sports car team. Despite not having fully competitive cars, he distinguished himself in several important events in various forms of motorsport, including rallying. In 1954, when he bought a Maserati 250F with financial assistance from his father and was subsequently drafted into the Maserati team, his career progressed rapidly. By the time he came to Mercedes, Moss had made a name for himself as a major talent. He was welcomed into the German team as a successor to his countryman Dick Seaman, one of the greatest pre-war Mercedes drivers, who was killed in the 1939 Belgian Grand Prix.

GRAN PREMIO DE LA REPUBLICA ARGENTINA

On 16 January, the temperature at the 'Fangiodrome' was 36°C in the shade and over 50°C on the track. Several drivers collapsed from heat exhaustion, and of the 21 who started only two stayed in their cars for the full three hours and two minutes it took to complete the race. Whenever an overcome driver came into the pits he was relieved by a team-mate who had stopped earlier and had had a chance to recover. In all, there were sixteen substitutions, and of the seven cars that made it to the finish line three had two different drivers, one of them had three and another had four. The two solo survivors were Robert Mieres, a native of Mar del Plata, who drove his Maserati from start to fifth-placed finish, though he made several pit stops to be doused with buckets of water, and his Balcarce-born countryman, whose heroic victory was the stuff of legends.

From the start, having been outqualified by the González Ferrari and the Ascari Lancia, Juan deliberately set a terrific pace in pursuit, hoping to wear down his rivals, whose cars were lighter and more nimble but less reliable than his Mercedes. But this was a day to test the stamina of men more than their machines, and Juan's superior conditioning and sheer mental fortitude proved unbeatable. Ascari, disorientated by the mirage effect produced by the shimmering heat, soon spun his Lancia out of the race, leaving González in front for only a few laps before he came into the pits and fell out of his Ferrari suffering from heat stroke (he eventually recovered and shared the second-placed Ferrari with Farina and Trintignant). In the meantime, Juan just kept on circulating. Several times, before he realised the burning sensation on his neck, arms and shoulders was being caused by the searing wind, he thought his Mercedes must surely be on fire. That conflagration was imaginary, but the reality was nearly as bad. A red-hot chassis tube, heated by the exhaust system and pressing against his leg in the cockpit, caused pain so intense that he cried out in anguish. His calf was being roasted like a piece of meat – he would carry the scar for the rest of his life – but still he drove on.

As word of his epic performance spread throughout Buenos Aires, thousands more of the city's citizens rushed to the circuit; over 400,000 were there to see Juan's historic finish. It would have been so easy to stop, as so many others did, and deny them, himself and his team the moment, but Juan's sense of responsibility overpowered the thought of any such shameful desertion of his duty. He was, after all, a Mercedes-Benz dealer, and the company had just opened a factory in Argentina. But the racing team's boss wasn't sure his driver's loyalty ran deep enough to go the distance in Buenos Aires, and a few laps from the finish Neubauer signalled Juan to come into the pits and hand his car over to Moss, whose overheated car had earlier stopped with a vapour lock out on the track. When a somewhat groggy Moss climbed out of the car and lay down for a moment to recover, he was seized by a medical team and carried off to an ambulance. There, until Moss found an interpreter to express the true nature of his feelings, his loud protestations were diagnosed as heat-induced delirium. Having obtained a medical release, Moss walked back to the pits where Neubauer, after sluicing him down with several buckets of water, pronounced him fit and ready to take over the leading car. This, of course, would require the co-operation of his team-mate, but Neubauer's pit signals were studiously and deliberately ignored. Having come this far, Juan was not in a car-sharing mood. 'Fangio was like a bull on the racetrack, a bull with a mass of troubles in his head, and with enormous strength,' Neubauer said. 'You could throw bottles at him and he'd still drive cheerfully through.' Instead, Neubauer called in Hermann, whose car had already been driven by Kling, and Moss brought it home in fourth place, two laps behind the winning Mercedes.

'To be frank, I was at the end of my tether,' Juan admitted later. 'I won that race simply by staying in the car. My body seemed to be on fire and my leg was burning so badly I could smell it. To stop myself passing out, to avoid cracking up, I tried to imagine that I was lost in the snow, and that I had to keep going or I would die of cold. There was a time when I thought I couldn't do it, but then my morale came back, and the will to win. When it was all over they had to lift me out of the car. They laid me on the floor of the pits and gave me an injection.'

Two weeks later, this time driving in much cooler conditions, though with his leg still hurting, Juan won the non-championship Gran Premio Ciudad de Buenos Aires. Moss finished second.

Before heading back to Europe, Juan spent the month of February recuperating at home and attending to his growing business interests. Besides his Mercedes dealership in Buenos Aires, which had been expanded to accommodate a large workshop run by his brother José, the Fangio & Co. garage in Balcarce had also become a Mercedes distributor. Juan's property investments now included a 2,000-seat cinema in Mar del Plata, where he was able to indulge his passion for Western movies. Like his light reading, Juan saw the films – featuring whiskey-drinking cowboy heroes fighting snarling, dastardly villains, spectacular bar-room brawls, sweating horses galloping madly off in all directions and continual gunfire – as another form of escape. His predilection for such mindless activity did not mean he was an intellectual lightweight. What such diversions signified mostly was the need to rest a mind overworked from concentrating almost exclusively on his profession. He also found solace in nature, and from time to time he bought landscape paintings, several of which adorned the walls of his flat in Buenos Aires. He seldom took time off, from either racing or business, but when he did he preferred to visit seaside resorts such as Mar del Plata in Argentina or Pescara in Italy, where he swam and enjoyed cresting the waves in motor boats.

Though by now quite skilled socially – and when meeting new people his relaxed, easy-going charm, positive outlook and naturally generous nature invariably won them over immediately – Juan preferred the close company of friends and family. Even with them, he never raised his voice or tried to monopolise conversations, and he actively disliked aggressive confrontations. Self-taught in the ways of the world, and hugely successful in them, he showed no trace of a superiority complex and was always willing to offer wise words of advice to the many who sought it. 'Instead of coming up with some theory about life, Juan made the practical side of his life into a theory,' said his brother Toto. 'All his knowledge of life, both motor racing and personal, is practical. He has suffered hard knocks and success, which made him the man he is.' Stirling Moss was just one beneficiary of Juan's happily shared worldly wisdom. 'He treated all those he met, from the highest to the lowest, with equal dignity and importance,' Moss recalled. 'When he was talking to you, you were the only one that mattered.'

In their first race as Mercedes team-mates in Europe, Juan was beaten by Moss in what became known as one of the

Englishman's greatest drives. For the 1955 Mille Miglia, Juan invited his old Alfa Romeo mechanic Giulio Sala to ride with him in the Mercedes 300SLR. But during their practice runs for Italy's longest race, Sala found the constant buffeting of his helmet against the two-seater's headrest more than he could bear and he reluctantly chose not to join Juan in the race. Though disappointed at the disadvantage this conferred since nearly every other competitor had a passenger, Juan thought it might be for the best. Ever since the death of Daniel Urrutia, for which he always felt responsible, Juan had preferred to drive alone. In the end, despite the handicap of having his Mercedes firing on only seven of its eight cylinders, he finished a distant second.

Juan's worthy solo effort was eclipsed by his record-setting team-mate, who became the first Englishman to win Italy's classic race. Moss was accompanied in his Mercedes by the British journalist Denis Jenkinson, whose pre-race preparations included eighteen pages of painstakingly accurate pace notes arranged on a roll, and from which he communicated directions to Moss throughout the race by means of hand signals. The Moss-Jenkinson car, having raced for ten hours, seven minutes and 48 seconds for 976 miles, won the race at an astonishing average speed of 97.9mph.

GRAND PRIX DE MONACO

Having been dropped from the calendar following Fagioli's fatal accident in 1952, the resumption of championship racing through the dangerous streets of Monte Carlo was marked by the 1955 event also being designated as the Grand Prix of Europe. The dramatic weekend that followed made it worthy of its twin titles, and then some.

Mercedes entered three cars, two special shorter wheelbase versions for Juan and Moss and a third, standard version for Hans Hermann, who was for this race called in to replace Karl

Kling, who had been injured in a crash during the Mille Miglia. Unfortunately, Hermann's appearance in Monaco also ended in an accident. With Juan and Moss trading fastest times in practice, Hermann's attempts to keep up proved beyond the capabilities of either himself or his car. On the high-speed entrance to Casino Square, he lost control and his Mercedes ploughed head-on into a stone wall. The German was taken to hospital with broken ribs, a punctured lung and other internal injuries that would keep him out of racing for a long time. To replace him in Monaco, Neubauer appointed the French privateer Andre Simon, who qualified the repaired Mercedes mid-field among the twenty cars. Meanwhile, on this tightest of all circuits, where good grid positions were vitally important, the fight for front-row honours was intense. Juan took pole with a time that beat by over six seconds the circuit record set in 1937 by the Mercedes star Rudolph Caracciola. Only a second slower than Juan was Moss, though the team-mates were separated at the front of the grid by the Lancia of Alberto Ascari, who was credited with a time equal to Juan's.

That evening, several of the drivers, including the three on the front row, went to the cinema. On the way back to their hotels, they took a stroll around the track. As they walked along the harbour-front chicane, someone pointed to the barrier and prophesied that whoever touched it the next day would end up in the water. Ascari, though well known for his superstitions, took this as a dare and deliberately touched the barrier. 'There followed in the race one of the most extraordinary accidents in the whole history of motor racing,' Gregor Grant reported in *Autosport*. 'Ascari skidded wildly at the chicane, and the Lancia bounced off a stone bollard and disappeared in a great cloud of steam into the harbour. Ascari surfaced, and was dragged to safety by frogmen stationed in boats at that point in case such an unlikely thing should occur.'

Ascari's unlikely mishap took place just nine laps from the end of the race, by which point he had inherited the lead following the retirements of the frontrunning Mercedes teammates; Juan had stopped on lap 50 with a broken axle, and Moss's engine had broken 31 laps later, though he pushed the car across the line and was classified ninth (and last). The unexpected winner was Maurice Trintignant, whose victory in a Ferrari was his first in a championship Grand Prix.

But the 1955 Monaco event was forever after known as the last race of Alberto Ascari. His injuries were comparatively slight – a broken nose and a severe shaking – and when Juan visited him in hospital that night Ascari joked that it was fortunate he could swim. Then, on a more serious note, the two-time world champion wondered out loud whether his star was setting, and if, after 32 championship Grands Prix, his total of thirteen victories (the last one in Switzerland in 1953) would prove to be unlucky for him. His father Antonio, Alberto knew all too well, had also won thirteen out of 32 before he was killed in 1925.

Though he had deserted him for a full-time Lancia drive, Enzo Ferrari retained a particular affection for Alberto Ascari. Ferrari knew he loved his wife Mietta and their two children dearly, but wondered why he didn't show it more often. Ascari replied that he didn't want his children, especially, to become too fond of him because one day he might not come back from a race. They would suffer less if he had kept them at arm's length. 'On the Thursday after falling into the sea at Monte Carlo,' Ferrari recalled, 'Ascari turned up at Monza where Castellotti was practising in one of our three-litre sports model they were due to drive that weekend in Germany. Alberto remarked that after an accident one must as soon as possible get back behind the wheel again in order not to lose one's nerve. During the midday break, he asked if he could take the car round the track a couple of times. He set off without bothering about his crash helmet, and with his tie fluttering over his shoulder. The second time round, he was killed on the big, sweeping bend that is hardly a bend at all. His death, on 26 May, came on the same day of the month as his father.'

All of Italy mourned the loss. On the day of Ascari's funeral in Milan the whole city fell silent as a procession carrying the fallen hero moved slowly through streets lined with an estimated one million people dressed in black. Fifteen carriages were required to carry the profusion of wreaths and flowers, and in the hearse, drawn by a team of plumed black horses, Ascari's familiar light-blue helmet lay on top of the black coffin. 'I have lost my greatest opponent,' Juan said. 'I deeply admired the graceful, pleasant style of Alberto's driving. He was a real champion, worthy in every way of his father Antonio.'

GROTE PRIJS VAN BELGIE

A week after their failure to finish in Monaco, Juan and Moss scored a one-two victory for Mercedes in the International Eifelrennen sports car race at the Nürburgring. Seven days later, and just across the border at Spa-Francorchamps, they repeated their performance in the Belgian Grand Prx. The principal opposition at Spa came from the Lancia driven by Castellotti, whose car was privately entered in what was to be Lancia's last Grand Prix. Devastated by the death of Ascari, and with his business also close to financial collapse, Gianni Lancia withdrew his cars from further competition and a month later handed them over to Ferrari. Determined to make the most of Lancia's last race, Castellotti put his car on pole with a record-breaking time. Starting second and third were Juan and Moss, both of whom overtook Castellotti on the opening lap. While the Lancia dropped back and eventually retired with gearbox failure, the two Mercedes cars went faster and faster.

Juan, who led for all 36 laps, eventually set a new lap record that averaged out to 121.227mph around the 8.75-mile circuit. After shadowing him closely for most of the race, Moss, whose car suffered a ruptured oil pipe towards the end, crossed the finish line covered in oil and 8.1 seconds adrift of the Maestro. 'It is hard to say how much I respect him as a man and as a driver, and how much I have learnt from him,' Moss said. 'At Spa in particular we would come past the grandstands as though tied together by a piece of string, but out on the course he would go really fast on a certain section, a good deal faster than I could at that time, just to show me what could be done. And then, after we had duly made our "team appearance" passing the pits, he would do it again on the next lap but over a different part of the course. It was a fantastic experience, following him weaving around the hills, way above 160mph. Neubauer gave us a stiff talking-to about racing so closely because he was worried about us colliding.'

Having saluted the victory with his by now traditional performance of throwing his hat under the wheels of Juan's winning Mercedes, Neubauer sat down with his drivers to work out a way to avoid them unduly risking their cars. Moss, though young and eager, was not about to challenge Juan's authority within the team, but nor would he forgo an opportunity to beat him; similarly, Juan's sense of fair play would not let him accept having Moss held back by team orders. The solution, which Juan suggested and the others agreed to, was to let every man race for himself from the start until a definite advantage had been gained over the opposition, at which point Neubauer would signal them to slow down and hold their positions to the finish.

These new team orders would not come into effect in the next race, where Juan and Moss were teamed to drive the same car. Unfortunately, with Juan in it at the time, the Mercedes came perilously close to being involved in the worst disaster in motorsport history.

24 HEURES DE LE MANS

For that ill-fated 24 Hours of Le Mans, Mercedes entered three 300SLR sports cars, modified especially for the round-the-clock race to include air brakes. These took the form of a hinged flap that automatically rose up behind the driver's head whenever second gear was engaged. To drive the German cars in the most important endurance race in the world, the team had six drivers. Alongside Juan and Moss were Kling and Simon (still filling in for the injured Hermann), and John Fitch and Pierre Levegh drove the third car. Fitch, an American, was the Daimler-Benz representative in the USA, while the Parisian Levegh was included so that the team could have a French driver on home turf, moreover one who had extensive Le Mans experience.

Levegh, just a few months short of his 50th birthday, was a wealthy industrialist whose real name was Pierre Bouillon. He raced under the surname of his uncle, who had been one of the pioneer French drivers. An excellent athlete, Levegh played tennis at a high level and also international ice hockey, though his primary passion was racing, which he first took up in 1938. He had some success, but in the 1947 Grand Prix de L'ACF at Lyon his Delage crashed into the crowd, killing four spectators and injuring eleven others. After finishing fourth at Le Mans in 1951, he very nearly won the race the next year with an epic solo effort that created a sensation at the time. Without a co-driver, Levegh had taken his Talbot into a massive lead by the 22-hour mark. Then, greatly fatigued, he missed a gear change and the engine blew up, enabling a Mercedes to win.

From the beginning, the Le Mans weekend seemed jinxed. On the first night's practice a pit lane accident involving Moss's Mercedes and another car injured three bystanders, among them

Jean Behra who was hospitalised and unable to drive for Maserati. The next evening Elie Bayol crashed his Gordini and suffered serious head injuries, and there were several other accidents out on the 8.5-mile circuit, where many lives had been lost in the 32 years since the race had first been held, and where on Saturday, 11 June over 200,000 spectators had gathered to watch the traditional four p.m. start.

As expected, following their fastest practice times, the race for top honours began as a tri-nation contest featuring the silver German Mercedes, the red Italian Ferraris and the green British Jaguars. Crossing the line first on the opening lap was Castellotti's Ferrari, followed by Hawthorn's Jaguar, then a high-speed procession that included the Mercedes of Levegh and Kling, whose team-mate Juan was back in fourteenth place having lost time when he jumped into the car and the gear lever slipped under his trouser leg. However, an hour later, the frontrunning trio comprised Castellotti, Hawthorn and Fangio, with Kling and Levegh in sixth and seventh. By six o'clock, with Castellotti's Ferrari having fallen back to third, the race at the front had settled into a straight fight between Hawthorn and Juan. They set a terrific pace, rushing side by side down Le Mans' long Mulsanne straight at close to 180mph (reminding the fans of their fabulous duel in the 1953 French Grand Prix at Reims), tearing down the pit straight at nearly 130mph, and trading fastest laps at speeds averaging well over 120mph.

'By 6.30,' Juan recalled, 'drivers were changing over and cars were being refuelled, and there was a lot of coming and going in the pits. There were five us going along the pit straight. In front of Hawthorn and I were Macklin [the Englishman Lance Macklin, several laps down in an Austin Healey], Levegh and Kling [both a lap down]. From behind, I saw it all happen as if on a cinema screen. Hawthorn passed Macklin, and then pulled rather violently to the right to get into his pits. Macklin, possibly surprised, pulled to the left. Levegh then raised his hand to signal to me that he was about to pull to one side. I saw this gesture clearly, as Kling went into the pits on our right. It all happened very quickly. I was doing about 135mph and Levegh must have been doing more than 125mph. Levegh had not left himself enough space, and ran up and over the rear of Macklin's car. I gripped my wheel hard. Levegh's Mercedes flew into the air and into the fence of the spectators' area, while Macklin's car went skidding along the road out of control. As I passed, I saw the sparks thrown up by a wheel of his car dragging on the ground. I kept going. The last thing I remember was an explosion behind me. At that instant, I felt no emotion. A few moments later, I realised that something terrible had happened. I was lucky to escape from that crash; it was by pure chance, destiny if you like. After I had passed through the crashing cars, without touching anything or anyone, I started to tremble and shake. I had been waiting for the blow, holding tightly on to the steering wheel. But the blow never came, and instead the way opened and I passed through. For a time I was shaking as I drove. When I came past the pits again there was nothing but smoke and flames. But until I came in three laps later so that Moss could take over, I had no idea of the full extent of the disaster.'

After being launched over the back of Macklin's car, Levegh's Mercedes flew towards the grandstand area in front of which was a packed spectator enclosure. The car ploughed along an earth bank, hit a post and rose higher into the air, spinning twice before crash-landing upside down, then executing a second airborne spin. On returning to the ground, the car hit a cement parapet and exploded in a ball of fire. The flaming front part of the car, including the engine, broke away and scythed sickeningly through the crowd. Poor Levegh died instantly, as did an estimated 80 spectators. Over a hundred more were injured.

Despite the appalling carnage, the race went on because the organisers felt that stopping it would hinder the firemen, gendarmes and medical personnel who were working feverishly to assist the victims and transfer them to ambulances. It was some time before the full horror of the calamity became apparent, and in the gathering darkness out on the track the Jaguar versus Mercedes battle continued at unabated speed. By midnight, the Moss-Fangio car was nearly two laps ahead of the Hawthorn-Bueb Jaguar, with the Kling-Simon Mercedes in third, but 'deep down', Juan 'felt happier at two in the morning when orders came from Stuttgart for Mercedes to pull out of the race as a gesture of mourning and respect. I knew that if we had won, it would have been a bitter victory with all those people killed. Before his Jaguar went on to win, Hawthorn came to me in the pits and he was crying, saying the accident was his fault. I told him it wasn't, and that these things can happen. Racing is like that.'

As a result of the Le Mans tragedy, all over Europe there were demands that motor racing should be banned, though the only country passing a law prohibiting it was Switzerland. The Swiss Grand Prix was cancelled, as were the 1955 World Championship events in West Germany, France and Spain. The races in Holland, Britain and Italy went ahead as scheduled, Juan and Moss continuing to dominate in what were little more than demonstration runs for Mercedes, though their personal battles were not without interest.

GROTE PRIJS VAN NEDERLAND

In the sand dunes at Zandvoort a week after Le Mans, Juan outqualifed Moss by four tenths of a second and preserved that margin to the finish of the Dutch Grand Prix. But Moss was learning from the Maestro fast, and enjoying it immensely. 'Normally, following someone close is a frustrating business, but following Fangio was not,' he said. 'The thrill of being able to keep up with a man at those heights of performance was deeply enjoyable. His precision was fantastic, he never put a wheel wrong, but sometimes he would deliberately tweak his car sideways into a corner and I'd run up alongside him and then I would pull a face at him and he would grin back and we would go hell for leather into the next corner. I tell you, it was fun.'

BRITISH GRAND PRIX

At his home Grand Prix, on the Aintree circuit near Liverpool, Moss got the better of Juan by two tenths of a second to put his Mercedes on pole. Juan got away first, but on lap three Moss overtook him, and just two laps later they began to lap the rest of the field. Towards the finish, with Moss still in front and an estimated 145,000 of his countrymen cheering the prospect of a British driver finally winning the country's Grand Prix, Neubauer signalled him to slow down. 'Fangio was right there,' Moss recalled. 'I took the chequered flag with his car's nose about level with my steering wheel. I don't know to this day if Juan let me win or not. There were suggestions Mercedes might have hinted it would be good for business to have a British winner. I like to think I could have won it fair and square, but in any case it was my first championship Grand Prix win.'

GRAN PREMIO D'ITALIA

In their next race, for sports cars in the Grand Prix of Sweden at Kristianstadt, Moss finished second to Juan for the sixth time that season. For the following championship race, the Italian Grand Prix on 11 September at Monza, where the circuit had been revised to include a section of banked bends that allowed speeds over 170mph, both drivers were given streamlined versions of the Formula 1 cars. Moss dropped out of the race with engine trouble, leaving Piero Taruffi, who had been drafted into the Mercedes team to give it an Italian flavour, as the closest challenger to Juan. But the Mercedes team leader, who started from pole, easily won the last championship race of the year to add yet more points to a total that underlined his dominance in 1955. In the final standings, Juan had 40 points and Moss had 23, leaving Castellotti, Trintignant, Taruffi and the rest lagging far behind.

Juan's last three races in 1955 were in sports cars. In the Tourist Trophy at Dundrod in Northern Ireland, the Mercedes he shared with Kling finished second to the sister 300SLR of Moss and Fitch. In the Targa Florio, Juan and Kling finished second to Moss, who this time had Peter Collins as his co-driver. For this race, the Mercedes team comprised sixteen drivers and 45 mechanics to service the eight cars. A week later, on 22 October, Daimler-Benz announced that the Mercedes-Benz cars were withdrawing from both the Formula 1 and sports car championships, and that the company would henceforth concentrate on producing road cars. The decision was based partly on the adverse publicity created by the Le Mans disaster, but also on the huge expense incurred by the racing effort.

Over a season and a half, the Mercedes-Benz W196s had started fifteen Grands Prix and won twelve of them, seven times finishing one-two. In sports car racing, the 300SLRs had won every time out except at Le Mans, where the team had withdrawn while leading. In the team's twenty major championship races, Juan won thirteen times, including eight championship Grands Prix en route to his two successive driving titles. It was some record, but now the three-time world champion was out of a job. 'The fact is,' the 44-year-old Juan claimed, 'I was going to get out of racing. When Daimler-Benz announced it was pulling out, I thought the time had come for me as well. I wanted to return to Argentina for good.'

Before going home, Juan accepted an invitation to race a Maserati 300S sports car in the Grand Prix of Venezuela at Caracas. Because it was run in a Spanish-speaking South American country, he felt obligated as the world champion to put on a good show. This he did, winning the race despite a strong challenge from the second-placed Ferrari driven by the Marquis de Portago. But Juan had found the 85-lap race, run in very hot weather, exhausting, and he was vexed when a Maserati executive tried to take the winner's trophy from him, claiming it belonged to the team, not the driver. Juan got the trophy, a handsome gold-plated cup, but then received a worrying phone call from friends in Buenos Aires.

Six days after he had won his third driving title in Italy, the Argentine government of General Juan Domingo Perón had been overthrown and replaced by a new regime that had now decreed that the affairs of those closely linked with the deposed president were going to be investigated. Anyone who had obtained 'in an illicit manner' gifts, goods, services or money would have the offending items confiscated and face prosecution. Of course, having been sent to Europe in the first place under the auspices of the Perón government, Juan Manuel Fangio's name featured prominently on the list of those under suspicion. His friends recommended that Juan should avoid returning until the heat died down, but he told them he was coming back, he had nothing to hide, and they could arrest him if they wanted to. Still, he was shocked that the country whose flag he had flown so proudly abroad should now be so ready to incriminate him.

Leaving Caracas in a melancholy mood, Juan passed through Peru on the way home and stopped off at the village of

Huanchasco, where his friend Daniel Urrutia had died in their crash in 1948. At the accident scene, Juan found that the local people had erected a small shrine with a cross. He knelt beside it for a few moments, in effect saying a silent goodbye to Daniel and all those who had been close to him in a sporting career he now felt was over. He had started racing ten years before Daniel's death, and so much had happened since then; so many miles covered, so many risks taken. Instead of it becoming easier as time went by, the reverse had been true. Juan had had enough. 'The strict self-discipline I had to practise in order to go on being champion made me think I was past my peak and going downhill,' he said. 'But my view of reality was in conflict with the Argentine reality.'

When he arrived in his homeland, the country's most famous citizen was subjected to a series of indignities. At Buenos Aires airport, customs officials went through all his luggage, something that had never happened before in all his travels. The shamefaced officer in charge trembled throughout and whispered to Juan that he was only following orders. At the Fangio Mercedes dealership in the city, government inspectors moved in. A couple of them were corrupt and demanded money and special favours in return for giving Juan's business a clean bill of health. He refused to comply, but they sat in on meetings with Juan and his partners and tried to influence any decisions that were made, and Juan was not allowed to sign any cheques. The business stagnated, finances floundered, and Juan needed to find cash fast. As the investigation into his affairs dragged on – he wasn't completely exonerated of any wrongdoing until four years had passed – Juan became increasingly fed up and decided that there was no way out but to return to Europe and resume the profession he had been ready to abandon. But those under investigation were not allowed to leave the country. Juan went directly to the Minister of Foreign Affairs and told him he had been given another opportunity to race in Europe and had to say yes or no as soon as possible. The minister told him he was free to go, so Juan headed back to Italy to sign a contract with Enzo Ferrari.

Chapter Fourteen

1956: Fourth World Championship (Ferrari)

'Ferrari was a hard man. He wanted victory for his cars, and this suited me, for I never raced only for myself. I raced for the car and the team.'

ENZO FERRARI HAD FIRST contacted Juan when he was taking a few days' holiday in Pescara following the 1955 Targa Florio. They spoke on the telephone about the likelihood of a Mercedes withdrawal and Ferrari asked him to think about joining his team for 1956. Ferrari said he knew Juan would cost a lot, but he needed him. At the time, Juan was more interested in an offer from Maserati, but after his annoyance about the squabble over the winner's trophy in Caracas he became more warmly disposed to dealing with Ferrari. To help negotiate with the notoriously hard-nosed team owner, Juan used as an intermediary an Italian journalist/entrepreneur, Marcello Giambertone, who had befriended Beba. Eventually, though Juan had never had one before and was somewhat reluctant to have an outsider represent him, Giambertone effectively became Juan's manager.

Though Juan later completely disowned it, Giambertone wrote an unauthorised Fangio autobiography which was highly critical of Ferrari. The controversial book created a long-standing rift between the fiery team owner and the driver who had hardly ever said a disparaging word about anyone. Nor had anyone before formed such a negative opinion of Fangio. They didn't patch up their differences until the team's 40th anniversary in 1987, the year before Ferrari died, but the Ferrari–Fangio relationship was an uneasy one almost from the outset.

'I first met Fangio at the Modena autodromo in the spring of 1949,' Ferrari recalled. 'There were a number of other drivers and cars there. I saw him go round a couple of times and then began to watch him more closely because of his unusual style: he was perhaps the only driver who came out of the bends without shaving the bales of straw on the outer verge. This Argentinian, I told myself, knows his job; he comes out of the bends like a cannon-shot and keeps right in the middle of the track. A little later that day he came to see me, accompanied by an official of the Argentinian Automobile Club and another man. I had quite a long talk with them, although Fangio himself did not volunteer more than a dozen words. Rather put out by his persistent silence, I began to look at him with some curiosity, wondering whether he was shy, slow on the uptake or just a deep one. He avoided my glance, answered in monosyllables in a strange, tinny voice and let his two companions speak for him, all the time maintaining an inscrutable expression marked by the shadow of an indefinable, squinting smile.

'At that first meeting, I came to two conclusions about Fangio: that he would be world champion within a year and that it would be some time before I could make out his personality. I was wrong on both counts: he was world champion not in 1950, but a year later, and while I came to understand something of his personality, it came only when it was too late.

'Our subsequent conversations were no more fortunate than that first one: he continued to avoid looking me in the face and my questions always received enigmatic answers given in that small, metallic voice. Whenever he was in my company he invariably let his companion do all the talking. Juan Manuel Fangio has thus remained something of a mystery in my memory.'

And Enzo Ferrari's memories went back a long way. He was born in 1898, just after the birth of motorsport. His father operated a small ironworking shop in Modena, a town where the coming of horseless carriages was met with great enthusiasm and where their sporting capabilities were soon fully exploited. But before he gave in to what would become his great passion, little Enzo wanted to be an opera singer or a sports journalist. All that changed when he was ten years old and saw his first motor race. 'That day I felt profound emotion,' he said.

After serving with the Italian Army in the First World War, during which he shod mules, he went to technical college in Turin, then travelled to Milan to work for Alfa Romeo. There, he tested cars and competed in them, winning thirteen of his 47 races. It was during his driving days that Ferrari, then 25 years old, adopted as his emblem Il Cavallino Rampante, the prancing horse, which had been the personal insignia of Francesco Barraco, Italy's leading fighter pilot in the war; after one of Ferrari's race victories, the aviator's family presented it to him as a symbol of courage and audacity. To make it his own, Ferrari added a yellow background, the colour of his home town of Modena, thus creating the shield that would later become famous on the cars bearing his name.

When Ferrari stopped racing in 1939, at his wife Laura's insistence after their son Dino was born, he took over running the Alfa Romeo teams which, with such great drivers as Nuvolari and Varzi, won many victories all over Europe. In

1939 he formed Scuderia Ferrari to campaign Alfas for a variety of drivers. After the Second World War, in which the team's Modena premises were destroyed during an air raid, the 'Sorcerer of Modena' moved twelve miles away to Maranello, where he began to manufacture his own road and racing cars and became known as the 'Commendatore'.

Enzo Ferrari was a passionate man with a romantic view of racing. 'I race because I am an enthusiast,' he always said. 'Others do it as a business.' And when it came to cars, his affections lay with their motive power: 'I build engines and put wheels on them.' Yet he seldom went to see his cars compete, because, he said, 'It offends me to see the machines I have created being driven to death.' Above all, Ferrari loved winning. Though he was always accused of having much deeper affection for his cars than his drivers, he knew that having the right man behind the wheel could make the difference between victory and the defeats that had come his way in recent years. Following the team's first World Championship win courtesy of José Froilán González in 1951, Alberto Ascari's Ferrari dominated the 1952 and 1953 seasons, but since Ascari's death Ferrari had been searching for a driver capable of emulating the exploits of the legendary Tazio Nuvolari.

In Ferrari's opinion, Nuvolari was by far the greatest racing driver of all time, and though he had retired before Ferrari's teams reached full flower, Nuvolari remained in Enzo's mind the ideal prototype for all his future drivers. 'The Little Man from Mantua' had manhandled the mighty machines of his day with great flair and gusto, and had always looked as if he was on the verge of an accident – and he had many of them. Even when the cars he drove were not necessarily up to the task of winning, Nuvolari's tremendous fighting spirit enabled him to triumph. 'Nuvolari,' Ferrari said, 'was a driver who, in any type of car, in any circumstance on any track, always gave everything and ended up, on the whole, the best. In contrast with many drivers of yesterday and today, he never started out beaten because he had an inferior car.' Though Ferrari believed the likes of Nuvolari (who had died in 1953) would never be seen again, he thought he saw in one of Nuvolari's greatest admirers enough of the same tenacious qualities. 'Fangio was a man who never gave in,' Ferrari said. 'If he could not be first, he would battle just as hard for one of the very last places. This is a noble trait in his character which I cannot but acknowledge.'

It was perhaps inevitable then, that two of the greatest names in racing would get together. And though the professional relationship between the Commendatore and the Maestro was productive in 1956, it was for Juan his hardest ever Formula 1 season. In keeping with his policy of pursuing progress by playing his drivers off against one another, Ferrari hired six others to team up with Juan, and, hopefully, even to oppose him (Giambertone, much given to conspiracy theories, suggested in his book that Ferrari recruited the others in the hope that they would beat the great Fangio and thus demonstrate the superiority of Ferrari cars). There were no holdovers from 1955, and the newcomers were a colourful, multinational group: the dashingly handsome Italians Eugenio Castellotti and Luigi Musso, the photogenic blonde British 'Golden Boy' Peter Collins, the suave Belgian aristocrat Olivier Gendebien, the swarthy Spanish nobleman Alfonso de Portago, and the dapper little French vineyard owner Maurice Trintignant. Other than Trintignant, who was born in 1917, the new recruits were much younger than Juan; Collins was twenty years his junior. 'Ferrari would not say who was to lead the team,' Juan recalled. 'The young men told me it was me, because I was the world champion.'

In 1956, Ferrari's Maranello factory had a workforce of 260 who annually produced the 100 road cars that brought in the finance necessary to field a team of ten sports racing two-seaters and ten Formula 1 cars, the latter being developments of the 1955 Lancias that had been turned over to Ferrari. For the new seven-race World Championship season, in which the British Connaught, Vanwall and BRM teams were also entered, Ferrari's main opposition would come from Maserati. Leading the Maserati team were Stirling Moss, on the rebound from Mercedes, and holdover Jean Behra. They would be joined on occasion by González, whose enthusiasm for racing had remained dimmed since the death of Onofre Marimón, by his fellow Argentine Carlos Menditeguy, by various privateers and, when their cars weren't ready, drivers from the British teams.

GRAN PREMIO DE LA REPUBLICA ARGENTINA

There was this year no heatwave to contend with in the opening race of the season on 11 January, though Juan still had a torrid time in his home Grand Prix. The race at the 'Fangiodrome' featured a battle with his former Mercedes team-mate, the now Maserati-mounted Moss, and also included a squabble over the rules. The reigning world champion started his Lancia-Ferrari from pole, but then had to stop with a fuel pump failure. At this point, his team-mate Musso was called in and Juan took over his car, which was a lap behind the race leader, Moss. In his haste to catch up, Juan spun off the track and became stuck. Two people, one of them a track marshal and the other a bystanding driver, pushed him out, but since the rules allowed only authorised personnel to give assistance to a stranded car, Maserati protested that Juan should be disqualified. Juan was informed of this and fully expected to be black-flagged, but the flag was not shown and he caught up Moss, who held him off valiantly for several laps. On the 80th lap, the Lancia-Ferrari overtook the Maserati, which retired two laps later with a broken engine, and Juan crossed the finish line first, nearly half a minute ahead of Behra's Maserati. Later, Maserati's protest was disallowed and Juan's win (shared with Musso) went into the record books as his third in succession in his home Grand Prix.

A week later, again at the Autodromo Buenos Aires, the Fangio-Castellotti Ferrari Monza sports car retired with mechanical failure from the 1,000-kilometre race, and the Moss-Menditeguy Maserati went on to win. The following weekend, at the Mendoza circuit, 650 miles west of the Argentine capital, and back in their Formula 1 cars again, the Fangio–Moss fight in the Grand Prix of Buenos Aires ended again in victory for the local hero. In this race, Juan's team-mate Castellotti crashed heavily and was lucky not to be hurt. A month after that, Castellotti joined Juan in Florida where their shared Ferrari Monza convincingly won the 12 Hours of Sebring. Halfway through the race, Menditeguy lost control at high speed and his Maserati somersaulted, pitching the unfortunate driver out on to the road where the impact left him with a badly fractured skull. After the podium ceremonies, commemorating his first win in the USA, Juan rushed to Menditeguy's bedside and remained in Sebring for several days to make sure he was going to fully recover (he did, and raced for several more years).

Before he set off for the beginning of the European season, Juan went back to Buenos Aires, where the meddling by government investigators was seriously hampering his business, which urgently needed financial assistance. Though he personally never discussed it in public, news of his predicament spread abroad and into the racing world. By now, having seen first-hand his incredible prowess as a driver, his young Ferrari team-mates had come to regard him with the greatest respect and admiration; moreover, they were moved by his personal warmth and generosity of spirit. When they heard about his money problems, they decided to do all they could to help improve Juan's fortunes on the financial front. Though they kept it from him, their plan was to help him win races.

The ringleader was Luigi Musso, who, like the others, came from an affluent background. His father was a successful diplomat, and Musso was brought up in luxurious surroundings; the Collins family in England had a highly lucrative car dealership, Castellotti came from a family of landed aristocrats, Gendebien's titled ancestors had helped found Belgium, and the 17th Marquis de Portago's inheritance made him one of the richest men in Europe. Trintingant, the prosperous winegrower, was also happy to assist the balding, middle-aged, bandy-legged former mechanic from Argentina in his time of need. Had he known about it, their Ferrari boss might have disapproved of such collusion, since he was paying Juan a retainer reported to be close to $40,000 – much more than any other racing driver was then earning. Ferrari was also obligated under the terms of their contract to give Juan a major share of whatever prize money he earned. As the season developed, Juan's continuing superlative performances showed he was worth every penny of whatever Ferrari was paying him; indeed, his success in the forthcoming races showed he was entirely capable of collecting more than his share of prize money and that he didn't actually need anyone's help to earn it.

Juan's fourth victory in the five-race-old season came at the non-championship Formula 1 Grand Prix at Syracuse in Italy on 15 April. It was here that the Musso-led charity drive was supposed first to come into play. Indeed, the race proved to be a Ferrari runaway: Juan planted his car on pole, then set by far the fastest race lap while overtaking Castellotti, who later crashed heavily, and easily led Musso and Collins across the finish line to win the race at a record-breaking average speed of 97.07mph.

The 1956 Mille Miglia was another Ferrari benefit, the team cars of Castellotti (in eleven hours, 37 minutes and ten seconds),

Collins, Musso, Fangio and Gendebien taking the top five places. All were exhausted at the finish of what was regarded as the worst-ever driving conditions in a European open road race. Violent hailstorms, cloud-covered mountain roads and torrential rain throughout led to many accidents as a result of which five people – two drivers and three spectators – were killed and sixteen others seriously injured. Of the 373 cars that started the 23rd running of the 1,000-mile classic, only 178 made it back to Brescia.

Perhaps the most heroic of the drives that day was made by the man in the fourth-placed Ferrari, for whom 'it was the worst Mille Miglia I ever raced in. Never in my life have I suffered so much as that day.' Juan's problems were caused by a hole that had been cut in the rear of the cockpit in order to make last-minute repairs to a leaking fuel tank. The race and the rain started directly after this task was performed, so from the start cold water was pumped by the rear wheel directly into the cockpit, where it soaked Juan from the waist down and rose steadily to a depth of several inches on the cockpit floor. At the Ravenna checkpoint, Juan asked the Ferrari mechanics to cut a hole in the floor to drain the standing water, but when he sailed off again into the storm, a new stream of water shot vertically like a geyser from the newly cut drainhole and was blown directly into his face by the wind. He had trouble seeing, it was perishingly cold, and he gradually began to lose feeling in his extremities.

Once he had passed Pescara and headed up into the Abruzzi mountains, low-lying cloud decreased visibility even further. Juan passed several accident scenes, and at one of them, near the checkpoint at L'Equila, he recognised the remains of the Maserati driven by last year's race winner Stirling Moss, who was again accompanied by the journalist Denis Jenkinson. Moss had lost control on a mini-river of water crossing the road in the middle of a corner and the car had skidded into a stone wall, climbed over it, dropped down a hillside and hit a small tree, around which the car was wrapped, swaying precariously about 300 feet above a rock-strewn gorge. Juan stopped and asked them if there was anything he could do. Moss was slightly cut on the forehead and Jenkinson had escaped with severe shock. 'Bless his Argentine heart,' Jenkinson recalled, 'Fangio offered us a lift in his passenger seat to the next town. We waved him on, indicating that he was supposed to be racing, but he smiled and shrugged, indicating that he was "touring" to the finish. The Maestro is too old and wise to hurry in impossible conditions.'

Promising them that he would try to get help sent back to them, Juan drove off again into the gloom. Several hundred miles later he was shaking and shivering so hard he could hardly hold on to the wheel. Near Modena, he slid the waterlogged Ferrari to a halt at a small taverna where he often used to eat. He ran inside and asked if he could borrow a coat. A farmer's coat was quickly donated to his cause, as was a stiff slug of brandy. On the road again, the Ferrari's engine soon developed a misfire caused by water in the ignition. Juan's control over the car became increasingly tenuous, caused by fingers so frozen he could hardly grip the steering wheel. Though by now nearly delirious with fatigue, and quite probably suffering from an advanced case of hypothermia, Juan persuaded himself he could not stop because he had no dry clothes to change into. They were in his hotel room at the finish line, and he simply had to get there, which he did, after twelve hours, eleven minutes and 50 seconds of pure torture.

When he collapsed into a hot bath in his hotel room, his lips began to swell grotesquely. Whether it was an adverse reaction to the brandy or from the freezing rain smashing into his face, he didn't know, but the sensation was alarming and he knew he had pushed his nearly 45-year-old self too far.

The next weekend, Juan had recovered enough to put his Lancia-Ferrari on the front row for the non-championship International Trophy race at Silverstone. In the race, to the delight of the 100,000 British fans, he was overtaken by Hawthorn in a BRM and Moss in a Vanwall. Like Juan, Hawthorn dropped out with a mechanical problem, but Moss went on to win for Vanwall.

GRAND PRIX DE MONACO

Quickest throughout the three days of practice in Monaco in mid-May, Juan put his Lancia-Ferrari on pole with a time that was just 0.6 seconds faster than Moss in the Maserati. They finished the 100-lap race with their positions reversed, Moss having driven flawlessly to lead from start to finish and Juan having clipped kerbs and bounced off walls in one of the most hair-raising comeback performances ever seen in the storied streets of the principality. 'I drove like a madman,' Juan said after the race. 'When I finished, the car was junk.'

Juan's uncharacteristically untidy drive became necessary first of all because of a slow start, then a spin on a patch of oil at the Ste Devote corner that damaged his car's rear suspension and made the chassis lurch and yaw alarmingly around the circuit's never-ending series of corners. Having in a few laps overtaken three cars on the tightest of all tracks where even a single such manoeuvre is rare over a full race distance, Juan was soon up to second again behind Moss, whereupon the Lancia-Ferrari's clutch began to play up and the gears became difficult to engage. On lap 42, he missed a gear, and the car slid wide going into the Bureau de Tabac corner and smashed into the kerb. With a front wheel now askew, the car's handling took an even greater turn for the worse, and Juan had no choice but to come in and park it in the pits. It being a Ferrari tradition that a team-mate should hand over his car to a team-mate with a better chance of winning, it was decided in the pits to call in Collins, who was now running a worthy second to Moss.

While the changeover was made, on lap 54, Behra's Maserati assumed second place, so Juan resumed racing in third, with Moss in front by nearly a minute, still pushing hard. 'Even if you had a minute lead over Fangio you could not relax,' Moss said later, 'for you never knew what the Old Man would pull out.' Going through the Gasworks corner on lap 60, Juan elbowed his way past Behra by means of a breathtaking full-opposite lock slide, and then tore away in an increasingly desperate pursuit of Moss. There followed a furious exchange of lap records between the leader and his chaser, whose spectacular forward progress took the form of a series of sideswiping incidents wherein both the front and the back of his car came into sharp contact with concrete and stone. By lap 78, Juan had reduced the gap to 39 seconds. On lap 86, Moss dented his Maserati's nose as he barged by a backmarker; in the remaining laps, Juan several times used similar methods to move tardy also-rans out of his way. On the 100th and last lap, during which Juan broke the Monaco lap record for a final time, the Moss Maserati sped past the finish line, followed 6.1 seconds later by the battle-scarred Lancia-Ferrari.

During the podium ceremony, Juan congratulated Moss on his second World Championship victory. 'As always,' Moss remarked, 'he was wonderful in defeat. He just seemed pleased for me.' Juan then sought out Collins, to whom he expressed his gratitude for donating his car to his cause. Their shared second place gave them three points apiece, meaning that Juan, who collected another point for the fastest race lap, was after the first two races of the season leading the championship by just one point over Moss.

The Moss versus Fangio battle then moved to West Germany, where their sports cars, shared with team-mates, dominated the

1,000 Kilometres of the Nürburgring. After they took turns leading for most of the nearly eight-hour-long endurance contest, the win went to the Moss-Behra Maserati when the Fangio-Castellotti Ferrari had to make a late stop for fuel.

GROTE PRIJS VAN BELGIE

For the Belgian Grand Prix at Spa at the beginning of June, Juan put his Lancia-Ferrari on pole with an incredible lap that was nearly five seconds faster than the Moss Maserati. Demonstrating both that the Ferraris were on form and that he was rapidly coming of age, Peter Collins recorded the third fastest time which was less than a second slower than Moss. In the race, Juan was in a commanding lead when his car's oil-deprived differential locked up, the rear wheels seized solid and he was forced into retirement. Moss, who survived a frightening moment when a wheel fell off, took over the Maserati of privateer Cesare Perdisa, set the fastest race lap and finished third, behind the worthy winner Collins, who had driven flawlessly to score his first championship Grand Prix victory. On the rostrum, as 'God Save the Queen' was being played for the beaming new winner whose arm was held aloft by his grinning countryman Moss, the scorekeepers noted that for the first time in history two British drivers were leading the World Championship, with no less a personage than the four-time champion lagging a point behind.

Two weeks later, Collins won again, sharing a Ferrari with his good friend and co-driver for the day Mike Hawthorn. Second in this Supercortemaggiore sports car race at Monza was the Moss-Perdisa Maserati, which finished two minutes ahead of the Fangio-Castellotti Ferrari. Seven days later, Collins extended his winning streak to three in a row, while his increasingly disenchanted older team-mate had another troubled race.

GRAND PRIX DE L'ACF

A few days before the French Grand Prix, Enzo Ferrari's beloved son Dino lost a long battle with leukaemia. Ferrari seriously considered withdrawing his team from the event, but at the last minute he relented, though his drivers appeared at Reims wearing black armbands as a token of respect.

Obviously buoyed by the momentum from his hat-trick of wins, Collins beat Juan and Castellotti to pole position. However, by the halfway point in the race the running order in the Ferrari formation at the front was Fangio, Castellotti, Collins. Then the leading Ferrari began to fall back, and a few laps later it trickled into the pits. At the back of the fuel pressure gauge a connection had come loose; fuel had been sprayed all over the cockpit, and Juan's helmet and clothing were saturated with the volatile liquid. Despite the danger of an explosion, he remained in the cockpit while the leak was repaired, a frustrated man. 'The car let me down again in a silly way when I thought I was going to win,' he said later. Two minutes later, he went back out on the track, where his team-mates were exchanging the lead in a thrilling fight for victory. In the end, the flying Collins scored his second Formula 1 victory in a fortnight, with Castellotti second, ahead of Behra's Maserati and Juan's Ferrari, which had managed to set the fastest race lap despite its driver suffering from painful fuel burns.

In fact, Juan was now in a state of considerable physical disrepair. Having not yet fully recovered from the severe soaking and chilling he'd incurred a month earlier in the Mille Miglia, the fuel bath in France left his upper torso red-raw and painfully swollen. Moreover, he seemed uncharacteristically apathetic and depressed, so much so that his worried manager Marcello Giambertone took him to a neurological specialist in Milan. The diagnosis was that Juan had pushed himself too hard and was in a mentally weakened state. He was said to be suffering from a 'reactive neurosis' that made him 'emotionally anxious', and the prescribed cure was a lengthy period of rest, which of course the unwilling patient said he certainly had no time for. However, Juan was persuaded to take about ten days off, and he did not drive in the following weekend's race, a non-championship event at Rouen, where he was the guest of honour. From there, he travelled across the Channel to Silverstone, where he arrived with such a high fever that there were doubts he would be able to compete in the fifth round of the championship.

BRITISH GRAND PRIX

'In England,' Juan recalled, 'the doctors did not want me to race, but the organisers insisted, so they gave me pills to dull the pain and to make the fever go down. I raced and was lucky to win, but after that I felt dead.' Mike Hawthorn's BRM, from the front of the grid alongside the Moss Maserati (on pole) and the Fangio Lancia-Ferrari, led the first fifteen laps before retiring with an oil leak. The Maserati led for the next 53 laps, then stopped with a broken rear axle. The Ferrari-Lancia led from that point onwards, and won by over a lap. 'Let's face it,' wrote Gregor Grant in *Autosport*, 'he is still the great man! While his rivals fell out one by one, Juan Manuel Fangio pursued his relentless way to win the British Grand Prix at Silverstone.'

GROSSER PREIS VON DEUTSCHLAND

At the beginning of August, two weeks after his gritty, if somewhat fortuitous, British win, Juan was back on top form, and he needed to be, since the penultimate round of the championship took place on West Germany's mighty Nürburgring. Beginning with this race, Juan was also now being better served by Ferrari. With Giambertone acting as the intermediary, Juan had convinced the Commendatore to appoint one mechanic to be exclusively responsible for his car, instead of having all the mechanics service all the cars, as was the custom at Ferrari. Putting one man in charge, Juan contended, would help prevent the kind of shoddy workmanship that had led to the water bath in the Mille Miglia and the fuel shower at Reims. Moreover, as both a mechanic and a racing driver Juan knew from long experience that the two disciplines benefited from close personal relationships. A mechanic who believed in his driver would work harder for him, and the reverse was also true.

During qualifying on his favourite circuit, Juan tore around the tortuous 14.5-mile-long circuit in 9m 51.2s, breaking the track's absolute record set in 1939 by Hermann Lang in a 600bhp Mercedes. Collins was almost as quick, clocking a time only three tenths of a second slower, while their team-mate Castellotti and Moss in his Maserati also made it on to the first row.

Collins and Moss got the better start, but halfway around the first lap Juan overtook them, and the three championship contenders ran one-two-three for the next few laps. Since the point awarded to whoever set the fastest race lap could be critical to settling the championship, Collins sought it immediately by setting a new race lap record, only to have it beaten next time around by Moss, who was equally keen to make a point by going quickest around the greatest drivers' circuit of them all. On lap eight, Collins replied to Moss with a rousing 9m 45.5s, an effort that was cruelly negated by a split fuel pipe; a lap later he had to come into the pits half blinded and made dizzy by the effects of the fumes. While he was recovering, de Portago was signalled to bring in his fourth-placed Lancia-Ferrari for Collins to take over. Juan set a new lap record on the tenth tour, and he was leading the race at the time from Moss, who was now being followed by Collins, who had recovered fast. Too fast, as it turned out: on lap fourteen his Lancia-Ferrari skidded off at the Karussel corner and Collins was out of the race. On the same lap, Juan threw in the fastest lap in the long history of the Nürburgring, stopping the timing devices in a sensational 9m 41.6s. This time, which was almost ten seconds faster than his record-breaking pole position, meant that Juan had driven around the most difficult and dangerous track in the world at an astonishing average speed of of 87.731mph.

Juan won by almost a minute over Moss, whose Maserati team-mate Behra finished in third place for the fourth time that season. With only one race remaining, the championship standings showed Juan in front with 30 points, followed by Collins and Behra tied on 22 and Moss with 19. Moss was now out of the running for overall honours, but either Behra or Collins could take the title from Juan by scoring nine points – winning the race and setting the fastest lap – in the forthcoming showdown at Monza. Juan had to score only two points on the circuit where he'd nearly died in 1952 to be assured of his fourth World Championship.

GRAN PREMIO D'ITALIA

The grid for the Italian Grand Prix, which was this year also designated the Grand Prix of Europe, featured an all Lancia-Ferrari front row, with Juan on pole and Castellotti and Musso alongside him. The Maseratis of Behra and Moss were on row two, with the Lancia-Ferraris of Collins and de Portago behind them. Before the start, Juan cautioned Castellotti and Musso about the need to conserve their tyres on the high-speed Monza track. He told them to take it easy at first, that he would set the pace for the first 40 laps and that they should follow him until the final ten laps, when he would let them by to fight it out for the honour of winning their home race. It didn't matter to him, Juan said, because even if he came third or fourth he would still win the championship. 'But they both told me they wanted to do the race their way,' he said. 'From the start they forced the pace like madmen, locking their wheels under braking, burning their tyres, and I thought, "These two will not reach the finishing line." '

On the fourth lap, both Castellotti and Musso screamed into the pits for new tyres, then de Portago had a tyre delaminate on the Monza banking and his car slid out of the race. Meanwhile, the slipstreaming fight at the front was furious, with Moss, Juan, Collins and Behra joined by Harry Schell, who showed a surprising turn of speed until his Vanwall retired with a mechanical problem. Behind them, on lap nine, Castellotti had a tyre burst at 170mph on the banking and his Lancia-Ferrari spun spectacularly into retirement. Musso's comeback drive was more successful, and by lap fifteen he was up among the frontrunners. On lap nineteen, when he was running third, Juan came into the pits with deranged steering. A steering arm, drilled with holes to make it lighter, had snapped under the stress of braking. Juan got out of the car and sat on the pit counter while the mechanics set about the lengthy job of replacing the broken arm. 'I spent more than fifteen laps stuck in the pits,' he recalled, 'watching the race slip away from me. When Musso came in for a stop our team manager asked him to give me his car, but he refused. That I understood, because the team protocol was that I should take over a lower-placed car. It should have been de Portago's, but he retired before me.'

Out on the track, where Behra's Maserati had dropped out of contention with a steering problem, the race had settled down into a three-way fight involving Moss, Musso and Collins, who were very evenly matched. There was every possibility that

Collins could win and set the fastest race lap, which with Juan out of the race would make him the world champion (indeed, Musso was destined to drop out with broken steering, and Moss was forced to take the final lap at a snail's pace because of a badly worn tyre). All three drivers had to make another pit stop, and on lap 34, when he was in third place, Collins came into the pits for fresh tyres. 'When Collins came in,' Juan said, 'he saw me stuck there, and without being asked he got out of his car and offered it to me to finish in. That was a fantastic gesture. My anxiety and misery gave way to joy, so much so that I threw my arms around him and kissed him. After that I finished second to Moss, but it was enough, thanks to Collins and his English sense of sportsmanship. I don't know whether I would have done the same. Collins was a complete gentleman.' Later, Collins revealed the reason behind his magnanimity: 'All I could think of out there was that if I won the race and the championship I would become an instant celebrity. I would have a position to live up to. People would make demands of me. I would be expected at all times to act like "The Champion". Driving would not be fun any more. I wanted things to go on just as they were, so I handed my car over to Fangio. I would not have been proud of beating him through his bad luck. I am only 25 years old and have plenty of time to win the championship on my own. Fangio deserves it this year anyway.'

In *Autosport*, Gregor Grant thought this fourth World Championship consolidated the now 45-year-old Fangio's claim 'to be one of the greatest of all Grand Prix drivers, joining that band which includes Nuvolari, Caracciola, Varzi, Wimille and a few others. Fangio's presence in Scuderia Ferrari has definitely improved morale, and his leadership made the organisation a most formidable racing team.' For his part, Enzo Ferrari recognised as beyond dispute Juan's 'stature on the track. He was possessed of a decidedly superior insight into the significance of the vicissitudes of a race, while his judgement, diagnostic intelligence and driving confidence were altogether singular. I think it unlikely we will ever again see a champion capable of such a sustained series of successes.'

Chapter Fifteen

1957: Fifth World Championship (Maserati)

'*It was true that he always had the best car, and that was because he was the best damn driver! The cheapest method of becoming a successful Grand Prix team was to sign up Fangio.*'

STIRLING MOSS

F OR THE 1957 SEASON, Juan turned down an offer to stay with Ferrari and went back to his friends at Maserati, where their earlier dispute over the trophy in Caracas had soon been forgotten and the happy family atmosphere he preferred now prevailed. 'Fangio did not remain loyal to any marque,' observed Enzo Ferrari. 'He was conscious of his ability, he invariably used every endeavour to ensure that he should if possible always drive the best car available, and he was successful in this, placing his self-interest – which was quite legitimate and natural – before the affection which has, instead, kept other great drivers faithful to a certain marque through good and ill fortune.' But Juan's return to Maserati was not so much because he knew the cars were better as that he had found the complicated political environment at Ferrari trying, and his uneasy relationship with Enzo Ferrari wearing. Contrary to

Ferrari's opinion, Juan was prepared to sacrifice a mechanical advantage for a warm human environment, because he felt it brought the best out of him as a driver.

As it turned out, the 1957 Maserati, a much-developed version of the car with which he had started the 1954 season before switching to Mercedes, proved to be greatly to his liking. The updated Maserati 250F was lighter, had more power and was very well balanced. The latter factor in particular enabled Juan to fully demonstrate the art of cornering by means of his speciality – a wonderfully spectacular yet fully controlled four-wheel drift that he would deploy lap after lap after lap. 'If the absolute limit of adhesion of a car through a certain bend is 101.5 miles per hour,' the Marquis de Portago commented, 'the Old Man will go through at 101 every time. Not slower, not faster.' Juan's technique when entering a corner very fast was to lightly touch the brake pedal to settle the car before applying heavier pressure on the pedal while turning the steering wheel, an action that sent the car into a sideways slide. Using minute steering motions to correct the direction of the slide, he then provoked a more pronounced sideways motion by gradually feeding in more and more power via the accelerator, so that by the exit of the corner the car, its engine screaming at maximum revs and with wisps of blue smoke from burnt rubber curling up from the tyres, was often nearly at right angles to the track. To Juan, this was at the very heart of his romance with racing: the sensation of being at one with a machine, of coaxing the maximum peformance from it and employing consummate skill to control it. To onlookers, the control aspect seemed often in doubt, in what was very obviously a massively dangerous act of defiance against gravity, centrifugal force and quite probably several other laws of nature; still, as Denis Jenkinson observed, 'anyone who saw him in opposite-lock four-wheel slides at 150mph in a complete state of calm and balance knew they were seeing the ulitmate in high-speed driving and car control. It was Fangio, the complete master, at his best.'

Fangio's team-mates at Maserati for 1957 were Jean Behra and Harry Schell, with several other drivers contracted to race in selected events. Their chief opposition was expected to come from Ferrari, where Mike Hawthorn had returned to join his close friend Peter Collins alongside holdovers Luigi Musso, Eugenio Castellotti and Alfonso de Portago, who would be joined on occasion by Olivier Gendebien and Count Wolfgang von Trips. Though the perennially under-financed Gordini team had folded, and BRM would make only three ineffectual appearances, a strong challenger would also emerge in the form of the Vanwall team led by Stirling Moss and also featuring Tony Brooks, who would prove to be the most impressive newcomer of the season. Since Vanwall had no sports car team, Moss also continued to drive for Maserati in that series, and when Vanwall's Formula 1 car was not ready for the first race of the season at the 'Fangiodrome' on 13 January, Moss also became Juan's Maserati team-mate.

GRAN PREMIO DE LA REPUBLICA ARGENTINA

Having won in Buenos Aires with Maserati in pouring rain in 1954, with Mercedes in tropical heat in 1955, and with a mechanically troubled Ferrari in 1956, Juan's fourth consecutive victory at the 'Fangiodrome' was relatively straightforward. In a race run in fine weather, he waited until the likes of Behra, Castellotti and Collins had taken turns in the lead, played themselves out and dropped their guard. On the 25th lap, at quarter distance, the wily Juan overtook them all and went on to win easily, averaging 81mph over the 240-mile distance. Following the defending champion home were his Maserati team-mates Behra, Menditeguy and Schell. De Portago was fifth for Ferrari, but his team-mates retired with mechanical failures, including the early race leader Castellotti. Sadly, this was to be the last championship Grand Prix for both the Ferrari drivers.

In the following two races in Argentina, Juan's fortunes fluctuated between both ends of the success spectrum. In the Buenos Aires 1,000-kilometre sports car race, the Maserati 'Bazooka' 450S sports car, which he shared with Moss, lapped every car in the field except the Castellotti-Gregory Ferrari, only to have to retire with a broken gearbox. The next weekend, this time back in the Maserati 250F Grand Prix car, Juan dominated the first heat then eased off to finish third in the second heat to win the Grand Prix of Buenos Aires by a comfortable margin.

Before heading back to Europe, Juan travelled north from his homeland for two more sports car races and won both of them, albeit in two completely different environments. The Grand Prix of Cuba in Havana took place amid growing political unrest between the government of longstanding president Fulgencia Batista and the guerrilla movement led by Fidel Castro. There were rumours of kidnap threats, and Juan, Moss, Collins, Castellotti and de Portago were assigned bodyguards, as were visiting celebrities such as the Hollywood movie star Gary Cooper. The race boiled down to a battle between Juan's Maserati and the Ferrari of the Marquis de Portago. The Spanish aristocrat led most of the way, but with eight laps remaining he was delayed by a pit stop and the victory went to Juan. At the prize-giving, where he received $3,000 for winning to supplement a rumoured $5,000 in appearance money from the Batista government, Juan typically downplayed his achievement and said it had really been de Portago's race.

A month later, sharing a Maserati 'Bazooka' with Behra, Juan led the 12 Hours of Sebring in Florida for all except the first few of the 1,050 racing miles. However, this latest Maserati triumph was overshadowed by sad news from Italy, where the 27-year-old Ferrari driver Castellotti had been killed a few days earlier. 'Eugenio Castellotti was a handsome country gentleman from the agricultural town of Lodi, where his family owned estates,' Enzo Ferrari recalled. 'He had got into motor racing at his own expense, paying for his first sports cars out of his own pocket. It cannot be said that he was a driver of outstanding class or impeccable style, but none can deny that he was a big-hearted and extraordinarily generous young man with great determination and pluck. Castellotti was killed in a banal accident during a test run in one of our latest cars on the Modena track. He was going through a confused and conflicting time emotionally, and it is probable that his end was brought about by a momentary slowness in his reactions. He had asked his fiancée, the beautiful actress Delia Scala, to give up her career, which she didn't want to do. At Modena he was bitter, and absent in his manner. On only the second lap, his car crashed into one of the concrete barriers, and poor Castellotti was thrown out headfirst into a stone wall.'

Then, on 14 May, just a few days before the European Grand Prix season was due to begin, two more Ferrari drivers lost their lives. The 17th Marquis de Portago, Alfonso Cabeza de Vaca, Count of Mejorada, known to his friends as 'Fon' – who once said that he didn't believe a racing driver was necessarily a brave man so much as a man who wasn't afraid – was killed along with his American friend and co-driver Edmond Nelson in a horrendous accident during the 24th running of Italy's historic Mille Miglia. Running fourth at the time, and within thirteen miles of the finish line at Brescia, de Portago had a tyre burst while his Ferrari sports car was travelling at 170mph. The car flew off the road, snapped off a telephone pole, careered through a group of spectators, flipped over a bank and somersaulted back on to the road, throwing its now lifeless occupants into a ditch. The death toll – nine spectators (five of them children), de Portago and Nelson – caused public outrage, and the classic Mille Miglia was never run again as a race.

On 16 May, a memorial service was held for de Portago and Nelson in a small parish church at Guidizzola near Mantua. An immense crowd gathered outside in the brilliant sunshine and stared solemnly at the two hearses that would take the two fallen heroes on their last ride. Inside the dimly lit church, where the smell of burning incense and flickering candles filled the air, heavily veiled women stood quietly sobbing in front of the two flower-draped coffins. Among the mourners sitting in the front row was Enzo Ferrari, who remembered de Portago as 'a man possessed of a high degree of physical courage; he was to be found on bobsled tracks, steeplechases, motor races or anywhere else where you can risk your neck. On the whole, he was an unusual type, followed wherever he went by his fame as a vastly wealthy Don Juan, looked upon everywhere as a sort of "magnificent brute" on account of his air of personal neglect.' Alongside Ferrari were four of his drivers: Piero Taruffi, who had won the tragic Mille Miglia, Olivier Gendebien, Peter Collins and Count Wolfgang von Trips (the latter two of whom were also destined to die in Ferraris). Sitting alone and almost unnoticed in a back row of the darkened church at Guidizzola was one of the too often deadly sport's longest survivors: Juan Manuel Fangio.

GRAND PRIX DE MONACO

'My opponents were now all young fellows – Moss, Brooks, Collins and Hawthorn,' Juan reflected. 'They called me the Old Man, and I suppose I was. They could have been my sons, but they did not have the experience in racing that I had, and experience is very important.' And in Monaco the Old Man beat the youngsters to pole position by means of his superior speed and went on to win the race using a combination of speed and experience.

Sensing that the keen rivalry among the youthful Englishmen might interfere with their judgement in the claustrophobic confines of the narrow street circuit where the slightest mistake can lead to disaster, Juan was ready for trouble. On the fourth lap, when the running order was Moss, Collins, Fangio, Brooks, Hawthorn, Moss braked too late going into the chicane on the entry to the harbourfront and his Vanwall smashed terminally into the sandbags and wooden posts that at this point bordered the track. A too closely following Collins misjudged his avoiding action and his Ferrari ploughed into the barriers next to the harbour. As Juan came out of the tunnel, he saw debris flying into the air from the carambolage in front, braked carefully and was able to negotiate his way safely through the chicane. Behind him, the oncoming Brooks braked hard, whereupon his Vanwall was hit from behind by the Hawthorn Ferrari, which bounced off it and crashed heavily into the wrecked car of Collins, who was already exchanging points of view with Moss. Though their friendships were for the moment strained and their pride wounded, the disgruntled British trio miraculously escaped injury and were left to spectate as the Old Man administered another driving lesson in the Riviera sunshine. 'All the young English boys were out except Brooks,' Juan said, 'who made it through the troublespot and was really driving hard. The tempo of the race was very fierce, and he started gaining on me. The best weapon a leading driver has is to show his rival that he is stretching himself for nothing, so I decided to pile on the pressure so he would lose heart. As the laps went by, Brooks saw from the Vanwall pit signals that he was not gaining, and he eased off and left me alone.'

A fifth-place finish in a shared Maserati (Juan teamed up with three other drivers in two different cars) at the 1,000-kilometre sports car race at the Nürburgring followed, then there was a sterling solo effort in the Grand Prix of Portugal at Lisbon which rewarded Juan with his fifth win from seven races. But the season was already beginning to exact a toll on the now 46-year-old champion. 'To be the world champion and maintain that position is a very difficult task,' he said. 'I used to arrive at a track, no matter what type of race it was, thinking I had to demonstrate why I was the world champion.'

GRAND PRIX DE L'ACF

For 1957, the venue for the championship race in France changed from Reims to the Rouen-les-Essarts circuit, situated in a forest south of Rouen between two bends in the river Seine. The 4.5-mile track featured several taxing curves, in particular the sharp New World corner, which was approached by a steep downhill gradient. It was there, having to make up lost ground because of a rare poor start, that Juan resorted to a cornering technique that was even more aggressive than usual. Lap after lap he sped down into the New World corner at a seemingly suicidal speed, each time retrieving the situation at the last moment by throwing his Maserati into a huge tyre-smoking powerslide that served the dual purpose of scrubbing off speed without using the brakes while also positioning the car for full application of the throttle throughout the remainder of the corner, which he exited at an astonishing velocity. By means of this other-worldly progress through the New World, Juan soon worked his way back to the front. Once in command, he never let up. Olivier Merlin, a Fangio biographer, remembered Juan 'coming by regularly' at Rouen 'as if sitting in an armchair in his Maserati, with the three Ferraris driven by Musso, Collins and Hawthorn struggling hard in vain pursuit'.

BRITISH GRAND PRIX

Despite Juan's superb driving, the 1957 championship was by no means a foregone conclusion. Following a mechanical failure on 14 July in a non-championship round at Reims, Juan, who was also suffering from a gastric complaint, was beset by another Maserati malfunction in the British Grand Prix at Aintree a week later. His having to stop when his engine blew up was of little consequence to the partisan British crowd, since the race win was shared by Brooks and Moss (who took over from his team-mate when his own car broke down) for Vanwall. It was an historic occasion – the first shared win by Englishmen in their country's championship race and the first Grand Prix victory for a British-built car since Sir Henry Segrave won the 1923 French Grand Prix in a Sunbeam. 'The first one to congratulate us, as usual, was Juan,' said Moss, 'ever the great sportsman whether he won or lost.'

GROSSER PREIS VON DEUTSCHLAND

The mighty Nürburgring, the brooding giant of a track lying in the midst of the Eifel Mountains, had so many twists and turns along its 14.5-mile length that their number could not be determined with absolute accuracy. It was generally agreed that it had about 90 main corners that turned left and only slightly fewer corners that went in a right-hand direction. Some of the turns were long and sweeping, but about 30 of them were acutely sharp hairpins. The sections of road linking them were seldom straightforward either; in fact, aside from the 1.24-mile-long run preceding the start-finish line, there were no straights worthy of the name. Many of the more complicated corners did have names, and these – such as Butcher's Field, Swedish Cross, Pick Axe Head, Park of Wild Animals and Enemy's Garden (translated from the German) – were testimony to their Teutonic fierceness. Complicating the task for those who tackled the track in speeding cars was the fact that the undulating obstacle course, which encompassed changes in elevation of over 1,000 feet, included many pronounced bumps and several humpback bridges that launched the cars six feet into the air for distances as much as 25 feet. For the drivers, the Nürburgring was as much a test of courage as of skill, though it had to be treated with the utmost respect because an excess of bravery had been the major cause of the approximately 125 deaths in the 30-year history of this most dangerous track.

But Juan loved it. 'There was always fear at the Nürburgring,' he said, 'but fear is not a stupid thing. Winning is not a question of courage, but of faith in oneself and in the car. The Nürburgring was always my favourite track, from the first day I drove on it in an Alfetta in 1951. A circuit that was dangerous was good for me, because there you could tell the difference between us all, and my luck never let me down.' When he won the 1956 event in his Lancia-Ferrari, Juan had established a new race lap record of 9m 41.6s; this time, during practice for the 22-lap, 310-mile German Grand Prix, he hurled his Maserati 250F around the course in a breathtaking 9m 25.6s. Next fastest, and just three seconds slower, was Hawthorn's Ferrari, with Behra's Maserati a further two seconds adrift, and then the Collins Ferrari, which was nine seconds slower than Juan's pole position time. The Vanwalls of Brooks and Moss were respectively eleven and sixteen seconds off Juan's pace.

For the British Grand Prix winners, their cars' rock-hard suspension and resultant poor handling proved to be entirely unsuitable for the tortures of the Nürburgring in the epic race that followed. Indeed, it was one of the greatest races in the history of motorsport, and for the victor, the finest of his superlative career.

'From the start,' Juan recalled, 'the two Ferraris of Hawthorn and Collins took the lead. I let them do so, and in fact I was surprised at the way they kept passing each other instead of working together as a team. Instead of thinking about how to get out in front together, they were playing around for the lead.

I kept behind for the first two laps, and that allowed me to study their style of racing. On the third lap, I took advantage of the fact that they had stopped dicing with each other, and challenged them both.' Denis Jenkinson wrote in *Motor Sport* that Juan, 'improving on the lap record on every lap, passed Collins at the beginning of lap three and overtook Hawthorn on the descent to Adenau. From now on there was only one man on the Nürburgring. Increasing his lead by seven seconds a lap from Hawthorn and Collins, who were in close formation, Fangio on lap twelve drew into the pits, where his Maserati mechanics took a disgustingly long time by Grand Prix standards to change the rear wheels and refuel.'

'When I came into the pits,' Juan continued, 'I had a 28-second lead. I stopped the car and got out. While I was having a drink, my mechanics were working away, but they weren't doing a good job. I don't know whether they were nervous or what, but the fact is that I lost all the advantage I had gained, plus another 48 seconds. While they were working, I heard the two Ferraris pass, one very close to the other. When the mechanics finally lowered the jack, there were ten laps left of the 22-lap race. When I set out again I felt quite disappointed, as I was losing a race that could win me the championship.

'I had to get the tyres bedded in, so on the next lap I was 51 seconds behind. After that, the car really began to perform to my liking. The Nürburgring is one of those tracks where you lose touch with things; you think you're going fast and you're not going fast at all. I began to use higher gears. I had learnt from experience that if you left the car in a higher gear for some of the faster curves, and as long as you went in at the correct angle, you came out with the engine revving at a faster rate on the following straight, which made a difference in terms of time. It wasn't very comfortable, feeling the lack of grip as the car went round, but after all, I had to win. I began to take nearly all the bends in a higher gear than I would have normally used.

'That's how I was driving when I came to the dip below the bridge, where I had passed González in 1954 in order to gain the lead in the first lap. This time, I didn't lift my foot off the accelerator. Normally, we took that place in fifth, trying to skim rather than jump the car so as not to jolt it too hard and allow a margin for error when it landed. This time I took it without slackening at all, with my foot down. I tried to stick well to the inside of the dip, where the car took off, and I touched the ground on the opposite side of the track, uncomfortably close to the fence. There were no guard rails in those days. In my mirror I saw the cloud of dust I'd raised at the edge of the track, but it was a risk worth taking. The curve linked two straights, and I had treated it as if it were just one straight. I knew I'd make up some seconds there. They told me afterwards that there had been quite a stir in the Ferrari pits. As I seemed at first to be losing rather than gaining after my pit stop, they had told their drivers to reduce their pace. But when they looked at their stopwatches after the first lap in which I'd used the higher gears, they couldn't believe their eyes. I had made up ten seconds.'

Jenkinson confirmed that 'the Ferrari pit became frantic and urged the two Englishmen to greater things, but there was nothing they could do. When the Old Man gets into a record-breaking groove there is no one to stop him, especially on the Nürburgring. On lap nineteen he lowered his lap record to 9m 23.4s. At the end of lap twenty, Hawthorn led Collins over the line, both straining all they knew how, and then the crowds rose in acclamation, for Fangio was right behind them. Then came the most shattering development of the whole race. Fangio had just lapped in 9m 17.4s! An unbelievable record, but obviously true because he had gained eleven seconds on Hawthorn in fourteen and a half miles.'

'On that lap,' said Juan, 'I saw a red blur disappearing round a bend among the trees, and I said to myself, "I'll certainly catch that Ferrari." The pits had signalled to me that there were not two cars in front of me, but only one; I had no idea that the other was only a few metres in front of the one I had seen. On the Adenau descent, I saw the two red cars, one behind the other. I knew I was going to catch them. By the time we passed the pits, I was tailing them. We came into the second to last lap, passed the semi-circle, on to the straight behind the pits, and on the way into the left-hand North curve I got on the inside of Collins. I had pressed the Maserati a bit too hard, and it was too far over coming out of the curve. Collins gained some yards on me, overtook me again, and placed himself strategically for the next curve. I didn't want him to think he had got the better of me, so I stuck to his tail through a series of bends until we reached a short straight that led upwards to a bridge. I got alongside him. At the speed we were going, it seemed that there wouldn't be room for two cars. Collins gave way, and I got in front of him at the little bridge and went down the toboggan run that followed it.

'And there was Hawthorn's Ferrari, right in front of me. I started tailing him, and was beginning to work out how many chances I had left to overtake him when the opportunity suddenly presented itself. After a series of curves came a short straight which ended in a 90-degree turn to the left, followed by an equally sharp turn to the right. On the straight stretch, Hawthorn pulled to the right to get his angle. I saw my chance, and cut in on his inside. Hawthorn must have suddenly seen a red blur to his left, because he quickly pulled over as if startled.'

'It was a straight fight with Fangio,' Hawthorn said, 'and I was driving right on the limit as we rushed through the endless tree-lined curves to Hocheichen and on to the Quiddelbacher Hohe, but just as I was going into a slow right-hander Fangio cut sharply inside me and forced me on to the grass and almost into the ditch. If I hadn't moved over I'm sure the old devil would have driven right over me!' Stirling Moss thought it 'remarkable to see anybody get past two such great drivers as Collins and Hawthorn in single moves, and with such relative ease. I already had great admiration for him, but to see Juan do that underlined my knowledge of his greatness.'

'The Englishman Hawthorn then collected his wits again,' Juan said. 'I made a point of getting away from him before reaching the final straight, because there he might have taken advantage of my slipstream and passed me. On that last lap my seat came loose, and I had to drive pressing my knee against the side of the car and holding on to the steering wheel hard to stop myself rolling around in the cockpit of the bouncing car. My lead was sufficient for Hawthorn not to be able to stick close to me. I kept it up for the whole of the last lap.' Hawthorn conceded that as they started that last lap Juan 'had the vital yards in hand which prevented me from getting to grips on the corners, and he crossed the finishing line 3.6 seconds ahead of me. This race had been every bit as exciting for the drivers as the spectators, and even though Peter and I had been beaten, we enjoyed every moment of it.'

'What a celebration there was!' Juan recalled. 'I was carried here, there and everywhere on people's shoulders. When I managed to get to the podium, Hawthorn and Collins were ecstatic, as if they had been the winners. They never stopped congratulating me and shaking me by the hand, even though my car had thrown up a stone and broken one of the lenses of Collins's goggles. They were both very good lads. Both appreciated me, and their congratulations were sincere.'

'It was one of the classic drives of all time,' Moss concluded, 'by perhaps the greatest driver of all time. I was witness to it; in fact I finished fifth in that German Grand Prix. I know the word "incredible" is much devalued these days, but what Juan Manuel Fangio did on 4 August 1957 was, and remains, absolutely that.' Denis Jenkinson agreed. 'His average speed of 88.7mph for the entire three and a half hours, pitstop included, had been faster than the lap record he had set the previous year. It had been a truly great race in which Fangio had surpassed himself, secured the World Championship for 1957, and put everyone in their place on the toughest Grand Prix track in the world.'

'That day,' said Juan, 'I had everything turned on and firing on all cylinders. I was ready to do anything. Whichever way you look at it, it was an extraordinary race. When it was all over I was convinced that I would never be able to drive like that again – never. I had reached the limit of my concentration and will to win. Those were the two things that allowed me to take the risks I did that day. I knew I could win, but I knew equally I could lose. I was stretching myself to the limit, and afterwards the car was covered with grass and dirt. I was trying out new things, pushing myself further at many blind spots where I had never before had the courage to go to the limit. I was never a daredevil, never a spectacular driver. I would try to win as slowly as possible. Until that race, I had never demanded more of myself or the cars. But that day I made such demands on myself that I couldn't sleep for two nights afterwards. I was in such a state that whenever I shut my eyes it was as if I were in the race again, making those leaps in the dark on those curves where I had never before had the courage to push things so far. For two days I experienced delayed-action apprehension at what I had done, a feeling that had never come over me after any other race, a feeling that still returns to me this day when I think about that time.'

Juan's conviction that he 'would never be able to drive like that again' was an accurate one, for this Homeric triumph at the Nürburgring, his 24th win in a World Championship Grand Prix, was to be his last major victory.

GRAN PREMIO DI PESCARA, GRAN PREMIO D'ITALIA

In the final two championship races of 1957, both of them in Italy, Juan's Maserati finished second to Moss's Vanwall. On the podium after winning the Grand Prix of Pescara, which was run in a heatwave, Moss playfully sprayed a bottle of mineral water over the Old Man and rubbed it into his bald head. On the podium following their hard-fought battle in the Italian Grand Prix at Monza, Juan appeared with his face badly pockmarked and cut from stones thrown up by the rear wheels of Moss's victorious Vanwall.

The evening after the Monza race, 9 September, several of the top drivers and their companions got together on the roof garden of the sumptuous Palace Hotel in Milan for a post-season celebratory banquet. Among those attending was Stirling Moss with his then fiancée the Canadian Katie Molson, his mother and his father. Also on hand was Peter Collins, accompanied by his new American wife Louise Cordier and his best friend Mike Hawthorn, who as usual had an attractive female companion on one hand and a strong beverage in the other. The raucous group also included Wolfgang von Trips, Harry Schell and Olivier Gendebien, even the retired Piero Taruffi. Conspicuously absent from the festivities was the five-time world champion Juan Manuel Fangio, who that night dined quietly with his 'wife' Beba and a few close friends in his favourite humble trattoria near his Milan headquarters, the comparatively downmarket Colombia Hotel.

A few days later, Juan made headlines around the world when he was involved in a spectacular and potentially deadly accident. At eight o'clock in the evening, while driving his Lancia Aurelia road car from Milan to Modena where he was

scheduled to compete in a non-championship race, Juan suddenly came upon a large truck that was in the process of making a
turn and was sideways across the narrow road. Travelling at
120mph and with no time to stop, Juan deliberately spun the car
to avoid the truck, but the Lancia sideswiped a telegraph pole
and its doors burst open. Driver and front-seat passenger were
thrown out; remaining in the back seat was Gary Laughlin, a
35-year-old Texas oil baron and air force veteran who had
served in both the Second World War and in Korea to whom the
world champion had offered a ride to Modena. 'The car stopped
inches from the truck,' Laughlin said. 'I jumped out without a
scratch to see Fangio and his wife lying in the roadway.
Amazingly, although they were both scratched and bleeding, he
had only a sore left hand and she had the skin burnt off her left
arm and leg from skidding across the road. Then the berserk
truck driver came for me: who did I think I was driving at that
speed in the darkness. Was I crazy? Did I think I was Fangio?
"No," I replied, "but he is," pointing to the bloodstained figure
staggering across the road. The truck driver was aghast, stood
there looking for a few seconds, then burst into tears.'

Juan's banged-up hand prevented him from competing at
Modena, and in his next race, the Grand Prix of Morocco in
Casablanca, he was among several drivers afflicted by a serious
bout of flu. A fluless Behra won the race, but a feverish Collins
and Hawthorn both had to drop out; Juan hung on grimly to
finish fourth. To complete his seventeen-race season and bring
his victory total to ten, Juan went on to win two sports car
races, at São Paulo and Rio de Janeiro in Brazil, where he felt
he had to uphold his country's honour 'because of the rivalry
between Brazil and Argentina . . . The risk was not great, but
the responsibility was heavy.'

When at last he returned to Argentina in mid-November,
Juan was received with full state honours by a government that

had by now decided his gains, certainly in the world of racing, were not ill gotten but fully deserved. Preceded by a military motorcycle escort and followed by a long procession of dignitaries in limousines, Juan was paraded through the streets of Buenos Aires in an open Cadillac. Back in Balcarce, the people's champion was fêted at a banquet attended by 400 people.

In Europe, too, more laudatory prose was being churned out than ever before. 'For the third successive year, Juan Manuel Fangio carried off top honours in the World Championship,' Gregor Grant wrote in *Autosport*'s seasonal survey. 'His is an imposing record. The great Argentinian has won the title no fewer than five times since it was instituted in 1950, the others being Nino Farina and the late Alberto Ascari. His achievements this year are all the more remarkable when one considers that Fangio is in his 46th year.' In the *Automobile Revue*, Gunther Molter also thought Juan 'a phenomenon. His younger colleagues will now look up to him as someone unsurpassed, the grand old master of Grand Prix racing who can drive like no one else. And let them look up to Fangio, who from being a poor mechanic from a little pampas township in Argentina racing in dilapidated cars in very minor events has now become king of the world's famous racing circuits. He is a man who will be esteemed wherever he goes, who will remain the same in spite of his fame – what the British refer to as "a decent chap" and his own people "Muchacho".'

Chapter Sixteen

1958: Farewell to Racing

'I thought that if I went on, I might only prove that I was stupid.'

DESPITE JUAN'S SUCCESSES for the team the previous year, Maserati was close to insolvency and there was no budget for a full 1958 season, when rule changes would require the building of new cars and starting money offered by race organisers would be drastically reduced. Since 1947, when the Maserati brothers (whose father had founded the firm in 1927) sold out their interests to Count Adolfo Orsi, the company had concentrated mainly on making machinery for industry; the race team continued only because the owner's son Omer Orsi was a racing enthusiast. Given the financial situation, Maserati was able to prepare Grand Prix and sports cars only for a few private entrants, and it was in these cars that Juan began the 1958 season, albeit with considerable misgivings.

'Before the first race,' Juan revealed, 'our family doctor told me, "Be careful, your father and mother are not so strong any more. After one of your races last year I found them very agitated." ' Juan's devotion to his parents in their declining years became stronger than ever. The guilt he felt about leaving them behind to worry over him was compounded by his deliberate failure to contact them during the European racing season. Over the years he had hardly even sent them a postcard, because, he said, it would make him so homesick it would interfere with his racing. Now, he felt, he had gone on long enough. 'It had been many years since I started racing. I had already nearly stopped in 1955. I had never thought much about winning, only competing, and I had won five World Championships, so what else was I looking for? In any field – racing, singing, acting, sports – if you become a name you must know to recognise the moment when to retire. That is an essential thing.'

For the moment, though, he decided to approach 1958 with a wait-and-see attitude, taking opportunities when they presented themselves to race as an independent in selected events. The first of these was on 19 January in his home Grand Prix, for which a wealthy enthusiast provided him with a 1957 vintage Maserati 250F.

GRAN PREMIO DE LA REPUBLICA ARGENTINA

Determined to do well in what might be his final appearance in a championship race at the 'Fangiodrome' in Buenos Aires, Juan put his Maserati on pole. Beside him on the front row were the Ferrari team-mates Hawthorn and Collins, but it was the presence on the second row of Moss in a flimsy, quaint-looking rear-engined Cooper-Climax that was causing a sensation. The car, entered by privateer Rob Walker, was much smaller than the traditional front-engined Formula 1 machinery, and in the skilful hands of Moss (whose Vanwall team had not entered the season-opener) it won the race.

Having taken the lead from Hawthorn's Ferrari on the ninth lap, Juan looked in his mirrors and saw 'Moss coming at me in that little thing'. He began driving harder than ever to discourage his pursuer, and set the fastest lap of the race – even quicker than his pole time – but the Cooper persisted. Juan's tyres began to wear badly, his Maserati's engine began to overheat and lose power, and he fell back to fourth at the finish, behind the Ferraris of Hawthorn and Musso. The victory for Moss, the first in a championship race for a rear-engined car, heralded a move to that configuration that would within two years make the front-engined cars obsolete.

The next weekend, Juan made an embarrassing exit from the 1,000-kilometre sports car race at the 'Fangiodrome'. Sharing a Maserati 300S with the Spanish privateer Francisco Godia-Sales, Juan was lying third early in the race when he spun on some oil and crumpled the car's nose. His intentions had been honourable – he was trying to conserve the engine by taking the corners in a higher gear than usual – and he made no excuses when he brought the damaged car back into the pits and apologised profusely to its owner for letting him down.

Two weeks later, in the Gran Premio de Buenos Aires, the third and final race of the Argentine season, Juan won for what was to be the final time in his career. Starting his Maserati 250F from pole, he finished second to Hawthorn in the first of two heats, both of them run in torrential rain. In the second heat, showing all his old mastery in the difficult conditions, Juan set the fastest race lap and overtook the Ferraris of Hawthorn, Musso and von Trips to win comfortably and score the overall victory on aggregate time. But for the winner, a most trying time lay ahead.

On 23 February, the eve of the Cuban Grand Prix for sports cars, Juan was among several drivers surrounded by a crowd of onlookers gathered in the lobby of Havana's Lincoln Hotel. Having been given for this race a Maserati 450S by an American enthusiast, Temple Buell, Juan had put it on pole and was the centre of attention. As the most popular sporting personality in Latin America, his autograph was much in demand, and, as usual, Juan was happy to sign the pieces of paper. Suddenly, instead of a pen, a bearded, nervous-looking youth produced a Colt 45 pistol and pressed it into Juan's ribs. At first, Juan thought it was someone playing a joke, but the gunman expertly disarmed the personal bodyguard assigned by the Batista government to protect Juan and ushered him to the door where a second armed man stood holding a pistol levelled at the astonished onlookers in the hotel lobby. The other drivers also had armed guards, and Juan was worried that a shootout might start at any second. 'The fellow who had the gun on me was shaking a bit, which frightened me,' he said. 'I said I would go with him. As we walked out, I was waiting for gunfire, ready to throw myself to the ground, as in action films. But nobody fired. At the door, the second kidnapper shouted out, "Nobody leaves this hotel for five minutes." Outside there were four men with machine guns pointing at the door.'

Juan was put into the back seat of a waiting car, where another man held a sub-machine gun in his face. Juan told him to put it down, that he would offer no resistance. He was then told to crouch down out of sight, otherwise they might be spotted and there would be shooting. They drove off through the streets of Havana and eventually stopped at a house in a quiet suburb. 'We went into a room where there was a woman with a small child. The woman asked me to give an autograph to her son. I put down the date and the child's name and signed it. We went by car to a second house, then a third, where I was kept overnight. There were several men and women. We got along quite well, considering the situation. They fed me some fried eggs and potatoes, and the others ate with me and explained their situation.'

The kidnappers told Juan they were members of Fidel Castro's revolutionary 26th of July Movement and that they had tried and failed to capture him a year earlier in order to draw attention to their fight against the Cuban dictator Batista, whose spendthrift ways in the midst of the country's general poverty had to be stopped. Juan listened sympathetically as the kidnappers, most of them young students, listed a string of government-sponsored crimes which included murdering several of the relatives and friends of the insurgents. Before he went to bed, Juan asked his hosts to telephone his family and say that he was all right. They did this, adding that they did not intend to harm him.

At breakfast the next morning, the kidnappers showed Juan the enormous publicity his capture had created in the local newspapers, which reported that an all-out manhunt was underway for the missing driver. In the afternoon, while he watched the race on television with his captors, Juan came to realise that they might have done him a favour. The start of the race had been delayed by two hours in the vain hope that the rebels might release the star attraction, whose expected presence was largely responsible for attracting a crowd of over 150,000 people to the race through the streets of Havana. When Juan failed to show up, his Maserati was taken over by Maurice Trintignant. On the sixth lap, a Ferrari driven by an inexperienced Cuban driver, Armando Garcia Cifuentes, skidded on some oil and ploughed into the crowd. The toll was six dead and 30 injured, among them the driver. The race was stopped immediately, and Stirling Moss, whose Ferrari was leading at the time, was declared the winner.

Back in the house where Juan was being held, his captors wondered how to set him free. Having gained the desired publicity, there was no point in keeping him any longer, but they were worried that if they released him Batista's people might kill him and accuse the rebels of doing it. They asked Juan for his opinion, and he suggested that the safest way would be to deliver him to the Argentine ambassador in Havana. Late that night, Juan was taken to the flat of an Argentine Embassy employee where the ambassador, Guevara Lynch, was waiting. His captors bid Juan a fond farewell and again apologised for inconveniencing him.

For the Batista government, the Fangio kidnapping and the failure of a full-scale manhunt to find any trace of him was an acute embarrassment; for the followers of Castro, who would eventually overthrow the government, it was a huge publicity coup; for Juan, it brought unexpected fame elsewhere. 'There is no doubt that the people in the movement got what they wanted by kidnapping me,' Juan reflected, 'but they had no idea how popular this was going to make me in the United States. From Havana, I went to Miami to rest for a few days, and the mayor met me and handed me the keys to the city. Then I was given $1,000 to go to New York and appear on television on *The Ed Sullivan Show*, along with the champion boxer Jack Dempsey. I had won the World Championship five times, and I had raced and won in Florida, but what made me big in the United States was being kidnapped in Cuba – which I thought was a bit strange.'

Mainstream America had first become aware of Juan Manuel Fangio the year before when, after he won the Sebring sports car race for the second time, he was featured in a cover story in the country's most popular publication, *Life* magazine. In the article, Juan said that the most famous US race, the Indianapolis 500 on the 2.5-mile oval track, was so specialised and the cars so different from road-racing machines that it would be difficult for him to race there competitively without a great deal of practice, which his busy schedule would not allow. In response to this, the American publisher of the Indianapolis 500 year-book, Floyd Clymer, wrote that foreign drivers were afraid of the admittedly dangerous Indy race and of being dominated by the American Indy stars, and that Juan was a phoney world champion. Clymer issued a challenge to Juan – who, he declared, drove only for money – offering him $500 if he passed the traditional rookie test and was allowed to enter the 1958 race; $1,000 if he qualified in the 33-car field; $2,500 if he finished the 500 miles better than fifth in an American-made car; and $5,000 if he could do it in a foreign car. Juan's response was that the money did not interest him and that it was not as champion of the world that he refused to go to Indianapolis, but as the representative of all European-based drivers and their road-racing discipline. The Indianapolis Motor Speedway, home of 'The World's Greatest Race', was completely different, comprising four steeply banked high-speed left-hand turns connected by two long 150mph straights. The cars were purpose-built for the task, with rudimentary chassis, four-cylinder Offenhauser engines offset to the left to help centrifugal force, almost horizontal steering wheels, two-speed gearboxes and basic brakes that were hardly ever used during the flat-out run. Still, despite his unfamiliarity with this form of motorsport, Juan had always been intrigued by it, and he now said that because he had the time available he would consider contesting the 1958 race if he was given a competitive American roadster.

Once he had declared himself, and after he had appeared with Ed Sullivan on TV, he was invited to test a roadster on the short oval at Trenton, New Jersey. In only three laps he set a time just off the track record, whereupon an Indycar owner offered him a 'Dayton Steel Foundry Special' for the forthcoming Indianapolis 500 at the end of May. Juan easily passed the compulsory rookie test, working his way up to a 142.8mph lap that would have comfortably qualified him for the race, but the car was a handful and on one occasion he spun wildly because the crew had, without telling him, topped up the fuel tank and upset the balance of the chassis. Once he'd got to grips with that, Juan found there were other problems, with the car and the crew. 'I was trying to go faster,' he said, 'but the car would not respond. I found out that the car was three years old and there was little speed left in it. First there was a steering problem, then an engine problem. The garage had no spare magneto, and I had to go and borrow one myself from another team. When I saw that the mechanics assigned to my car couldn't get a four-cylinder engine in trim, which is the simplest thing in the world, I knew the whole thing was going to be a flop.'

Luckily for Juan, there were also some difficulties over fuel contracts; Juan was committed to using British Petroleum products, but the American car's owners were contracted to Mobilgas. This proved a convenient out for Juan, and before official qualifying began he withdrew his entry, donated the $500 paid by Clymer for having passed the rookie test to the Damon Runyon Cancer Fund, and flew to Europe, where he became a reluctant participant in another New World versus Old World confrontation.

The 'Two Worlds Trophy' race at Monza, using the banked section of the track, had first taken place at Monza in 1957. The intention of the organisers was to have a 500-mile contest run under Indianapolis rules and featuring the best American Indy drivers in their roadsters and the top Formula 1 stars in specially prepared Grand Prix machinery. But none of the European teams had taken it seriously, and the Americans dominated. For the 1958 race, Ferrari entered two much-modified Formula 1 cars for Hawthorn and Musso, Moss was given a specially prepared Maserati, Jaguar had several cars for British drivers, and Juan was provided with a US-built 'Dean Van Lines Special' roadster. The continental contingent's opposition comprised twelve American cars and drivers.

The three-heat race was again a New World triumph. Despite heroic efforts by Musso, who started from pole with a fastest lap of over 174mph, and Moss to keep their Ferraris in contention, they were beaten by the 'Zink Leader Special' of Jim Rathmann, who won from the 'Belond AP Special' of Indianapolis 500 winner, the cigar-chomping Jimmy Bryan, who had won the famed race at an average speed of just over 134mph. Rathmann's winning average at Monza was 166.73mph, making this the world's fastest ever race.

It was, however, another non-event for the five-time world champion, whose car went nowhere fast. After being fastest in opening practice at a speed of 171mph, Juan's time was subsequently equalled by another US car, which then broke a piston. The following morning, Juan arrived at his team's garage to find his car's engine in pieces, while the car that had broken a piston was repaired and ready to run. While his car was being fixed, Juan had to sit out the first two heats. In the third and final heat he did only a few laps before two pistons broke and he had to retire the car, at which point he seriously began to consider doing the same himself. 'Everything was persuading me that the time had come,' he said. 'I found myself thinking of Nuvolari as I had seen him in my first races in Europe, just a shadow of the genius I had read about at the height of his brilliance. I'd promised myself that I'd never go out like that. When I was no longer able to show my best, I should retire at the top – no hanging on.'

GRAND PRIX DE L'ACF

The weekend after the Monza fiasco, in early July, Juan arrived in France for the fifth championship round of the season. Having missed him in the Grands Prix in Monaco, Holland and Belgium, the Formula 1 fraternity welcomed the Old Man back in jocular fashion. For the race at Reims, most of the drivers stayed in the city's Lion d'Or Hotel. While Juan was out of his room, a group of drivers, led by the great practical jokers Musso and Collins, emptied the Fangio suite of every single item of furniture that could be removed. That prank was followed by their lugging Harry Schell's tiny Citroën 2CV up to the door of Schell's third-floor room. In the evening, everyone met in the lobby, and Juan happily joined in the general laughter. His rivals might have been half his age, but at 47 the Old Man could still hold his own in the light-hearted banter and appreciate the camaraderie. Still, he retired early and went up to his room, to which the hotel staff had returned the missing furniture. They had also removed Schell's car. He lay down on the bed with his arms folded behind his head and wondered again if he might have come to the end of the racing road. 'The youngsters had the road in front of them, and I had run it already,' he said. 'I had known the feeling of not being able to wait for the day of the race, for the contest to begin. What a contrast, the eve of this French Grand Prix, when I shut myself up in my hotel room as I had done before so many other races, looking after myself, going without all sorts of things in order to be physically and mentally fit, wondering which of the boys would give me the most work to do, wondering how I'd last the three hours in the car. Racing no longer gave me satisfaction. It had become an obligation.'

It was five months since he had driven a Maserati 250F, and during the first practice laps Juan found that the car had been drastically changed for the worse. He came into the pits and asked the mechanics what they had done. They explained that Maserati now had a contract with a new shock absorber manufacturer whose products were now on the car. 'Things were changing,' Juan mused. 'For me, the atmosphere was not like before, when it was a sport for enthusiasts. During my first seasons in Europe I often had to repair my own car with my own hands. Now, everything was done by proxy. Since 1956, I had been discussing contracts, advertising, and all that sort of thing. Me, who'd started racing never thinking about the money I'd win. I only wanted to race, and win if possible. But even this was becoming more and more difficult.'

During qualifying, the best performance he could extract from the ill-handling Maserati was only good enough for eighth on the grid in the field of 21 cars. On the front row were the Ferraris of Hawthorn and Musso and the BRM of Schell; behind them was the Ferrari of Collins and the Vanwall of Brooks, followed by Moss in a Vanwall and Trintignant, whose BRM lined up alongside the five-time world champion whose racing future was in grave doubt. 'What a splendid sight that first lap was,' wrote Gregor Grant, 'with Hawthorn, Schell, Musso, Collins, Moss, Brooks and Fangio bunched together, screaming into the fast bend after the pits in one solid mass. There followed some real motor racing that brought the crowd to its feet howling with excitement, as the top-liners flew by, trusting each other's judgement within an inch of their lives. The slightest mistake, and anything could happen. Fangio was revealing the great mastery of his craft, pushing his Maserati as no Maserati has ever been pushed since Nürburgring 1957. Past the pits, there was a scare-making moment as Juan Manuel decided to take the inside of the group and came out ahead, scattering those terrified folk who were foolishly hanging around in front of the pit wall. Then, on lap ten, the leaders came through, strung out and looking tense. Tragedy had struck at Scuderia Ferrari, and Luigi Musso was the victim.' Juan was behind Musso at the time. 'I saw how he went level with another car on the entry to the fast bend beyond the pits. He didn't leave himself enough track. There was a low barrier at the end of the curve. His front wheel must have touched it, and he went out of control and went off. I didn't realise then how serious an accident it was.'

On the 24th lap, while he was running third behind Hawthorn and Behra, Juan peeled off angrily into the pits and threw his car's clutch pedal at the feet of the embarrassed Maserati mechanics. The pedal, having been drilled full of holes to lighten it, had broken in two. Juan briefly considered stopping then and there, but decided to continue. 'I did so without using the clutch for the rest of the race, changing gear by ear. I thought of the public out there. They had no idea what was wrong with my car, but they could tell I wasn't making quick gear changes and that I was driving like a beginner. I thought I was letting down those who had paid for a ticket to come and see the world champion, when he didn't look like one on the track.

'On the long straights at Reims, I had time to think. I had started here in 1948 and originally planned to stay in Europe for only a year or two, but I had been there ten years running. Many things went through my mind. I thought about my father and mother and how they worried for me. I thought of all that had gone wrong lately: the kidnap in Cuba, the failure at Indianapolis, the frustration at Monza. Something was wrong, I told myself. I believe in fate, and I had a terrible feeling I was forcing it. I had always considered myself a lucky man, yet I wondered if my luck would soon run out. As champion, I was under an obligation to drive the fastest laps, but to do so I had to take risks. I was thinking about all this as I drove. It was then that I realised I had every excuse for quitting.'

But there was still the remainder of the race to be run at Reims. Juan had fallen to seventh place because of the delay in the pit, but by the penultimate lap he'd hauled the clutchless car up into fourth place, though still nearly a lap down on the race leader, Hawthorn. 'As we headed to the finish,' Hawthorn recalled, 'I decided out of respect not to lap the Old Man, but instead to watch him. He had all his old skill, and his placing of the car for a corner was, as it always had been, immaculate.' Juan appreciated the gesture, and finished fourth. 'I had told Maserati that I would drive as long as the car went well,' he said, 'and it was going less than well. I stopped the car in the pits and the decision was made. I would stop racing. But there was no ceremony for me, and no joy for Hawthorn. I then went to the hospital to see Musso. But it was too late. Poor Musso was gone.'

Enzo Ferrari found himself having to deal with the death of yet another of his drivers. 'When eagerness for victory grips a determined driver, he is liable to take incalculable risks,' Ferrari reflected, 'especially when his direct rival is animated by the same stubborn will to win. At Reims, there were two men, Musso and Hawthorn, at the wheels of two equally powerful cars, each equally anxious to win. I do not think there was any personal animosity between them. They admired each other and were good friends, even though they were of widely differing temperaments. Musso had won at Reims the previous year. The circuit was one that suited his style and he was therefore full of confidence. Like Hawthorn, Musso was after the World Championship, and he had a good chance of winning it. But on that bend, they probably engaged in a brief, ruthless battle, Hawthorn in front and Musso about twenty yards behind him. I am convinced that, in the excitement of the chase, Musso kept his foot down. He was travelling at over 130mph when he went off the road, and the car cartwheeled, catapulting him out into a wheat field.'

Less than a month later, Ferrari lost another driver in similar circumstances, during the German Grand Prix at the Nürburgring. While chasing his team-mate and best friend Hawthorn, Peter Collins lost control of his Ferrari, which flew into a ditch then somersaulted into a tree. Collins was thrown out and died shortly after being admitted to hospital. 'I had a very high opinion of Peter Collins,' said Ferrari, 'both as a driver and as a man. There is no better example of his generosity of character than when he willingly gave his car to Fangio at Monza in 1956. My last memory of poor Collins is when I shook his hand before he left for the Nürburgring. Looking at him, I was suddenly seized by a strange feeling of sadness. As we parted, I could not help wondering whether it was some sort of presentiment. His death was a great blow to us all, none more so than to his friend Hawthorn.' The Collins accident happened in full view of Hawthorn, who was devastated. At the end of the season, after he had clinched the 1958 driving title, he announced his retirement from racing. Early in the new year, he too would be killed, in a road accident in England.

Hawthorn had only just edged out Moss in the 1958 World Championship battle, which was finally resolved at the last race of the season, the Grand Prix of Morocco in Casablanca on 19 October. Sadly, during that race Stuart Lewis-Evans was dreadfully burnt when his Vanwall caught fire; he died six days later. The year had exacted a terrible toll. The deaths in 1958 of Musso, Collins and Lewis-Evans were particularly shocking as they were the first in World Championship races since 1954, when Juan's protégé Onofre Marimón had been killed at the Nürburgring. Juan's final appearance at a Grand Prix had come at Monza in September, where he was the honorary starter for the Italian Grand Prix. 'It was a good race,' he commented laconically. 'No one was killed.'

The official announcement of Juan's retirement came the evening after the Monza race at a gathering organised by his racing comrades at a hotel in Milan. On hand were Tony Brooks, who had won the Italian race, Mike Hawthorn, Stirling Moss, Harry Schell, Wolfgang von Trips, Jean Behra, Jo Bonnier, and most of the other drivers and their wives and girlfriends. When Juan and Beba – he looking dapper in a sharp new suit, she radiant in a silver satin dress – arrived they received a standing ovation. Veteran retired driver Louis Chiron, president of the Professional Drivers Union, gave a short speech and presented to Juan a golden globe of the world to commemorate his five World Championships. In response, Juan thanked everyone and announced that his racing days were over. 'I am now 47 years old,' he said, 'though in my heart I feel as if I were younger than any of you. But it is time to stop. I have always gone in for motor racing with a passion. I have struggled very hard and have had some success. Wherever I have been, I have made a cult of friendship and an obligation of sincerity. I may have made mistakes with my head, but never with my heart. Only time will tell if my sporting campaigns will be remembered. What I will remember most is the friends I have made, and also sadly those that were lost in our sport. I wish all of you well. For myself, a new life has begun.'

Part III: Fangio

The Legend Lives On

Chapter Seventeen

Life After Racing, 1959–95

'He is someone out of the ordinary. His kind pop up once in several lifetimes. Some streak across the sky like a comet, and are as rapidly forgotten. The greatness of Fangio will be forever remembered, and in the years to come his name will become a legend.'

GREGOR GRANT, A TRIBUTE IN *AUTOSPORT*

I T WAS ONLY AFTER he retired that the full impact of the Juan Manuel Fangio phenomenon – the magnitude of his racing achievements and the compelling nature of his character – became more widely known and appreciated. As the years went by and more racing history was made, and as it began to be covered widely by the international media, his place at top of the pantheon of the sport's personalities was confirmed and celebrated. When statistics were compiled and compared, a much wider audience became aware of his remarkable record of success in motorsport. In the world at large, only a few dedicated enthusiasts had known about his fabulous exploits in many years of racing in South America before he even came to Europe.

In a career spanning 20 years, Juan competed in 200 races, winning 78 times, finishing second 69 times and retiring on 53 occasions. He won races in eighteen countries, driving over a dozen makes of cars in half a dozen different categories of motorsport. In seven full seasons of Formula 1 racing, he contested 51 Grands Prix, starting from pole position 29 times, from the front row 48 times, and setting 23 fastest race laps. He finished on the podium in 35 races and scored 24 victories. In 1950 and 1953 he finished second in the standings; otherwise he won five World Championships, in 1951, 1954, 1955, 1956 and 1957. Having been such a fixture on the scene for such a long time, and such 'a natural gentleman, a driver without parallel', Gregor Grant felt that 'his departure from the circuits leaves a gap that may never be filled. It is to be sincerely hoped that his association with the sport he loves will not be severed, and that this fine man will continue to be seen around the places where his name will be forever remembered.'

Temptations to race again were certainly put in Juan's way, as he admitted. 'They tried to get me all enthusiastic about driving again, but very painfully I managed to get racing out of my system, though I never tired of going back for visits.' Indeed, following his retirement Juan increasingly assumed a role as an unofficial roving ambassador for motorsport. He travelled around the world, making appearances as the guest of honour at races, giving driving demonstrations, participating in parades in historic cars, opening exhibits, attending ceremonies, charity events, receptions and banquets given in his honour, unveiling statues and commemorative plaques celebrating his achievements, and so on. He was, over the years, the recipient of a plethora of awards, decorations, honours and distinctions. In 1958, he was made an Officer of the Order of Merit of the Italian Republic, with the rank of Commendatore, which was in 1969 raised to the rank of Grand Officer. Also in 1958, he was declared by the French Academy of Sport as the Achiever of the World's Most Outstanding Sporting Feat. In 1976, he was awarded the Order of Merit of the Federal Republic of

Germany, with the rank of Commander. In 1980, he was made an Honorary Member of the Fédération Internationale du Sport Automobile, the governing body of world motorsport, and the members of the International Racing Press Association voted him the Best Driver of All Time (Juan received 278 votes to Jackie Stewart's 255, Jim Clark's 253, Stirling Moss's 99 and Niki Lauda's 66).

When he wasn't travelling abroad, Juan attended to his varied business interests in Argentina, which prospered and made him a very wealthy man. 'I could easily have had businesses and lived on in Europe,' he pointed out, 'but I was always wanting to go back to my own people. Life was better among family and friends.' His dispute with the government was forgotten, and he became for his countrymen a symbol of hard work being rewarded by financial success. He invested in property, cattle ranches and farms, and became the biggest landowner in Balcarce. His affiliation with Mercedes-Benz grew stronger, he opened other dealerships around the country, and was eventually appointed chairman of the board of Mercedes-Benz Argentina, after which for many years he held the position of honorary chairman. He was still an excellent salesman, and among his biggest group of customers were the taxi drivers of Buenos Aires, nearly all of whom bought Mercedes diesel cars. Despite his strong ties with the German manufacturer, Juan was also at various times appointed to the board of directors of General Motors and Renault in Argentina. His services as a consultant were also much in demand by car manufacturers. Mercedes valued him as an adviser when developing new models, as did the Italian automotive stylists Bertone and Pinin Farina. When Lamborghini developed its new Miura sports car, Juan was the first person outside the firm to drive it.

Another major source of income for Juan was from companies wishing to cash in on his celebrity status and use him as a figurehead in advertising and publicity campaigns. Because he felt it would be dishonest to endorse a company or product he didn't know, he would go to great lengths to personally evaluate them. Before signing on with Goodyear to advertise a new type of tyre, for instance, he went to the company's Luxembourg factory and watched them being made. He then had the tyres mounted on a car and tore around a test track at 125mph for several hours. After subjecting them to this rigorous test, he agreed to advertise them. Testimony to his all-around appeal to both advertisers and consumers was the fact that Juan was always closely allied with rival tyre manufacturer Pirelli, on whose tyres he had won many races.

Despite his lifelong involvement with cars, Juan drove hundreds of thousands of miles without a licence to do so. When he learnt to drive as a boy in Balcarce, in the interior of the country, a licence was not required and very few people had them. For years, the only driving document he had was a sporting one, given him annually by the ACA and entitling him to drive racing cars. It was only in 1961 that he obtained an official permit to conduct vehicles on public roads, though the piece of paper did not affect careful driving habits that were deeply ingrained. 'Someone who is driving should never let themselves be distracted,' Juan said. 'At one time or another passengers riding with me must have wondered if I was rude or deaf, as I didn't reply to questions when driving. When I drive I concentrate on that alone. There are those who go out on the road and admire the countryside and point things out to those with them. When something catches my attention during a journey, I stop at once. A driver should be concentrating only on what he, his car, and other drivers are doing.'

When it came to offering advice to would-be racing drivers, Juan was exceedingly generous with his time. Though the death of his protégé Onofre Marimón remained one of his saddest memories, Juan's love of the sport was such that he was always willing to offer encouragement to those he felt sincerely shared his passion for it. It was natural that he should help promote the career of his nephew, Juan Manuel Fangio III (the son of Juan's younger brother Toto), who became quite a successful professional driver, but Juan also went out of his way to assist a completely unknown driver.

In 1959, he was approached in a Mar del Plata restaurant by 26-year-old Juan Manuel Bordeau, who said he wanted to go to Europe and see how far he could progress as a racing driver. To Bordeau's surprise, the great Fangio took him under his wing, inviting him to accompany him on one of his trips to Italy, where he introduced him to influential racing people as his new protégé. Under the world champion's guidance and through his connections, Bordeau made rapid progress and was on the verge of making it into Formula 1 only to have his promising career effectively ended by injuries received in a sports car crash in England.

What struck Bordeau most were the qualities of Fangio the man, whose lessons in life he found more valuable than the advice he gave about the intricacies of racing. Juan often invited Bordeau to travel with him in Italy, where he witnessed several character-revealing episodes. Despite his busy schedule, Juan was happy to do favours for those less fortunate than him. On one occasion, Bordeau recalled, Juan interrupted a journey to find some rheumatism pills he had promised to get for a boy who was ill back in Balcarce. Another time, they drove all around Milan looking for a wheelchair for an invalid of Juan's acquaintance. Bordeau also once accompanied Juan on a 250-mile journey to a small village in the mountains above Turin where they visited for a few hours the humble home of a very poor family Juan had befriended during his racing days. 'He decides to act a certain way, and then he acts,' said

Bordeau. 'He never leaves anything undone, he never puts anything off, not even for an hour. If something has to be done, he does it. What's more, he never complains. You never hear him say that it's cold, that it's hot, that he's sleepy, that he's tired. He hardly ever says what he feels. He's a stoic. He opens his mouth in order to breathe. He will always give you a hand, push you forward with a pat on the back, saying, "Don't give up, old friend, don't give up." '

In Milan, Bordeau noted, Juan still stayed at the modest Hotel Colombia, which he treated as a home from home and where the staff fawned over their old friend and the elderly chambermaid treated him like her son. Juan said he felt more at ease here than in such prestigious establishments as the Principe di Savoia Hotel, where he had turned down a sumptuous suite offered to him free of charge for as long as he wanted by the hotel's very rich owner Count Giovanni Volpi di Misurata. 'Whether he is with rich or poor people,' Bordeau continued, 'Fangio never changes. I have seen him with the humblest and poorest Italians, and with Count Volpi and with the Agnelli family in Turin. He chats easily with them all. Power doesn't impress him, and his respect for people has nothing to do with their wealth. He particularly respects those who do plain and simple work: the mechanic, the carpenter, the builder – which his father was.'

Juan's beloved Papa and Mama had continued to work until near the end of their long lives in Balcarce. They didn't need the income, since their famous son shared his wealth with them to a most generous degree, as he did with his brothers and sisters, but they possessed a highly developed work ethic, which was one of the several admirable traits Juan had inherited from his parents. Their influence on Juan's character was noted by another of the racing people Juan became involved with after he retired. In 1966, Juan agreed to help promote a Formula 3 team sponsored by *Automundo* magazine and run by Enrico Vannini, an Argentine journalist and entrepreneur and a friend of the Fangio family. When Juan travelled in Europe with the team, Vannini was deeply impressed at how he pitched in to help with even the most menial chores, such as sweeping the floor of the garage, as well as taking engines apart and repairing them himself. But what most struck Vannini were Juan's mental strengths. 'One of Fangio's greatest virtues is his intelligence,' he said. 'And I often wondered where that intelligence came from. Don't forget, Fangio only went as far as the sixth grade in school. I've studied a lot more than he has, but I've learnt more from Juan than any teacher. One of his fundamental abilities is to reduce to their proper size any great economic, financial, political, family or social problem. To get the view into perspective, he narrows his eyes like a countryman, to see further, to where the city dweller's eyes don't reach, and with amazing speed he reduces the problem to the bare minimum by means of a mental capacity others simply don't have. Where does all this come from? I say it comes first from an intelligence he was endowed with by nature. To this, you must add the wisdom he inherited from his mother, and his father's high principles. And no doubt the way he was brought up went a long way to making Juan the man he is.'

Loreto Fangio, who finally retired from the building trade when he was 71, passed away in 1980, shortly after his wife Herminia. They were a loving couple until the end, which brought home to their devoted son a sadness over his own failure to have a family. His relationship with Beba Espinosa ended shortly after he retired from racing. 'I didn't marry, firstly because I loved motor racing so much, and secondly because we all make mistakes in life,' he said. 'It is true that at one time I knew a woman I might have married. I believed she loved me, and that I loved her, but because of our stupidity, we ended it.

We were not married, but we spent twenty years together. We parted in 1960, but not because I wanted to. When I retired from racing I thought, "Now we can start a happy life without problems." But something changed. We were beginning to argue, and the arguments got a bit rough. When a man and a woman lose mutual respect, the time has come to finish. One day we had a discussion, and she said if I didn't like being with her I could leave. So I left.' Their parting was acrimonious, though Juan gave Beba a generous financial settlement. When they were together, he had allowed her son Cacho to use his name, but after Beba and Juan parted company Cacho tried and failed to have his name legally changed to Fangio in a court of law.

There would be more women in Juan's life, as there had been on occasion during his time with Beba, though his trysts with others in his racing years were carefully kept secret from the fiercely jealous 'Mrs Fangio' by a few trusted team-mates and friends who were aware of Juan's roving eye. Always discreet about such matters, he would invariably respond to questions from outsiders about his female friendships with a raised eyebrow and a sly smile, and remain silent. His inscrutability only fuelled rumours about romantic relationships with women such as the glamourous Belgian lady racer Gilberte Thirion, and Juan took with him to the grave the truth about whether or not he ever had an affair with Evita Perón. His keen interest in women, and theirs in him, remained even in his later years. In 1991, he came to London to attend a function introducing a book about his career, sponsored by Mercedes-Benz and Pirelli and written by Stirling Moss with the racing historian Doug Nye. In the audience at the book launch, and carefully kept separate from one another by knowing friends of Juan's, were no fewer than three girlfriends of the Maestro, then in his 80th year, the twinkle in his eye undimmed.

But his real love affairs, as Stirling Moss noted, were 'his affairs with motor cars'. In 1970, Juan used his influence to have an enclosed race circuit built on the outskirts of Balcarce. His main motivation was to provide a safer place for racing following the deaths of several competitors and spectators in an open road race around the town in 1968. Juan wanted the circuit named 'Balcarce', but he was overruled and it became the 'Juan Manuel Fangio Regional Autodrome'. But to really celebrate his love of racing, not long after he retired Juan began thinking about establishing a museum in Balcarce where the townspeople to whom he felt he owed so much could see some of the cars, trophies and mementos from his racing career. In particular, he wanted young people to learn how it was possible for someone from the humblest of origins, by means of struggle and sacrifice and no small amount of luck, to achieve the tangible results the museum would display. He wanted it to show a range of cars, beginning with those in which he'd started racing and continuing through to examples of the Formula 1 cars he drove.

In 1979, a committee of influential citizens was set up in Balcarce to develop the Fangio museum project, and over the following years it gained momemtum to extend far beyond Juan's original idea. A disused civic building in the centre of Balcarce, just around the corner from the Fangio family home, was elaborately converted into a showcase for Juan's career, as well as a wider range of automotive matters. Arranged over six display levels connected by a spiralling ramp in a central atrium, the Technological and Cultural Centre and Juan Manuel Fangio Motor Museum was opened in 1986 and heralded as one of the finest specialised museums in Latin America. In addition to more than 500 trophies and a huge assortment of memorabilia from Juan's career, there were over 50 cars on display, ranging from his primitive Negrita and the famous Balcarce Chev coupé to the Alfa Romeo Tipo 159 Alfetta and the Mercedes-Benz W196, both loaned by the manufacturers in honour of the Boy from Balcarce who had brought them so much glory. 'The museum in my town represents what little I am able to pay back what I owe,' Juan said. 'Through it I express my gratitude to the people of Balcarce, to my family, to the friends of childhood and youth. Only through them did I get to where I am now.'

One main reason why Juan was so pleased to see his dream of a museum become reality was that when he awoke in hospital after a second serious heart attack he recognised that the museum was the only unfinished business left in a life about whose fragility he was becoming increasingly aware. His first heart attack had occurred in Buenos Aires in 1970. He had been stricken with an acute pain in his chest as he was about to set off after a particularly stressful day at the office to watch an evening football game at the River Plate stadium. Instead, he was taken immediately to the Guemes Sanatorium, where a cardiac team gave him a blood transfusion, assessed the damage and gave Juan some advice. 'The doctors told me to take my foot off the gas a bit, not to stop taking exercise but to deal with problems and approach life in a calmer and less hurried way.' Juan's heart then held out until December 1981, when he suffered a second attack while demonstrating a Mercedes-Benz in a historic car event in the capital of the Arab Emirates, Dubai. From West Germany, Mercedes sent a medically equipped executive jet with a doctor on board and flew Juan back to the heart clinic in Buenos Aires. There, it was determined that the previous attack had scarred his heart and restricted the blood supply. Juan was referred to Dr Rene Favaloro, a renowned Argentine heart surgeon, who recommended a bypass operation.

Since the doctor and his team had already performed a successful double bypass operation on his brother Toto, Juan willingly placed himself in their hands. He compared it to 'when one's car has been worked on by a very good team of mechanics. You go into the race calmly, not worrying about what might go wrong. I was in the hands of a good heart team. I thought of it as another race to be run. I went out under the anaesthetic one day and woke up three days later with a new engine.' In fact, he had very serious surgery, a delicate and complicated quintuple heart bypass operation, and he remained in intensive care in the sanatorium for some time. Dr Favaloro and his team of doctors and nurses would not take payment for their services, feeling that it was reward enough to have restored to health Argentina's most famous citizen.

After the death of his parents, Juan's next family loss came when his elder brother José died of lung cancer. Juan had been prepared for the deaths of his elderly parents, but José's death, a harsh reminder of his own mortality, Juan said, was the worst experience of his life. He became increasingly more family-conscious, and more frequently visited the Fangio home in Balcarce, where Toto and his family lived and where the clan of brothers and sisters and their offspring gathered as often as possible. Sunday lunch was a particularly happy occasion for Juan, who would take time out from playing with the throng of children to look fondly at the fading photographs on the walls of the dining-room. They ranged from baby christening photos, including his own from 1911, to family portraits of the happy children and their proud Mama and Papa. There was a photo of Juan with his football team, another taken during his confinement with pleurisy, another with him in his army uniform, and several of him at the wheel of various racing cars.

Since racing was for Juan in many ways a metaphor for life, after having raced so far for so long he remained philosophical about taking a chequered flag for a final time. 'I think the life of a man who has not achieved his aims must be very miserable when death approaches. Also that of a man who says on his deathbed, "What mistakes I made in my life!" And we shouldn't believe we are not going to die. In very long races, I learnt to take things in stages, because if you thought about the total number of laps to go it would have seemed much longer and you would feel defeated before you started. So you have to look at targets: first as far as there, then to the next stage, and so on. It is the same in life. When I was young I thought that the longest years of one's life must be when one is old. Now I know that this is not so, and that life is a hill that you have to climb and climb. And when you reach the top, you want to stay there, as you have no brakes for the way down. But life runs at great speed. I always drove with prudence and serenity, not like an ill-tempered person going to the cemetery. I always wanted to finish first in everything, but in death I preferred to finish last.'

During the last couple of years of his life, Juan's health deteriorated quickly. He developed kidney problems that required frequent dialysis treatment. In mid-July 1995, three weeks after his 84th birthday, he was taken to hospital in Balcarce suffering from severe pneumonia. On 17 July, at four o'clock in the morning, Juan Manuel Fangio died.

'I was playing golf in England when I heard the news about his death,' Sir Jackie Stewart remembers. 'The funeral was the next day, and I moved heaven and earth to get there. I finally made it to Buenos Aires, where Stirling Moss had also arrived, and we were whisked through immigration and flown by private plane to Balcarce, where Fangio's brother Toto was waiting for us. We changed into dark suits and only just made it in time to see Fangio lying in state in the church in the main square. The family asked Stirling and me to help carry the coffin, along with Toto, José Froilán González, Carlos Reutemann and the president of Mercedes-Benz Argentina. We attended the service in the church, which was incredibly packed with mourners, and then the six of us carried the coffin down the aisle and outside to the hearse. I'll never forget what happened that day. There must have been 10,000 people gathered outside in the square, standing there in total silence. Absolutely amazing. And suddenly they just started to clap – 10,000 people clapping in slow motion. I mean, overwhelming emotion, absolutely riveting. They were all in tears – 10,000 people in tears – and they all just wanted to touch the coffin of Fangio. I would never have forgiven myself had I missed that. It was one of the most important things I have ever done in my life. I was an enormous fan of his. More than a fan, a great admirer of the manner in which he conducted his life, presented himself and represented the sport. Juan Manuel Fangio was very special to me, as he was to who knows how many millions more.'

He was one of the most important people in the life of Sir Stirling Moss. 'I was a pallbearer at his funeral because I respected him so much, to the point of almost loving him, like my father. For me, Juan was like a second father. Not only was he a great driver, he was a very lovely man. He had a dignity about him. The Italians have the word "simpatico" – a very kind and warm person to speak to. Of course I couldn't speak to him because he could only understand a few words of English and I only knew a little Spanish and Italian. We talked with our hands. But we had a very close relationship in our love for what we were doing – motor racing. Of course, he was by far the best of us all. I mean, here was a man who could take a wheelbarrow and make it fly like Concorde. As impressive as he was, he was the nicest guy imaginable. Most of us who drove quickly were bastards, but he was unique. I can't think of any facets of Juan's character which one wouldn't like to have in one's own. He was such a humble person – which is of course an unknown word today. For me, Fangio the man is even greater than the myth.'

Chapter Eighteen

The Legend Admired

AFTER HE RETIRED, when he was in Europe, he would often take the opportunity to visit a Grand Prix. On these occasions, years and years after his last race, his presence was still magical, and 'Fangio!' was the word that rippled through the crowd and along the pit lane. He would make a tour of the pits with various officials, pausing to greet familiar faces from his old teams and to shake hands with drivers like Stirling Moss, Jim Clark, Graham Hill, Jackie Stewart, Alain Prost or Ayrton Senna. They all loved him. Fangio was Fangio. There was no need to embellish his name. It was powerful enough on its own.

Denis Jenkinson (journalist)

More than 30 years after he last acknowledged a chequered flag, fans who had never seen him would jostle to glimpse the unprepossessing little Argentine who, by most available yardsticks, had been the greatest racing driver of all time. His achievements made him a legend, but his modesty made him loved.

Richard Williams (journalist)

He commanded awe. When he entered a room, it went quiet. His whole bearing was almost like royalty, but it was accompanied by considerable modesty.

Tony Brooks (driver)

I don't think I knew a more softly spoken man, yet he still had real presence. You were always aware of him when he entered a room, even if you couldn't see him.

Phil Hill (driver)

You came into a room full of racing personalities, world champions and so on, and then Fangio comes in. All eyes turn towards him, all else is forgotten.

Sir Jackie Stewart (driver)

The great thing about him is that he won five world titles in four different cars and he never had a row with anyone.

John Cooper (team owner)

His manners were as refined as his driving. As a competitor, he was necessarily ruthless, but he was never callous. He was revered by his contemporaries, none of whom ever presumed to question his place on the pedestal.

Nigel Roebuck (journalist)

He was recognised not only as the best driver, but also the fairest. I never heard a single complaint about his behaviour, in or out of the cockpit, and there aren't many world champions you can say that about.

Tony Brooks (driver)

He was always so willing to share what he knew. It was a heck of a quality. At the Nürburgring, he once asked me what gear I was using through a certain section. I told him third; he said try fourth. I did, and I picked up three seconds.

Phil Hill (driver)

He was always the leading figure and centre of attraction among the travelling entourage of drivers, mechanics, organisers and journalists. But never did he allow this to affect him in any way, never did he become a prima donna, and always he somehow succeeded in shunning the publicity which nowadays is so often thrust upon public figures and idols. In private life he was the best, the most loyal and sporting friend, unanimously respected and loved by all the drivers, who do not generally waste time in being nice about one another.

Olivier Merlin (Fangio biographer)

Fangio, the driver, is a man who loves cars with an almost physical passion, who considers sport like a religion, and to whom speed is an expression of human beauty. Fangio is a born gentleman, in every meaning of the word. I have never heard him raise his voice or be aggressive to gain the upper hand in a discussion. Fangio would stay calm and control himself even in situations which made others shout with anger. He has never been a snob. He is natural with everybody. He has no inferiority complex. For the former modest mechanic, shaking hands with a ruling monarch is as pleasing as shaking hands with a pump attendant, so long as the handshakes are sincere.

Marcello Giambertone (Fangio manager and biographer)

Anyone who has been fortunate enough to talk to Fangio, or to be close enough to him to observe his eyes, cannot have helped but notice their remarkable sharpness. There is no doubt that eyesight plays a very vital part in Fangio's success. There are times when he appears to be taking no interest in his surroundings and appears to be in a sleepy and lethargic mood, but watch his eyes closely and you will see that they are observing everything going on around him. Though he moves his head very slowly, mostly due to the neck injury he received in the crash at Monza in 1952, and in normal everyday life his whole body moves slowly, his eyes will flash from one thing to another with great rapidity, which is made all the more noticeable by these slow body movements.

Denis Jenkinson (journalist)

It is his eyes, more than any other single feature, that distinguish him from his fellows. He possesses steely blue, penetrating, rapid eyes shielded by heavy eyebrows, which can also occasionally, merely by winking an eye, give some remarkably youthful glances.

Olivier Merlin (Fangio biographer)

He was of average height, stocky of build, slope-shouldered, thinning hair. He walked with a sort of rolling, bandy-legged gait. His voice was traditionally described as thin and reedy. Like any description of Fangio, it falls short of the truth because what must be immediately understood about Fangio is that his ordinariness is an extraordinary disguise. And all the more extraordinary because it is totally seamless. Never can you catch Fangio out of character. He is completely what he seems to be, wholly centred within his own being. No quirks for the camera. He is modest, direct and without artifice. He is humble in the exalted sense of the word.

Denise McCluggage (journalist)

I admire him so much because he has been a great champion. He was so calm I used to say he had distilled water instead of blood in his veins. A fantastic boy, not only for his great class but his simplicity. Few of them know how to remain themselves, once having attained fame and success. Their heads seem to expand and they can't wear their crash hats naturally. But Fangio, who could give all the young ones lessons even today, has stayed simple, sincere and loyal. He is a great gentleman, in spite of his modest origins, and I am very fond of him.

Louis Chiron (driver and race official)

I got his autograph as a wee lad, and when I started racing he was there one year when I won at Monaco and he came up to me after and spoke to me in his quiet, squeaky voice. Through an interpreter, he said he had watched me and I had driven a good race, not made any mistakes, all the things you want to hear. Another year when I won at Monaco, we went to dinner with him and some friends in Menton. And he drove, a Mercedes it was, and Helen and I were sitting in the back, and I couldn't believe I was in a car being driven by Juan Manuel Fangio.

Sir Jackie Stewart (driver)

I had the opportunity to meet Fangio in Vienna in the 1960s as he opened the Racing Car Show. Later, I had the honour of driving with him in a Mercedes 6.3 – it was a 350hp touring car, a heavy touring car – around the old Nürburgring. This was about 1967, I think, and he told me about his greatest race there ten years earlier, when he drove the Maserati and beat loads of young guys. He showed me where he had cut the grass and where he was drifting nearly to the trees, and it was a fantastic lap – quite mad, really. As he was talking to me he was driving very quickly, and the tyres on the Mercedes were smoking. But I was not afraid and felt very comfortable because he was so relaxed behind the wheel. I drove with him again in 1984, when Mercedes was introducing a new model of car and he was demonstrating them on country roads in Austria. By this time he was 73 years old and he was wearing glasses and looking his age. But Fangio seemed as fast as ever, and he was still really quick in the way he drove, braked, shifted gears, accelerated, turned the steering wheel. It was for me significant for this man to be able to still have such sensitivity, such feeling for the car in every move he made. You could see his outstanding class. And then we arrived near this village and rain started and the road was really slippery, and we drove at 120kph around a corner and suddenly one of these farmer's trucks was crossing the road right in front of us. Fangio never panicked and hardly slowed down. He braked a bit, slid the Mercedes right and left, corrected the slide and went easily around the farmer, whose eyes we could see were bulging. Fangio had a smile on his face, and he was murmuring something in Spanish. For me, this was fantastic to see such brilliant reaction time, really marvellous. This was the Maestro at work.

Helmut Zwikl (journalist)

He was the most natural driver around at the time. He was so good that he could produce outstanding performances without exceeding his personal safety margins. Some of his qualities were anticipation, judgement, sensitivity in his hands and the seat of his pants, and of course great mental strength. He read a race very carefully and drove very intelligently. He was always one step ahead. But when you try to analyse exactly what gave him his edge, you come up against a stone wall.

Tony Brooks (driver)

The greatness of the Maestro lay in a combination of many things: flawless timing, great speed, near-perfect judgement, phenomenal sensory and extra-sensory perception, self-discipline, patience and wisdom in the heat of battle, and an amazing ability to conserve equipment. These are the abilities one can put into words, but the degree to which he possessed them is indescribable, as are a collection of other abilities which can't even be identified.

Marie Heglar (journalist)

You could see that he was a very, very accurate driver. Lap after lap, if you were to put a coin on the road, he would put his tyres on that coin lap after lap. He was extremely precise. But the real reason why he was so special I could not see. However, in those days when they were sliding their cars, Fangio was of course fantastic at that. I remember I once had a rather boozy evening with Jean Behra and I asked him why Fangio was the better driver. Jean said that while he could slide his car up to about 200kph, Fangio could slide his at much faster speeds and hold his slide for considerable distances. That suggests he had more car control, probably through better reflexes. I don't think Fangio had more bravery than Behra, who after all died from an overdose of bravery. It's just that while Behra thought he knew his limit, Fangio's limit was higher.

Jabby Crombac (journalist)

To begin with, El Chueco is a driver born, just as there are great musicians, painters and sculptors born. He is a natural with a highly developed sixth sense which behind the wheel resolves itself in a combination of super-sensitive balance, hair-trigger reaction and faultless judgement. He seems touched by magic, almost infallible and invulnerable behind the wheel of a race car. His eye is dead true, his evaluation of chances a cold, detached, objective process, entirely unaffected by feelings of the moment. The secret of his very high percentage of finishes is that he knows instinctively just how much any machine will take. The calm and casual style that cloaks El Chueco's absolute mastery behind the wheel is actually a carry-over of his everyday existence, from which all unnecessary activity has been eliminated. He is the most relaxed individual imaginable, and, partly perhaps because of his low blood pressure, he simply does not know the meaning of emotional crisis.

John Bentley (journalist)

At the height of his racing career, adjectives singing his praises had as good as run out. When he was nearer 50 than 40, and beating drivers young enough to have been his sons at the time of his fifth world title in 1957, his feats put in the shade what those with long memories recalled of Nuvolari, Varzi, Rosemeyer, Caracciola and Wimille. At that age, drawing from his vast experience and knowledge, he was able to remain one step ahead of anything that happened, to anticipate his rivals' manoeuvres and beat them by whatever cunning or stratagem was necessary.

Roberto Carozzo (Fangio biographer)

For his admirers, the 'Old Man' symbolised the heroic age when racing drivers went about their business in cork helmets, polo shirts, string-backed gloves and suede loafers, forearms bare to the wind, faces streaked with hot oil. It was an age when chivalry played a part, and when the physical danger was such that each race seemed to thin the ranks of the participants. Perhaps the two were not unconnected.

Richard Williams (journalist)

There is no way you can compare me with him. What he achieved, at the wheel of fairly basic cars in just shirt sleeves and with no helmet, hardly bears thinking about. It wasn't even the same sport. No, I could never do what he did. That man was a hero.

Michael Schumacher (driver)

Racing Record

NB Formula 1 World Championship races in bold type

1938

27 March: Asociación de Fomento de Nechochea – Ford V8 – 7th

13 November: 400 Kilómetros des Tres Arroyos – Ford V8 – 8th

1939

7 May: Automóvil Club Argentina filial La Plata Circuito – Ford V8 – 8th

19–20 October: Gran Premio Argentino de Carretera – Chevrolet TC (Turismo de Carretera) – 22nd

29 October–25 November: Gran Premio Extraordinario – Chevrolet TC – 5th

19 December: Mil Millas Argentinas – Chevrolet TC – 13th

1940

27 September–12 October: Gran Premio Internacional del Norte – Chevrolet TC – 1st

14 December: Mil Millas Argentinas – Chevrolet TC – 8th

1941

22–29 June: Gran Premio Presidente Getulio Vargas – Chevrolet TC – 1st

13 December: Mil Millas Argentinas – Chevrolet TC – 1st

1942

21 January–3 February: Gran Premio del Sur – Chevrolet TC – 10th

2 April: Circuito Mar y Sierras – Chevrolet TC – 1st

1947

15 February: Premio Ciudad de Buenos Aires – Ford T-Chevrolet – 3rd

1 March: Automóvil Club Argentina filial Rosario – Ford T-Chevrolet – 1st

1 March: Automóvil Club Argentina filial Rosario – Ford T-Chevrolet – 6th

6 April: Premio Ciudad de Necochea – Ford T-Chevrolet – retired

20 April: Premio Vendimia, Circuito Parque General S. Martin – Ford T-Chevrolet – 3rd

13 July: Premio Fraile Muerto, Bell Ville, Córdoba – Volpi-Rickenbacker – 6th

13 July: Premio Ciudad de Bell Ville, Córdoba – Volpi-Rickenbacker – 5th

17 August: Gran Premio Ciudad de Montevideo – Volpi-Rickenbacker – 1st

17 August: Gran Premio Ciudad de Montevideo – Volpi-Chevrolet – retired

20 September: Gran Premio Primavera, Circuito 'El Torréon' –
Volpi-Chevrolet – 1st

21 September: Gran Premio Primavera, Circuito 'El Torréon' –
Volpi-Chevrolet – 5th

29 October: Doble Sierra de la Ventana – Chevrolet TC – 1st

22–30 November: Gran Premio Internacional de Carreteras –
Chevrolet TC – 6th

21 December: Mil Millas Argentinas – Chevrolet TC – retired

1948

17 January: Premio Ciudad de Buenos Aires, Circuito de
Palermo – Maserati 1500cc – retired

25 January: Premio Ciudad de Mar del Plata, Circuito 'El
Torreón' – Maserati 1500cc – 5th

1 February: Premio Ciudad de Rosario, Circuito Parque Independencia – Simca-Gordini 1200cc – 8th

14 February: Premio Dalmiro Varela Castex, Circuito de
Palermo – Simca-Gordini 1200cc – 8th

28–29 February: Vuelta de Pringles – Chevrolet TC – 1st

21 March: Premio Otoño, Circuito de Palermo – Volpi-
Chevrolet – 1st

28 March: 100 Millas Playas de Necochea – Volpi-Chevrolet –
3rd

11 April: Circuito Mar y Sierras – Chevrolet TC – 11th

24–25 April: Vuelta de Entre Rios – Chevrolet TC – 1st

2 May: Premio Ciudad de Mercedes – Volpi-Chevrolet – 1st

18 July: 2nd Coupé des Petite Cylindres, Reims, France –
Simca-Gordini 1430cc – retired

18 July: Grand Prix de L'Automobile Club de France, Reims, France – Simca-Gordini 1430cc – retired

20 October: Gran Premio de la América del Sur – Simca-Gordini 1430cc – retired

1949

16 January: Mil Millas Argentinas – Chevrolet TC – 2nd

29 January: Gran Premio Internacional Juan Domingo Perón, Circuito de Palermo – Maserati 4CLT/48 – 4th

6 February: Premio Jean-Pierre Wimille, Circuito de Palermo – Volpi-Chevrolet – 1st

13 February: Premio Ciudad de Rosario, Circuito Parque Independencia – Simca-Gordini 1430cc – retired

27 February: Premio Ciudad de Mar del Plata, Circuito 'El Torreón' – Maserati 4CLT/48 – 1st

20 March: Premio Fraile Muerto, Bell Ville, Córdoba – Volpi-Chevrolet – 1st

3 April: Grand Prix of San Remo, Circuit Ospedaletti, Italy – Maserati 4CLT/48 – 1st

18 April: Grand Prix of Pau, Circuit Parc Beaumont, France – Maserati 4CLT/48 – 1st

8 May: Grand Prix of Roussillon, Perpignan, France – Maserati 4CLT/48 – 1st

22 May: Grand Prix of Marseille, Circuit Parc Borély, France – Simca-Gordini 1430cc – 1st

2 June: Grand Prix of Rome, Circuit Caracalla, Italy – Maserati A6GCS – retired

19 June: Grand Prix of Belgium, Circuit Spa-Francorchamps – Maserati 4CLT/48 – retired

26 June: Grand Prix of Monza, Autodromo, Italy – Ferrari Tipo 166 F2 – 1st

10 July: Grand Prix of Albi, France – Maserati 4CLT/48 – 1st

17 July: 3rd Coupé des Petite Cylindres, Reims, France – Ferrari Tipo 166 F2 – retired

17 July: Grand Prix de L'Automobile Club de France, Reims, France – Maserati 4CLT/48 – retired

5–27 November: Gran Premio de la Republica de Carreteras – Chevrolet TC – 2nd

18 December: Premio Juan Domingo Perón, Circuito de Palermo – Ferrari Tipo 125 – 2nd

1950

8 January: Premio Maria Eva Duarte de Perón, Circuito de Palermo – Ferrari Tipo 166C – 4th

15 January: Premio Ciudad de Mar del Plata, Circuito 'El Torreón' – Ferrari Tipo 166C – retired

22 January: Premio Ciudad de Rosario, Circuito Parque Independencia – Ferrari Tipo 166C – retired

19 March: Grand Prix of Marseille, Circuit Parc Borély, France – Ferrari Tipo 166C – 3rd

10 April: Grand Prix of Pau, Circuit Parc Beaumont, France – Maserati 4CLT/50 – 1st

16 April: Grand Prix of San Remo, Circuit Ospedaletti, Italy – Alfa Romeo Tipo 158 – 1st

23 April: Mille Miglia, Italy – Alfa Romeo 6C/2500 Exp. (Sport) – 3rd

7 May: Grand Prix of Modena, Italy – Ferrari Tipo 166F2 – retired

13 May: **British Grand Prix,** Silverstone, England – Alfa Romeo Tipo 158 – retired

21 May: **Grand Prix de Monaco** – Alfa Romeo Tipo 158 – 1st

28 May: Grand Prix of Monza, Autodromo, Italy – Ferrari Tipo 166F2 – 1st

4 June: **Grosser Preis der Schweiz,** Bremgarten, Switzerland – Alfa Romeo Tipo 158 – retired

11 June: Circuit of the Ramparts, Angoulême, France – Maserati 4CLT/A6GCS – 1st

18 June: **Grote Prijs van Belgie,** Spa-Francorchamps, Belgium – Alfa Romeo Tipo 158 – 1st

24–25 June: Le Mans 24 Hours, France, partnered by José Froilán González – Simca-Gordini 1490cc Sport – retired

2 July: **Grand Prix de L'ACF,** Reims, France – Alfa Romeo Tipo 158 – 1st

9 July: Grand Prix of Bari, Italy – Alfa Romeo Tipo 158 – 2nd

16 July: Grand Prix of Albi, France – Maserati 4CLT/50 – retired (second in Heat 1)

23 July: Grand Prix of Holland, Zandvoort – Maserati 4CLT/50 – retired

30 July: Grand Prix of the Nations, Geneva, Switzerland – Alfa Romeo Tipo 158 – 1st

15 August: Grand Prix of Pescara, Italy – Alfa Romeo Tipo 158 – 1st

26 August: BRDC International Trophy, Silverstone, England – Alfa Romeo Tipo 158 – 2nd

3 September: **Gran Premio d'Italia,** Monza, Italy – Alfa Romeo Tipo 158 – retired

12 November: Premio Ciudad de Paraná, Circuito Parque Uriquiza – Ferrari Tipo 166C – 1st

18 December: Gran Premio Presidente Arturo Alessandri Palma, Chile – Ferrari Tipo 166C – 1st

24 December: 500 Millas Argentinas, Rafaela, Santa Fe – Talbot Lago 4500cc – 1st

1950 World Championship standings: Farina 30, Fangio 27, Fagioli 24, Rosier 13, Ascari 11

1951

18 February: Premio Ciudad de Buenos Aires, Circuito Costanera Norte – Mercedes-Benz W163 – 3rd

24 February: Premio Eva Perón, Circuito Costanera Norte – Mercedes-Benz W163 – retired

5 May: BRDC International Trophy, Silverstone, England – Alfa Romeo Tipo 159 – final abandoned (first in Heat 1)

13 May: Grand Prix of Monza, Autodromo, Italy – Ferrari Tipo 166 F2 – retired

20 May: Grand Prix of Paris, Circuit Bois de Boulogne, France – Simca-Gordini 1490cc – retired

27 May: **Grosser Preis der Schweiz**, Bremgarten, Switzerland – Alfa Romeo Tipo 159 – 1st

17 June: **Grote Prijs van Belgie**, Spa-Francorchamps, Belgium – Alfa Romeo Tipo 159 – 9th

23–24 June: Le Mans 24 Hours, France, partnered by Louis Rosier – Talbot Lago 4500cc (Sport) – retired

1 July: **Grand Prix de L'ACF**, Reims, France – Alfa Romeo Tipo 159 – 1st

14 July: **British Grand Prix**, Silverstone, England – Alfa Romeo Tipo 159 – 2nd

29 July: **Grosser Preis von Deutschland**, Nürburgring, West Germany – Alfa Romeo Tipo 159 – 2nd

2 September: Grand Prix of Bari, Italy – Alfa Romeo Tipo 159 – 1st

16 September: **Gran Premio d'Italia**, Monza, Italy – Alfa Romeo Tipo 159 – retired

28 October: **Gran Premio de España**, Pedralbes, Barcelona, Spain – Alfa Romeo Tipo 159 – 1st

1951 World Championship standings: Fangio 31, Ascari 25, González 19, Villoresi 15, Taruffi 10

1952

13 January: Gran Premio Ciudad de São Paulo, Interlagos, Brazil – Ferrari Tipo 166C – 1st

20 January: Gran Premio de Rio de Janeiro, Circuito de La Gavia, Brazil – Ferrari Tipo 166C – retired

3 February: Gran Premio Quinta da Boa Vista, Rio de Janeiro, Brazil – Ferrari Tipo 166C – 1st

9 March: Premio Presidente Perón, Inauguración Autodromo 17 de Octubre – Ferrari Tipo 166C – 1st

16 March: Premio Eva Perón, Autodromo 1 de Octubre, Buenos Aires – Ferrari Tipo 166C – 1st

23 March: Circuito de Piriápolis, Uruguay – Ferrari Tipo 166C – 1st

30 March: Circuito de Piriápolis, Uruguay – Ferrari Tipo 166C – 1st

14 April: Chichester Cup, Goodwood, England – Cooper-Bristol – 6th

4 May: Mille Miglia, Italy – Alfa Romeo 1900 (Touring) – 22nd

1 June: Grand Prix of Albi, France – BRM V6 MkI – retired

7 June: Ulster Trophy, Dundrod, Northern Ireland – BRM V6 MkI – retired

8 June: Grand Prix of Monza, Autodromo, Italy – Maserati A6GCM – retired, crash

1952 World Championship standings: Ascari 36, Farina 24, Taruffi 22, Fischer 10, Hawthorn 9

1953

18 January: **Gran Premio de la Republica Argentina**, Autodromo de Buenos Aires – Maserati A6GCM – retired

1 February: Gran Premio de la Ciudad de Buenos Aires, Argentina – Maserati A6GCM – retired

26 April: Mille Miglia, Italy – Alfa Romeo 6C 3.0 (Sport) – 2nd

3 May: Grand Prix of Bordeaux, France – Gordini 1987cc – 3rd

10 May: Grand Prix of Naples, Italy – Maserati A6GCM – 2nd

14 May: Targa Florio, Italy – Maserati A6GCS – 3rd

31 May: Grand Prix of Albi, France – BRM V16 MkI – retired

7 June: **Grote Prijs van Nederland**, Zandvoort, Holland – Maserati A6GCM – retired

13–14 June: Le Mans 24 Hours, France, partnered by Onofre Marimón – Alfa Romeo 6C 3 3.0 (Sport) – retired

21 June: **Grote Prijs van Belgie**, Spa-Francorchamps, Belgium – Maserati A6GCM – retired

5 July: **Grand Prix de L'ACF**, Reims, France – Maserati A6GCM – 2nd

12 July: Vue des Alpes Mountain Hill Climb, Switzerland – Maserati A6GCM – 1st

18 July: Formula Libre race, Silverstone, England – BRM V16 MkI – 2nd

18 July: **British Grand Prix**, Silverstone, England – Maserati A6GCM – 2nd

24–25 July: 24 Hours of Spa-Francorchamps, Belgium, partnered by Consalvo Sanesi – Alfa Romeo 6C 3.0 (Sport) – retired

2 August: **Grosser Preis von Deutschland**, Nürburgring, West Germany – Maserati A6GCM – 2nd

23 August: **Grosser Preis der Schweiz**, Bremgarten, Switzerland – Maserati A6GCM – 2nd

30 August: 1,000 Kilometres of Nürburgring, West Germany, partnered by Felice Bonetto – Lancia D24 (Sport) – retired

6 September: Grand Prix of Supercortemaggiore, Merano, Italy – Alfa Romeo 6C 3.0 (Sport) – 1st

13 September: **Gran Premio d'Italia**, Monza, Italy – Maserati A6GCM – 1st

20 September: Grand Prix of Modena, Autodromo, Italy – Maserati A6GCM – 1st

26 September: Woodcote Cup, Goodwood, England – BRM V16 MkI – 2nd

26 September: Goodwood Trophy, Goodwood, England – BRM V16 MkI – retired

19 November: IV Carrera Panamericana, Mexico – Lancia D24 (Sport) – 1st

1953 World Championship standings: Ascari 34.5, Fangio 28, Farina 26, Hawthorn 19, Villoresi 17

1954

17 January: **Gran Premio de la Republica Argentina**, Autodromo de Buenos Aires – Maserati 250F – 1st

31 January: Gran Premio Ciudad de Buenos Aires, Autodromo, Argentina – Maserati 250F – retired

7 March: 12 Hours of Sebring, Florida, USA, partnered by Eugenio Castellotti – Lancia D24 (Sport) – retired

20 June: **Grote Prijs van Belgie**, Spa-Francorchamps, Belgium – Maserati 250F – 1st

27 June: Grand Prix of Supercortemaggiore, Monza, Italy, partnered by Onofre Marimón – Maserati 250S (Sport) – retired

4 July: **Grand Prix de L'ACF**, Reims, France – Mercedes-Benz W196 – 1st

17 July: **British Grand Prix**, Silverstone, England – Mercedes-Benz W196 – 4th

1 August: **Grosser Preis von Deutschland**, Nürburgring, West Germany – Mercedes-Benz W196 – 1st

22 August: **Grosser Preis der Schweiz**, Bremgarten, Switzerland – Mercedes-Benz W196 – 1st

5 September: **Gran Premio d'Italia**, Monza, Italy – Mercedes-Benz W196 – 1st

11 September: Tourist Trophy, Dundrod, Northern Ireland, partnered by Piero Taruffi – Lancia D24 (Sport) – 4th

19 September: Grand Prix of Berlin, Avus, West Germany – Mercedes-Benz W196 – 2nd

24 October: **Gran Premio de España**, Pedralbes, Barcelona, Spain – Mercedes-Benz W196 – 3rd

1954 World Championship standings: Fangio 42, González 24, Hawthorn 24, Trintignant 17, Kling 12

1955

16 January: **Gran Premio de la Republica Argentina**, Autodromo de Buenos Aires – Mercedes-Benz W196 – 1st

30 January: Gran Premio Ciudad de Buenos Aires, Autodromo, Argentina – Mercedes-Benz W196 (three-litre engine) – 1st

1 May: Mille Miglia, Italy – Mercedes-Benz 300SLR (Sport) – 2nd

22 May: **Grand Prix de Monaco** – Mercedes-Benz W196 – retired

29 May: Eifelrennen, Nürburgring, West Germany – Mercedes-Benz 300SLR (Sport) – 1st

5 June: **Grote Prijs van Belgie**, Spa-Francorchamps, Belgium – Mercedes-Benz W196 – 1st

11–12 June: Le Mans 24 Hours, France, partnered by Stirling Moss – Mercedes-Benz 300SLR (Sport) – withdrawn

19 June: **Grote Prijs van Nederland**, Zandvoort, Holland – Mercedes-Benz W196 – 1st

16 July: **British Grand Prix**, Aintree, England – Mercedes-Benz W196 – 2nd

7 August: Grand Prix of Sweden, Circuit of Kristianstadt – Mercedes-Benz 300SLR (Sport) – 1st

11 September: **Gran Premio d'Italia**, Monza, Italy – Mercedes-Benz W196 – 1st

17 September: Tourist Trophy, Dundrod, Northern Ireland, partnered by Karl Kling – Mercedes-Benz 300SLR (Sport) – 2nd

16 October: Targa Florio, Sicily, partnered by Karl Kling – Mercedes-Benz 300SLR (Sport) – 2nd

6 November: Grand Prix de Venezuela, Circuito Los Próceres, Caracas – Maserati 300S (Sport) – 1st

1955 World Championship standings: Fangio 40, Moss 23, Castellotti 12, Trintignant 11, Farina 10

1956

22 January: **Gran Premio de la Republica Argentina**, Autodromo de Buenos Aires – Lancia-Ferrari V8 – 1st (finished with the car of Luigi Musso)

29 January: 1,000 Kilómetros de la Ciudad de Buenos Aires, Argentina, partnered by Eugenio Castellotti – Ferrari Monza 860 (Sport) – retired

5 February: Gran Premio Ciudad de Buenos Aires, Circuito General San Martin, Mendoza, Argentina – Lancia-Ferrari V8 – 1st

25 March: 12 Hours of Sebring, Florida, USA, partnered by Eugenio Castellotti – Ferrari Monza 860 (Sport) – 1st

15 April: Grand Prix of Syracuse, Sicily – Lancia-Ferrari V8 – 1st

28 April: Mille Miglia, Italy – Ferrari 290 MM (Sport) – 4th

5 May: International Trophy, Silverstone, England – Lancia-Ferrari V8 – retired

13 May: **Grand Prix de Monaco** – Lancia-Ferrari V8 – 2nd

27 May: 1,000 Kilometres of Nürburgring, West Germany, partnered by Eugenio Castellotti – Ferrari Monza 860 (Sport) – 2nd

3 June: **Grote Prijs van Belgie**, Spa-Francorchamps, Belgium – Lancia-Ferrari V8 – retired

24 June: Grand Prix of Supercortemaggiore, Monza, Italy, partnered by Eugenio Castellotti – Ferrari 500TR (Sport) – 3rd

1 July: **Grand Prix de L'ACF**, Reims, France – Lancia-Ferrari V8 – 4th

14 July: **British Grand Prix**, Silverstone, England – Lancia-Ferrari V8 – 1st

5 August: **Grosser Preis von Deutschland**, Nürburgring, West Germany – Lancia-Ferrari V8 – 1st

12 August: Grand Prix of Sweden, Circuit of Kristianstadt – Ferrari Monza 860 (Sport) – retired

2 September: **Gran Premio d'Italia**, Monza, Italy – Lancia-Ferrari V8 – 2nd (finished with the car of Peter Collins)

9 November: Grand Prix of Venezuela, Circuito Los Próceres, Caracas – Ferrari Monza 806 (Sport) – 2nd

1956 World Championship standings: Fangio 30, Moss 27, Collins 25, Behra 22

1957

13 January: **Gran Premio de la Republica Argentina**, Autodromo de Buenos Aires – Maserati 250F – 1st

20 January: 1,000 Kilómetros de la Ciudad de Buenos Aires, Argentina, partnered by Stirling Moss – Maserati 450S (Sport) – retired

27 January: Gran Premio Ciudad de Buenos Aires, Autodromo, Argentina – Maserati 250F – 1st

25 February: Grand Prix of Cuba, Circuito El Malecón, Havana – Maserati 300S (Sport) – 1st

23 March: 12 Hours of Sebring, Florida, USA, partnered by Jean Behra – Maserati 450S (Sport) – 1st

19 May: **Grand Prix de Monaco** – Maserati 250F – 1st

26 May: 1,000 Kilometres of Nürburgring, West Germany, partnered by Stirling Moss – Maserati 300S (Sport) – 5th

9 June: Grand Prix of Portugal, Circuito Monsanto, Lisbon – Maserati 300S (Sport) – 1st

7 July: **Grand Prix de L'ACF**, Rouen-les-Essarts, France – Maserati 250F – 1st

14 July: Grand Prix of Reims, France – Maserati 250F – retired

20 July: **British Grand Prix**, Aintree, England – Maserati 250F
– retired

4 August: **Grosser Preis von Deutschland**, Nürburgring, West
Germany – Maserati 250F – 1st

18 August: **Gran Premio di Pescara,** Italy – Maserati 250F – 2nd

8 September: **Gran Premio d'Italia**, Monza, Italy – Maserati
250F – 2nd

27 October: Grand Prix of Morocco, Casablanca – Maserati
250F – 4th

1 December: Gran Premio de Interlagos, São Paulo, Brazil –
Maserati 300S (Sport) – 1st

8 December: Gran Premio Circuito da Boa Vista, Rio de
Janeiro, Brazil – Maserati 300S (Sport) – 1st

1957 World Championship standings: Fangio 40, Moss 25,
Musso 16, Hawthorn 13, Brooks 11

1958

19 January: **Gran Premio de la Republica Argentina**, Autodromo de Buenos Aires – Maserati 250F – 4th

26 January: 1,000 Kilómetros de la Ciudad de Buenos Aires,
Argentina, partnered by Francisco Godia-Sales – Maserati
300S (Sport) – retired

2 February: Gran Premio Ciudad de Buenos Aires, Autodromo,
Argentina – Maserati 250F – 1st

29 June: 500 Miles of Monza 'Two Worlds Trophy', Italy –
Dean Van Lines Special – retired

6 July: **Grand Prix de L'ACF**, Reims, France – Maserati 250F –
4th

1958 World Championship standings: Hawthorn 42, Moss 41,
Brooks 24, Salvadori 15 (Fangio 6)

Bibliography

The following books, magazines and films were used for reference and/or quoted from in the preparation of this book.

Autosport (magazine, various issues to 1958, Haymarket Publishing)

Ball, Adrian (ed.), *My Greatest Race* (Granada Publishing Ltd, 1974)

Beaumont, Charles and Nolan, William F. (eds), *Omnibus of Speed* (Stanley Paul, 1961)

Bentley, John, *The Devil Behind Them* (Angus and Robertson, 1959)

Blunsden, John (ed.), *Jenks* (Motor Racing Publications, 1997)

Champion Fangio (video, Duke Marketing, 1992)

Cimarosti, Adriano, *Grand Prix Motor Racing* (Aurum Press Ltd, 1997)

Daley, Robert, *Cars at Speed* (G.T. Foulis & Co., 1961)

Daley, Robert, *The Cruel Sport* (Prentice-Hall, 1963)

Donaldson, Gerald (ed.), *Formula 1: The Autobiography* (Weidenfeld & Nicolson, 2002)

Fangio (film), directed by Hugh Hudson, produced by Giovanni Volpi (1973)

Fangio, Juan Manuel, with Marcello Giambertone, *My Twenty Years of Racing* (Temple Press Ltd, 1961)

Fangio, Juan Manuel, with Roberto Carozzo, *Fangio, My Racing Life* (Patrick Stephens Ltd, 1990)

Fangio Special (video, Warwick Video, 1995)

Fenu, Michel, *Ferrari's Drivers* (William Kimber, 1980)

Ferrari, Enzo, *My Terrible Joys* (Hamish Hamilton, 1965)

Frere, Paul, *Competition Driving* (B.T. Batsford Ltd, 1963)

Hansen, Ronald and Kirbus, Frederico B., *The Life Story of Juan Manuel Fangio* (Edita S.A. Lausanne, 1956)

Hawthorn, Mike, with Gordon Wilkins, *Challenge Me the Race* (Aston Publications, 1958)

Hayhoe, David, and Holland, David, *Grand Prix Data Book* (Duke Marketing, 1996)

Henry, Alan, *Autocourse: 50 Years of World Championship Grand Prix Motor Racing* (Hazleton Publishing, 2000)

Henry, Alan, *Formula One, Driver by Driver* (The Crowood Press, 1992)

Jenkinson, Denis (ed.), *Fangio*, based on the film *Fangio* (Michael Joseph, 1973)

Jenkinson, Denis (ed.), *The Racing Driver* (Robert Bentley Inc., 1969)

Lang, Mike, *Grand Prix!* (Haynes Publishing Group, 1981)

Lewis, Peter, *Dicing With Death* (a *Daily Mirror* book, 1961)

Ludvigsen, Karl, *Juan Manuel Fangio, Motor Racing's Grand Master* (Haynes Publishing, 1999)

McCluggage, Denise, *By Brooks Too Broad for Leaping* (Fulcorte Press, 1994)

Menard, Pierre, *The Great Encyclopedia of Formula 1* (Constable & Robinson Ltd, 2000)

Merlin, Olivier, *Fangio, Racing Driver* (B.T. Batsford Ltd, 1961)

Miller, Peter, *The Fast Ones* (Stanley Paul, 1962)

Molter, Gunther, *Juan Manuel Fangio, World Champion* (G.T. Foulis & Co. Ltd, 1956)

Moss, Stirling, with Christopher Hilton, *Stirling Moss's Motor Racing Masterpieces* (Sidgwick & Jackson, 1994)

Moss, Stirling, with Doug Nye, *Fangio, A Pirelli Album* (Pavilion Books Ltd, 1991)

Motor (magazine, various issues to 1958)

Motor Sport (magazine, various issues to 1958, Haymarket Publishing)

Nixon, Chris, *Mon Ami Mate* (Transport Bookman Publications, 2001)

Pritchard, Anthony, *The World Champions* (Leslie Frewin Publishers, 1972)

Purdy, Ken W., *The New Matadors* (Bond Publishing, 1965)

Rendall, Ivan, *The Chequered Flag* (Weidenfeld & Nicolson, 1993)

Roebuck, Nigel, *Chasing the Title* (Haynes Publishing, 1999)

Roebuck, Nigel, *Grand Prix Greats* (Patrick Stephens Ltd, 1986)

Schnall Heglar, Mary, *The Grand Prix Champions* (Bond Parkhurst Books, 1973)

Small, Steve (ed.), *The Grand Prix Drivers* (Hazleton Publishing, 1987)

Small, Steve (ed.), *Grand Prix Who's Who* (Travel Publishing Ltd, 1996)

Walker, Murray, with Simon Taylor, *Murray Walker's Formula One Heroes* (Virgin Publishing Ltd, 2000)

Williams, Richard, *Enzo Ferrari* (Yellow Jersey Press, 2001)

Williams, Richard, *Racers* (Viking, 1997)

Index